Kiffin Rockwell, the Lafayette Escadrille
and the Birth of the United States Air Force

Kiffin Rockwell, the Lafayette Escadrille and the Birth of the United States Air Force

T. B. Murphy

McFarland & Company, Inc., Publishers
Jefferson, North Carolina

LIBRARY OF CONGRESS CATALOGUING-IN-PUBLICATION DATA

Names: Murphy, T. B., 1979– author.
Title: Kiffin Rockwell, the Lafayette Escadrille and the
birth of the United States Air Force / T. B. Murphy.
Description: Jefferson, North Carolina : McFarland & Company, Inc.,
Publishers, 2016. | Includes bibliographical references and index.
Identifiers: LCCN 2016032466 | ISBN 9781476664019 (softcover : acid free paper) ∞
Subjects: LCSH: Rockwell, Kiffin Yates, 1892–1916. | World War,
1914–1918—Aerial operations, French. | France. Armée. Escadrille
Lafayette—Biography. | Fighter pilots—United States—Biography. |
Fighter pilots—France—Biography.
Classification: LCC D603 .M87 2016 | DDC 940.4/4944092 [B]—dc23
LC record available at https://lccn.loc.gov/2016032466

ISBN (print) 978-1-4766-6401-9
ISBN (ebook) 978-1-4766-2431-0

BRITISH LIBRARY CATALOGUING DATA ARE AVAILABLE

© 2016 T. B. Murphy. All rights reserved

*No part of this book may be reproduced or transmitted in any form
or by any means, electronic or mechanical, including photocopying
or recording, or by any information storage and retrieval system,
without permission in writing from the publisher.*

Front cover: Members of the Lafayette Escadrille with a French commander;
left to right: James McConnell, Kiffin Rockwell, Col. Georges Thenault,
Norman Prince and Victor Chapman (Dan Patterson Studio)

Printed in the United States of America

*McFarland & Company, Inc., Publishers
Box 611, Jefferson, North Carolina 28640
www.mcfarlandpub.com*

*To my wife Cortney,
who always believed I could write this book.
And to my children:
Jack, Eliana, Kiffin, Joseph and Daniel.*

Table of Contents

Acknowledgments ix
Preface 1
Prologue 7

1. The Early Years — 9
2. Leaving Home — 16
3. World War I Begins — 24
4. Training in the French Foreign Legion — 33
5. At the Front — 45
6. The Battle of Artois — 57
7. Kiffin's Recovery and New Hope — 68
8. Pilot Training — 75
9. The Creation of the Lafayette Escadrille — 88
10. Verdun — 98
11. The Lafayette Escadrille Comes of Age — 109
12. Passing the Torch — 120
13. The Climax of the Lafayette Escadrille — 132
14. The Transition to the U.S. Air Service — 144
15. The Dawn of American Air Power — 152
16. The Legacy of the Lafayette Escadrille — 160
17. Final Thoughts — 171

Chapter Notes 175
Bibliography 183
Index 185

Acknowledgments

Researching and writing this book took me over fifteen years, so I have many people to thank. I must first thank the U.S. Air Force Academy Library staff for the treasures I found in the special collections. My fascination with history started in those quiet rooms after trudging up the winding marble staircase to the sixth floor. It was there in the archive that I found Kiffin Rockwell's war letters, and his story has captivated me ever since. Thank you to my professors at the Academy: to Colonel Mark Wells for leading a demanding program in the history department; to Lt. Colonel John Farquhar for introducing so many bright-eyed cadets to the idea of air power; and to Lt. Colonel Vance Skarstedt for mercilessly teaching a hardheaded kid how to write. Thank you to my good friends who suffered with me at the Academy: Paul Davidson (who is now my brother-in-law), Kadeen Mansor, Darren Moore, Jamison Scheeres, Matt Strohmeyer, Josh Weed, and Paul Whitsel. You all definitely encouraged me in this project.

Thank you to all the pilots who served as the inspiration for this book. To the guys in pilot training: Scott Fann, Scott Gunn, Matt Roles, J.R. Williams, and many others—I thought of our experiences multiple times while writing this book. Thank you to my first squadron, the Gamblers of the 77th Fighter Squadron: particularly to "Bodhi" Bacon for being the finest tactician, instructor, and leader one could hope for; to my good friend "Nails" Acer; and to "Bruiser" Bryant, who made the ultimate sacrifice for his country. Thank you to the men and women of the 35th and 309th Fighter Squadrons as well as the Nickel pilots in the 555th Fighter Squadron, the Buzzards in the 510th Fighter Squadron, and the Lions of the 31st Operational Support Squadron. And to the greatest squadron on earth, the Warhawks of the 480th Fighter Squadron, you are all warriors cut from the same cloth as our ancestors in the Lafayette Escadrille.

My time at the National Defense University with the College of International Security Affairs was incredibly valuable to this book. The professors led a rigorous and mind-stimulating program that renewed my motivation to write this story. My specific thanks go to: Dr. Paul Miller, who has an uncanny ability to look at a problem from all perspectives and find unique solutions; to Dr. Sean McFate for his useful teaching style and enthusiasm; and to Dr. Michael Bell, who convinced me that anyone could write a book.

To the many friends who encouraged me to start writing: Wes Roberts, Justin Golart, Joe Kreidel, Ben Gunn, and many others. And to Vandal Mann, Major Mary, and many others who read the manuscript. Thank you to Major General Barre Seguin, who encouraged me to complete the manuscript and get it published. I can't thank all of you enough.

I also have to thank the Rockwell family for their kindness to an outsider like me and their full support for this project. The late Kenneth Rockwell, Paul Rockwell's son and Kiffin's nephew, was a pleasure to meet and an amazing source of knowledge about Paul and

Kiffin. Vance Brown, Kiffin's grandnephew, has been an incredible source of encouragement and is the man who found a publisher for this book—I owe you more than I could ever repay! Kenneth Rockwell's daughter, Sybil Robb, has also been a huge support and offered a wealth of pictures and research on Paul and Kiffin. Thank you!

Thank you especially to my family: to my Dad, who defined the idea of a fighter pilot to me at an early age and taught me so much about life; and to my Mom for her constant support, prayers, and nurturing home. My parents raised my sisters and me in a home centered on God, where learning, inquiring, and questioning were always present—I can't imagine growing up any other way! Thank you to my sisters Jenny, Megan, and Alison for putting up with your only brother and for taking an interest in Kiffin's story. Your little nudges over the years kept me going. I will always be thankful for my wife's family, the Johnsons. Mom and Dad, you have been such an encouragement for this book—your constant excitement about it was just what I needed to finally get it done!

My final thanks must go to my wife Cortney and our kids. Cortney, you have always been far more convinced that I would write this book than I ever was. You have heard snippets of this tale thousands of times over the last sixteen years, but you never stopped encouraging me to write them all down. I am happy to finally give you the full story, and I will be eternally grateful for all your support. My two older kids, Jack and Ellie, know a little about this project, but their sweet spirits motivated me more than they will ever know. My son Kiffin Fredric was the decisive inspirational force, however. I decided to finish this before his first birthday and completed the first draft just in time! And Joseph and Daniel were new additions during the edits and final drafts of the book for which I am forever grateful.

In closing, I again thank everyone listed above and the countless others who have been such a major part of my life. My highest thanks must always go to God, who has blessed my family and me in immeasurable ways and who gave me the strength and the endurance to write this book.

Preface

The history of mankind is a mystery in many ways—occasionally predictable, often baffling or perplexing, but sometimes extraordinary. And once every several generations, during these extraordinary times, an event occurs that cracks the foundation of society and ushers in a new era. These events lie almost exclusively in the realm of warfare, for it is human violence that has the greatest potential to fundamentally alter human society. Examples include the conquests of Cyrus the Great, his Greek counterpart Alexander, the civil war in Rome that left an empire in its wake, the Arab conquests after the death of Mohammad, the Mongolian invasions, and Western colonial conquests. None of these events occurred suddenly. Like a hurricane, ominous signs began to appear before the storm, and the storm's fury was occasionally broken by short periods of peace. And just as in the aftermath of a hurricane, the period following the event was defined by the damage that remained and the new structures that arose.

The First World War was such an event. Human society today is still grappling with the aftershocks of this terrible episode in history. World War I spawned two additional wars: the Second World War, more terrible than the first, and the Cold War, capable of destroying most of the world's population. The conflict also dealt a death blow to colonialism, even though its final breath came several decades later. The fact that nearly all modern conflicts have their roots in the transition from colonial empires to new nations underscores the significance of the first global war. A new era began after World War I, but it is difficult to define because we are participating in it and the act has yet to play out. We may not know the ending, but we can observe series of events that form unbroken lines from the dark periods of the war to modern times.

This book is about following one of those unbroken lines. The line starts with one person who lived and fought in the war, and it ends with a large, complex organization that plays a major role in global events today. This book is about the line between the United States Air Force of today and one man who has been largely forgotten. Kiffin Yates Rockwell of Asheville, North Carolina, was not solely responsible for the creation of the Air Force. Nor were the members of the group who fought with him, the Lafayette Escadrille. What the Lafayette Escadrille did create, and has never truly received credit for, is the character of the Air Force—its spirit. And Kiffin Rockwell, more than any other man in the group, epitomized the spirit that now defines the United States Air Force.

The story described in these pages is the culmination of over fifteen years of research on Kiffin Rockwell. While studying history at the U.S. Air Force Academy, I stumbled upon Rockwell and the Lafayette Escadrille during a trip to the library archives as part of an air power course I took my sophomore year. Kiffin's story fascinated me because it seemed larger than life and far more interesting than any of the novels or movies based on the early years of flight. Yet his life also left me stunned because I could not understand why his name (and those of his comrades) rarely appeared in official Air Force historical works or heritage pieces. It seemed as if a vital piece of Air Force history would remain hidden forever.

This is not to say that nothing has been written about the Lafayette Escadrille and Kiffin Rockwell. Several authors published books directly or indirectly about the extraordinary squadron, but most of them were written just after World War I and have since faded into the background. Even more important, however, is that none of the books adequately examined and demonstrated the enormous impact that men such as Kiffin Rockwell had on the eventual establishment and development of the U.S. Air Force.

As I began to unearth these stories up on the sixth floor of the Academy library, I promised myself that I would tell anyone who would listen about Kiffin Rockwell and his fellow pilots in the Lafayette Escadrille. It has taken me several years to put all of it together, and along the way I became a fighter pilot myself. I mention a small piece of my personal story on these pages only because flying aircraft has given me an even greater appreciation for Rockwell and the Lafayette Escadrille. I know that I have directly benefited from the fighting spirit that originated with these early pilots. I am proud to say that the courage, excellence, and commitment that characterized the Lafayette Escadrille over one hundred years ago still exist and thrive in today's U.S. Air Force.

Kiffin Rockwell and eight other pilots were the first members of a unique American squadron called the Lafayette Escadrille that fought under the French flag before the United States entered World War I. Rockwell was the first American pilot to record a kill in the squadron, and his early exploits laid the foundation for the fighting spirit that characterizes the U.S. Air Force today. Unfortunately, he and the others in the Lafayette Escadrille are largely forgotten heroes; their story must be told again and again until they receive the credit they are due. For Rockwell and his squadron mates did not just perform courageously and honorably under the French flag. When the U.S. finally entered the war, surviving members from the Lafayette Escadrille commanded flights, squadrons, and groups in the newly formed United States Air Service. Monumental figures such as Billy Mitchell observed and internalized their performance, while others such as Eddie Rickenbacker learned from commanders who had previously served in the Lafayette Escadrille. Numerous records indicate that the battle-hardened warriors of the Lafayette Escadrille had a profound impact on the untested American aviators who joined the war in 1918. The leadership and presence of the Lafayette Escadrille easily offset the inexperience of young American pilots who nervously flew over the front lines for the first time.

As the small group of weathered riders handed off the reins to the growing U.S. Air Service in Europe, a great legacy began to form. The pilots of the Lafayette Escadrille achieved remarkable success in the sky over France during their tenure, and the American Air Service quickly continued the pattern. As World War I ended, American aviators (like pilots in many other countries) began to exhibit a certain swagger and air of confidence. They lived and died where others could not go, soaring high above the battlefield and wreaking havoc on any enemy who dared to challenge them. Perhaps most important, however, is the fact that these men mastered a new dimension. By the end of the war, the Allies dominated the air and American pilots were justifiably proud of their part in achieving victory in Europe. The taste of success in a totally new arena of warfare created a thirst for future success. American aviators experienced the struggle for and ultimate achievement of air superiority, and from that point forward they would accept nothing less. The idea of mastering the air and the machines that fought in it began to form in the minds of everyone involved in American military aviation. After many years and many setbacks, the idea eventually became a tradition and the tradition ultimately became heritage.

People today often forget how young the U.S. Air Force is. The service is only sixty-nine years old as of 2016, but it has rapidly become an indispensable tool of national policy. The heritage that had its roots in a conflict one hundred years ago now defines the organization. The Air Force, like every other service, has experienced its share of difficulties and trials over the years, but one thing remains unchanged—the service has achieved superiority of the air *in every single conflict in its history*. That fact is astonishing in itself, but it becomes far more captivating after learning the story of where this desire was born. The United States did not just stumble upon air dominance. It was not inevitable due to America's industrial might and technological innovation. Incredibly intelligent people had to develop a vision for the new dimension. Brilliant designers had to take those visions and create machines that had the ability to achieve superiority. But most importantly, the pilots had to develop the skills to succeed and the belief that no one could challenge their mastery of the air.

The belief that mastery of the air could be achieved was the cornerstone of the spirit that the Lafayette Escadrille created and gave as an inheritance to the fledgling Air Service. The spirit of the Lafayette Escadrille was present during World War II in the Doolittle Raid, the treacherous daylight bombing campaign over Tokyo, and in the unparalleled success of the Tuskegee Airmen. It was deeply ingrained in the hearts of the aces who ushered in the jet age during the Korean War. This spirit repeatedly drove persistent tacticians back to the drawing board during the Vietnam War and enabled POW aviators to endure brutal torture and return home with honor. It played a crucial role in bringing the Soviet Union to its knees during the Cold War, and the same fighting spirit annihilated the Iraqi Air Force in a matter of days during the Gulf War. Serbia capitulated after an intense air campaign in the 1990s, and the 21st-century Air Force smashed down the walls of Afghanistan and Iraq to ease the advance of American and coalition ground forces. Even now U.S. Air Force aircraft provide invaluable intelligence and lightning-quick destruction of targets over the current battlefields in Afghanistan and across the Middle East. Perhaps the most powerful indication of Air Force air dominance is that it has literally been decades since an American soldier on the ground worried about an attack from an enemy aircraft.

Today, the fighting spirit that drove the men of the Lafayette Escadrille is known in the Air Force as excellence. And the unrelenting drive for excellence is not something that Air Force leaders assume will happen on its own. It is cultivated and protected through intense and unending training combined with innovative thinking at tactical, operational, and strategic levels. It is expected in *every* career field and required in everything from professional education to technical training. It is demanded in operational exercises and inspections. And, not surprisingly, it is enshrined in the third pillar of the Air Force Core Values, *Excellence in All We Do*. Some may view the idea of core values as little more than an advertising gimmick—I certainly entertained the idea in the past. But the longer I stay in the Air Force, the more I admit that the Air Force got this one right … in a big way. Ask any new pilot finishing pilot training if excellence was required and you will likely get a laugh followed by a sarcastically affirmative answer. Or ask the men and women of any career field attending the U.S. Air Force Weapons School. Ask them about excellence after they spend days pouring their hearts into the planning and execution of a mission and then failing because it just wasn't quite good enough. You may not even get an answer. The reality is that excellence is not just a slogan on a billboard. It is expected, demanded, and enforced at every level and in every individual. Excellence is truly what makes the Air Force great, and it is a direct reflection of the record and proud heritage that started with the Lafayette Escadrille.

However, this book is not intended to preach Air Force doctrine or infallibility in warfare. The U.S. Air Force is a human organization. It has made plenty of mistakes over the years and will certainly make additional mistakes in the future. What is indisputable is that the Air Force has managed to overcome those mistakes and achieve mastery of the air in every conflict. In addition, I readily acknowledge that this book only focuses on the roots of Air Force air power. Every one of the services contributes unique and essential capabilities in our nation's pursuit of aerial dominance during conflicts. The Army, Navy, and Marines can point to similar records of achievement during their long histories, but this book is about the origin of the Air Force's fighting spirit. The spirit created by Kiffin Rockwell and the men of the Lafayette Escadrille was unique and applicable to air combat. It provided the foundation for the Air Force's extraordinary pattern of success and should not be taken lightly.

I focus on Kiffin Rockwell in order to highlight the humanness of the unit that essentially started the Air Force as we know it today. A few books have been written about the Lafayette Escadrille, but they miss more than the connection between the Lafayette Escadrille and the modern Air Force. Previous books look at the subject broadly and only briefly touch on the souls, character, personalities, and ambitions of the men who fought in the Lafayette Escadrille. But these characteristics defined the men and the unit, so they must be addressed. Attempting to explore the full scope of every man's life in the unit would be a monumental task beyond the scope of one book, but it is possible to narrow the focus to one man. I chose Rockwell for three primary reasons. First, his own unit recognized him as "the best and bravest of us all" and the soul of the squadron.[1] He had an amazing drive to succeed that forced others to perform at his extraordinary level. Secondly, Kiffin's story was by far the most compelling of all the men who flew in the Lafayette Escadrille. This observation is quite remarkable in its own right because every single man, especially of the original core group, had a fascinating story. Finally, Kiffin's older brother Paul graciously compiled and published an extensive collection of the letters Kiffin wrote during the war. These letters provide a picture of a rare soul and one that demands further exploration.

There are, of course, other reasons I chose to study Rockwell's life. He dreamed big, knew no boundaries in the air, and inspired others to follow him. His love for his country, for France, and for his craft were highly contagious within the squadron. Rockwell was a humble man, but for those looking into the past, his actions and character now seem to scream for attention. To put it more simply, I wanted to write about Rockwell because his story is a noteworthy one, and great stories should not lie untended in the dust of history.

Thus, the critical emphasis of this book is following the life of Kiffin Rockwell in order

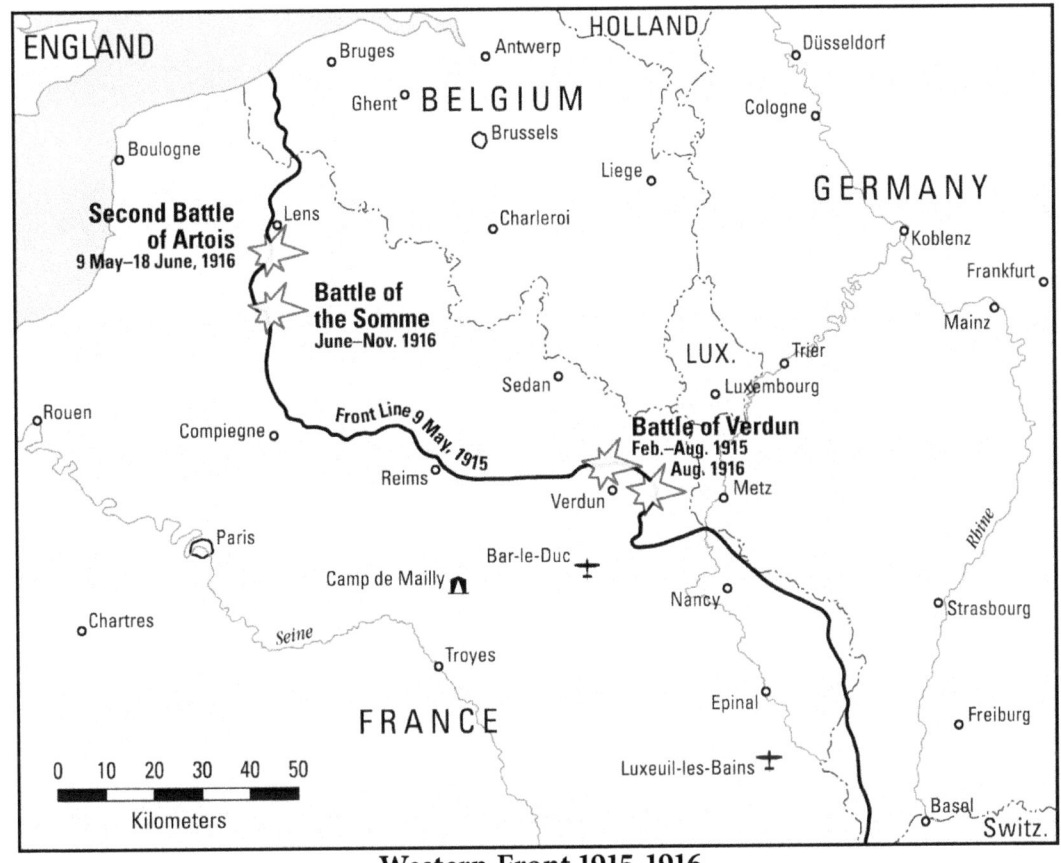

Western Front 1915-1916

The map depicts significant locations for Kiffin Rockwell and the Lafayette Escadrille. It includes most of the battle sites, airfields, and notable places mentioned throughout the book (map by Eureka Cartography, Berkeley, CA).

to demonstrate that the fighting spirit of the modern Air Force did not materialize on its own. It did not magically spread throughout the organization when Congress created the U.S. Air Force in 1947. The drive for excellence was not fashioned by members of the Army Air Corps, and it did not start when the American armed forces joined World War I, either. It started with the American men who first flew aircraft in combat. Excellence started when Kiffin Rockwell fired only five rounds at a German LVG, killing the pilot and the observer, and sending the aircraft down in flames. Excellence prospered as the men of the Lafayette Escadrille tirelessly advanced toward their goal of mastering the skies. My one wish is for readers to gain a deeper knowledge and understanding of what our first combat aviators did for our country and its air force. This book is written to show how Kiffin Rockwell and the Lafayette Escadrille gave birth to the fighting spirit that still exists and thrives in the U.S. Air Force. They deserve our long overdue honor and recognition. May their names never be forgotten again.

Prologue

A comforting breeze flowed peacefully down from the Swiss Alps through the open doors of a parlor in the center of a stunning French villa sprawled among the foothills of the Vosges Mountains. Nine men, all pilots, lounged around in the room, and one could almost feel a level of energy pulsing through the air on the cool spring evening. The men were not quiet, for pilots rarely are, but there was a certain sensation of gravity to the moment. They were clearly all waiting, anticipating some monumental event that no one seemed willing to discuss directly. The peaceful breeze belied the seriousness of their present situation, but something had occurred that sent the souls of these young men soaring.

The luxury resort that the men gratefully occupied was known as Luxeuil-les-Baines. Despite its picturesque scenery and air of royalty, it had not catered to wealthy Europeans or other affluent visitors for quite some time. The time was May 1916, midway through the dark conflict of World War I, and the grand villa's occupants were not Frenchmen, but patriotic, idealistic American pilots. These men were no ordinary fliers, either; in fact, one could hardly call them ordinary human beings. Nearly every single person standing in the parlor that night had left a life of affluence or academia in the United States. All of them answered the deep, primordial call echoing within their souls as they watched Europe descend into a conflict unprecedented in its scope and level of devastation. Some of them raced to France because they saw a fight and were inexplicably drawn to it. Others wanted a chance for adventure and an opportunity to master the world's newest machine. Still others felt an idealistic sense of duty to assist their European brethren even when their own country, the United States, openly refused to take sides. On this particular evening, the room buzzed with anticipation as these unique men enthusiastically shared their version of a remarkable event that had just occurred. The American pilots jealously awaited the arrival of Kiffin Rockwell, the one man who had accomplished a feat that had thus far eluded the rest of them. After the anxious pilots waited loudly and impatiently for several minutes, the twenty-four-year-old aviator finally entered the room and grinned sheepishly at the small crowd.

He did not like being the center of attention, but earlier that morning, only five days after his unit started flying at the Front, Rockwell had scored the squadron's first aerial victory. The rowdy pilots loudly welcomed him and applauded his recent success. They clapped him on the back, hugged him, and honored him the way young men honor one of their own. The pilots formed a semicircle around the victorious pilot and forced him to recount the story. With his typical mixture of aggressive eloquence, Kiffin recited his story. His eyes smoldered as he recounted his scouting trip and the disappointment he felt when his engine started to misfire, which forced him to turn for home. The pitch of his voice increased ever so slightly when he described seeing a lone German aircraft below him, just behind enemy lines. He completely glossed over his previous engine problems as he discussed his long, steep dive toward his prey. Kiffin's eyes flashed in synch with the bright blast of his machine gun in the story. With stunning detail, he described pulling away just before colliding with the German aircraft and seeing it arc toward the earth with a trail of smoke marking its final resting place.

The other men listened with bated breath, following every detail to its conclusion. They felt as if they had been there in the fight, and they somehow managed to suppress their twinges of jealousy with genuine happiness for their brother in arms. One of the pilots shoved a bottle into his hand and stood back to see his reaction. With all eyes on him, the young pilot fixed his gaze on the ancient bottle of alcohol perched firmly in the palm of his hand. The bottle immediately garnered the rapt attention of everyone standing in the room. Alcohol was not uncommon along the front lines, but this bottle was special. Kiffin was impressed when he saw 1835 etched on the bottle, but he did not know the complete story. The men excitedly explained that Kiffin's brother Paul, who also served as a soldier in France, had heard about his sibling's exploits and quickly sent the bottle as a gift. It contained eighty-year-old bourbon that had been preserved for an occasion such as this one. Rockwell beamed broadly as he recognized what an extraordinary gift his older brother had given to them. As he uncorked the bottle to share his prize with the other men, a lone voice called out, and another pilot calmly walked to the front of the room and began to talk.

"We can get plenty of liquor, but not like this. It's rare stuff. Let's save it for rare occasions." Naturally, the rest of the group heartily disagreed with him until he finished his thought. "Fellows, let's make it a real Bottle of Death … from now on every man who brings down a German is entitled to one good slug. It'll be something worth working for."[1]

After a short period of silence, all of the men agreed that it was a noble idea to reserve the bourbon only for those who tasted victory in the air, and from that day forward the Bottle of Death became a proud tradition of the unit. Unfortunately, the bottle lived up to its name in more ways than one. While many of the pilots eventually enjoyed a swig of the rare drink, most of them never lived to see the end of the conflict.

None of the men standing around the table that night knew what they had started, but the Bottle of Death marked the beginning of an epic story. The bottle they consecrated became a symbol for them. It represented the sacrifices they had made to come to France on their own volition and to fight for a foreign country. It represented their hope that their own country would one day join them on the side that they firmly believed was right and good. It soon represented those who had fallen in pursuit of their dreams. But most importantly, the bottle represented their relentless quest to control the skies.

One hundred years later, the men who drank from this bottle represent the spirit that now resides within the men and women of the United States Air Force. The relentless quest to control the skies is the central contribution of the Air Force to the defense of the nation. Excellence became the term to describe this unending pursuit. It started when Kiffin Rockwell took a sip from a bottle of bourbon and indirectly challenged everyone else to taste the fruits of victory. The Bottle of Death thus represents far more than the legacy of the fighter pilots whose signatures are inscribed upon it. It is in many ways the Holy Grail of the United States Air Force. The men who drank from the bottle started a tradition that defines why the Air Force is the premier air force in the world.

1

The Early Years

Today the name of Kiffin Yates Rockwell and the names of his colleagues remain locked in the prison of their own unique histories—largely forgotten by all but the most ardent aviation enthusiasts. They officially fought for France, and most believed they were fulfilling an obligation that their own government was unwilling to carry out. Their decision to fight for France was an intentional act of defiance against the United States government's proclamation of neutrality. The motives behind this willful defiance varied, but Kiffin's reasoning was both simple and nuanced at the same time. On one hand, Kiffin viewed the world in black and white. Germany's invasion of France was a gross injustice, and the United States was obligated to assist France in order to pay back the outstanding debt that remained after France helped the United States win its independence from Britain. On the other hand, the fact that such thoughts drove his actions indicates that Rockwell had a mind that operated in a much deeper realm than the mind of a normal human being. His reasoning about America's obligation to France was not entirely unique, but the actions that followed were as far from conventional as one could get. Letting such thoughts swirl in one's head is one thing, but volunteering to fight on the day war is declared is entirely another. Kiffin Rockwell was an incredibly rare person in an incredibly unusual time. But to fully understand what fueled his desires, we must look further back, for his character on the eve of World War I had been shaped by events that occurred years before he was even born.

Kiffin Rockwell came from a rather notable line of early American settlers. The Rockwell family settled in America during the very early days of English colonial settlement in the new land. Kiffin was from the family of William Rockwell of Somerset County, England—the exact same line as the famous artist Norman Rockwell. William was a member of an association that made the voyage to America in order to make settlements on the shores of New England.[1] They wanted land on which to make new homes and start new lives, so they sailed from England in the spring of 1630. William, a deacon of his church in England, and his fellow church members on the voyage planted their families and their faith in the rich new land. Hundreds of years later, remnants of their pioneering spirits lived on in the hearts of their kin.

During the early 1800s, Kiffin's family moved south into the Carolinas. His great-grandfather, Chester Rockwell, moved from Connecticut to North Carolina. He became a cotton and tobacco farmer who owned a plantation in what is now the town of Chadbourn, North Carolina, located just north of the South Carolina border. He was one of the richest men in his part of North Carolina, and he freely used his fortune and influence to help the cause of the Southern Confederacy during the Civil War.[2] Chester Rockwell was too old to fight in the war, but many of his sons fought, including Kiffin's grandfather, Henry Clay

Rockwell. Henry Clay had only been married for a year when the war broke out, and he felt compelled to join the Southern cause. His family's involvement in the Civil War would profoundly shape the life and character of Kiffin Rockwell.

Henry Clay's life in the Confederate Army followed the many ups and downs of the rebel force during the war. He received a commission as a captain in the Fifty-first North Carolina Infantry Regiment and saw a great deal of action. His regiment fought at Roanoke Island, Richmond, and Charleston, including the furious defense of Fort Wagner in 1863. A year later, Rockwell's regiment participated in a number of battles including Drewry's Bluff, Cold Harbor, Petersburg, the miserably failed assault at Fort Harrison, and Wilmington. During this period, the Fifty-First Regiment was reduced from a total of 1,100 officers and men to 145 men.[3] Captain Rockwell was indeed a very lucky man. He managed to survive the long and bloody conflict and surrendered with his regiment at Durham in April of 1865.

After the surrender, Captain Henry Clay Rockwell returned to a different world. With a heavy heart, Captain Rockwell trudged home "where the ravages of War were evident on every side and [he] began the struggle to restore his fortune and help upbuild his ruined State."[4] Unfortunately for his wealthy family, his father Chester lost almost everything he had after the war and died in 1871. For a young, formerly wealthy heir, this new turn of events was a calamity. His people had lost a war, his family had lost everything they owned, and Captain Rockwell now had to earn a living in an area that had been ransacked by the conflict. But Henry Clay Rockwell was not one to wallow in despair—the hopeful and pioneering spirit of his ancestors surged within him.

He cast aside any thoughts of self-pity and forged a new path that his son and grandson would follow unceasingly. Henry Clay chose to serve his community and spent his remaining years helping his fellow citizens recover from the destruction of the Civil War. His grandson Paul, Kiffin's brother, wrote, "Old inhabitants of Whiteville and Columbus County still remember and relate his kindness and generosity to less fortunate comrades and fellow citizens."[5] Unfortunately, Henry Clay soon followed his father in death, which began a cycle of untimely demise in the Rockwell family. Henry Clay died in 1874, leaving four sons and one daughter. James Chester Rockwell, Kiffin's father, was the second son of Henry Clay. He had no wealth, no land, and no specific skills to inherit from his father. His mother and siblings were barely over their husband and father's death before disaster struck again. James Chester's youngest brother and only sister also died before his fourteenth birthday. He and his mother and brothers had little choice but to keep moving forward.

It is difficult to imagine the sadness that must have characterized the life of James Chester Rockwell, but he wanted to follow his father's example in service to others. But before he could do anything, he knew he had to receive an education. As a boy, he quickly demonstrated a knack for scholarship and studied under Professor W.G. Quackenbush of Laurinburg, a man of immense talent who was revered by the local people. Professor Quackenbush was an orphaned and crippled Virginian who opened an academy offering a variety of courses to students after the Civil War. Up to a hundred children studied Latin, Greek, geography, history, math, English, grammar, and music with the professor. The town of Laurinburg "thought so highly of their professor that after his death in 1903 a monument was raised in his honor and placed in front of the courthouse on Main Street."[6] James Rockwell excelled at the academy, but he also read extensively on his own. Already regarded as a child prodigy, James sold his first poem at age eleven to a distinguished South Carolina poet named Paul Hamilton Hayne.[7] He continued writing and had his poems, essays, and book reviews published in a new journal called the *State Chronicle*, where his work began to win acceptance in northern publications.[8]

James Chester Rockwell finally found his calling after tragedy struck yet again. In 1886, his oldest brother William died. His older brother had always supported his writing endeavors, and the grief from his death caused James's health to decline as well.[9] James Rockwell moved to Old Fort, where he met a Baptist minister named the Reverend C.M. Murchison, who convinced him to enroll in the Southern Theological Seminary in Louisville, Kentucky. Before he even completed his studies, he knew his passion was in ministry. During seminary he discovered another passion as well. A young, high-spirited lady named Loula Ayres caught his eye and an engagement soon followed. James married Loula at her family home of Beachwood in Marion County, South Carolina. Unfortunately, the newly married couple could not stay in Louisville for long. The doctors advised Rockwell to move to the mountains due to his deteriorating health, and he was forced to leave seminary before completing his program.[10]

James Rockwell served first at a church in Waynesville, North Carolina, where he became known as a "preacher of great forensic power," and the *Waynesville Courier* reported that he left the congregation spellbound.[11] Rockwell was tall with a large black beard, and the former governor of Tennessee, Ben W. Hooper, described him as "somewhat like my conception of one of the Twelve Apostles."[12] After pastoring the Waynesville church and another in Morristown, Tennessee, James and Loula finally found a home in 1890 at the First Baptist Church in Newport, Tennessee. Loula had earlier given birth to their first son, Paul, and soon after arriving in Newport she gave birth to their daughter, Agnes.

Kiffin Yates Rockwell was born on September 20, 1892, and his parents' faith was manifested in the names they gave to him. The name Kiffin was given in honor of William Kiffin, an English home missionary in the fifteenth century, while the name Yates came from Matthew Yates, a foreign missionary from North Carolina in the nineteenth century.[13] Kiffin's older brother Paul had fond memories of his younger brother's entrance into this world: "I well remember the first time I saw Kiffin. I was about four years old, and my sister and I had been sent to spend the

Kiffin's father, the Reverend James Chester Rockwell, known as "a preacher of great forensic power." He was an accomplished poet who endured great hardships before dying at the age of twenty-five (from the Rockwell family collection, courtesy Sybil Robb).

night with some little friends," he wrote. "When we returned home in the morning, our father took us by the hand and led us into our mother's bedroom to see 'the present Dr. Snoddy had brought during the night.' As I looked at the tiny red mite my feelings were of pride and pleasure that I had a brother."[14]

Kiffin's earliest years were shaped by the beautiful vistas and difficult conditions of life in the Appalachian Mountains. Newport, Tennessee, was an interesting place to live in the years after the Civil War. The little town was nestled in the Appalachian Mountains about thirty miles from Knoxville, but its picturesque location belied the relatively turbulent history of the area. In the years leading up to the Revolutionary War, several clans of Scots-Irish chose the rugged landscape of the Appalachian Mountains as a new home for their families. Many of these men fought fiercely in the Revolutionary War and then continued to fight after the war. Newport was located along a Cherokee Indian route and thus was an area of conflict between American settlers and Cherokee Indians during the late 1700s.

After the Civil War, the area was somewhat isolated until enterprising companies began constructing railways through the mountains of eastern Tennessee. By the 1890s, Newport was still a quaint town of about 900 people with its share of mountain ruffians.

Some of those ruffians had an interesting encounter with their local preacher. Paul described his father as a man of great physical and moral courage and one who was equally content at home surrounded by his books as he was outside enjoying life.[15] The Rockwell home was on the outskirts of town near the main road leading off into the mountains, and on this particular day several drunken men from two enemy mountain clans began to fight outside their home. Preacher Rockwell went out to stop the fighting, but the men responded by striking him and threatening to kill him. James Rockwell held his ground, however, and eventually succeeded in convincing them to make peace. Paul clearly remembered that a few days after the fight, "men belonging to one of the clans appeared at the Rockwell home with a supply of chicken and eggs. They did not know how to apologize for their recent blows and threats, so they brought a good will offering to the peacemaker."[16]

James Chester Rockwell clearly left an

Loula Ayres Rockwell, Kiffin's mother. Loula was a strong woman who raised three children on her own after her husband's untimely death. She adamantly opposed Kiffin's decision to fight for France until she realized the cause for which he fought (from the Rockwell family collection, courtesy Sybil Robb).

enduring impression on his young children, and all three of them sought to replicate his example in their own lives. Unfortunately, the Rockwell children were not able to enjoy their father's company for long. A few days before Kiffin's first birthday, James Rockwell died of typhoid fever and they laid him to rest in Morristown.

Despite his limited time with his father, Kiffin's character was imprinted with the experience, talents, and character of James Rockwell. His father and grandfather had overcome immense personal and collective tragedy by focusing their efforts on others. Kiffin and his brother Paul inherited their father's gift of communication and love for life. They also inherited a sharp mind and an ability to lead other men. But above all else, Kiffin felt an irresistible pull toward service that he could never fully shake even when he tried to escape from it. His desire to serve a cause lay smoldering for years, leading to much uncertainty and dissatisfaction in his life until his destiny slammed headlong into an event preordained to change the world. Kiffin's destiny was shaped in large part by his father. James Chester Rockwell's most famous poem "The Poet's Story" is nearly a prophecy of Kiffin's future—his heart bled and sang, carrying a melody across a vast ocean:

> *The sweetest songs are those that spring*
> *From hearts that bleed, and, bleeding, sing;*
> *Through songs like these doth ever roll*
> *The mystic music of the soul.*
> *If we have weal, if we have woe,*
> *If we have rights, if we have wrongs,*
> *The world must all our feelings know—*
> *We tell our stories in our songs.*[17]

As strong as his father's influence was, two other individuals particularly shaped his future. The first was his mother Loula. After losing her husband, she had to scrape together a living in a depressed area where a working woman was unusual and often unwelcome. Raising three young children in her situation forced her to transform into a strict disciplinarian. She demanded swift obedience—something that would soon cause a seemingly irreparable break with her son. In the meantime, Loula decided to stay in Newport as a teacher and eventually founded a system of schools. While Agnes spent much of her time in her room reading books, Paul and Kiffin enjoyed their afternoon hours outside in the rugged hills around their home.

The Civil War still loomed large in their lives, largely because both of their grandfathers fought in the war. There still appeared to be a great deal of animosity between supporters of the North and those who sided with the South. The city of Newport tried to remain neutral during the Civil War, but apparently the two boys quickly learned the prevailing attitude of the Newport locals. Paul made no attempt to mask his partiality when he wrote, "The lowest class of East Tennessee mountaineers turned traitor to their State during the Confederate War, and sided with the North. Not many of them served in the regular Federal Forces, however, but forming gangs of bushwackers they stole the horses, cattle, and poultry of Confederate sympathizers, attacked the women, and plundered the houses of men who were away fighting in the Southern Army."[18] Paul went on to describe the enduring resentment towards these "scoundrels" and how the boys of Newport refought the "War between the States" on a frequent basis.

The boys certainly grew up with a rigid view of what happened during the Civil War, but then this is hardly surprising as the grandsons of Enoch Shaw Ayres. Enoch Ayres was the other major influence in Kiffin's life. Loula Ayres's father was born in 1835 and inherited a large plantation in Marion County, South Carolina, near the town of Nichols. Enoch grew cotton, tobacco, and rice on the plantation, and his estate resembled the average plantation of the type found throughout the South. When rumblings of war began to occur in 1861, Enoch (like Kiffin's paternal grandfather) chose to serve in the Southern army. He was one of the first to volunteer for South Carolina and received the rank of sergeant in Company 1, 8th South Carolina Infantry Regiment. Enoch's three brothers joined with him, and according to the naturally partial view of his grandson Paul, "his regiment was one of the finest in the Southern Armies, and was always there where the battle waxed fiercest."[19] In fact, the 8th South Carolina Regiment did see a great deal of action during the war. Enoch Ayres fought in some of the most famous battles of the Civil War, including the First Battle of Bull Run, Williamsburg, the capture of Maryland Heights, and Antietam. The 8th South Carolina fought valiantly but lost over half of its effective strength in the terribly bloody battle at Antietam.

Enoch's unit continued fighting in the Battles of Fredericksburg and Chancellorsville. Paul and Kiffin sat many times on their grandfather's knee and listened to him speak of how he "heard the volley fired which mortally wounded the noble Stonewall Jackson."[20] Whenever he spoke of that day, Enoch's voice would crack, and he would remain on the verge of tears as he related the story to his grandsons of Jackson's mortal wounding by "friendly fire." One of his brothers was killed in the Battle of Gettysburg, but Enoch continued fighting with General Longstreet's corps in Tennessee, in the Battle of the Wilderness, in Richmond and at Petersburg. Enoch's brother John fell wounded at Petersburg and was sent home, but as before, Enoch stayed with his unit and continued the exhausting campaigns. He fought with General Early in the Shenandoah Valley and then went back with his unit to South Carolina in order to reinforce Charleston in 1865. Amazingly, Enoch Shaw Ayres survived the entire conflict just as Kiffin's paternal grandfather, Henry Clay Rockwell, did. In fact, both of Kiffin's grandfathers fought in the Battle of Bentonville, and their units both surrendered at Durham in April of 1865. When Enoch Ayres returned to his plantation home in South Carolina, an utterly tragic scene awaited him. Just before the end of the war, his father, mother, brother John, and all his sisters and younger brothers had died during an epidemic of smallpox. Enoch and his surviving brother Thomas divided the plantation between them.

It is absolutely essential to grasp the significance of these stories in order to truly understand who Kiffin Rockwell was. Kiffin inherited a great deal from his father but was forced to grow up without him. In his young mind, his grandfather Enoch was one man who was truly larger than life. Loula Rockwell would pack up the kids and a few things every summer and travel to her parents' house in South Carolina. Every year, Kiffin spent months with his grandfather hearing the stories, picturing the events, and drawing his own conclusions.

Paul and Kiffin inherited the baggage that many white Southern men carried in the days after the Civil War. The men had lost a bloody internal conflict that took the lives of much of its young generation. They returned home to death and disease, and then they quickly lost much of the wealth that they had acquired before the war. The men of the South also had to deal with "carpetbaggers" who they believed were taking advantage of the dire situation, and they lost the slaves who were the foundation of their economic system. Today it is amply apparent that the South's stubborn refusal to give up the institution of slavery is appalling. However, through modern eyes, it is also easy to overlook the trauma that reigned in the lives of southern Civil War veterans. Their world was literally turned upside down. For the former slaves it was a moment of triumph and freedom because their world had been upside down for centuries. In light of the hundreds of years that slavery existed in America, it is difficult to sympathize with Southern plantation owners, but it is also necessary to see the world through their eyes in order to fully grasp their condition.

For a young boy like Kiffin, the tales of the Civil War were legends of contradiction. On one hand, his grandfather's stories were filled with moments of glory and fighting for their homeland. Kiffin would "listen for hours to his grandfather, his great-uncle Tommie, and other elderly men of the neighborhood recounting their battles, their marches.... His imagination and his ambition were constantly fired with desire to shine upon the battlefield for a worthy purpose."[21] Yet on the other hand, Kiffin clearly saw the destruction wrought by the Civil War and the societal divisions that continued after it. The men whom Kiffin adored also discussed "their sufferings from hunger and cold, and their disappointment and grief over the 'Lost Cause,' and their struggles after."[22] He understood his family's past suffering and triumphs, but he witnessed the aftermath. Kiffin loved his country dearly, and he saw what the Civil War had done in the South. But he learned from a young age what it was like to fight for a cause, and one has to wonder if he determined at that time to fight for a cause that the *whole* country could support.

Kiffin and Paul were certainly not immune to the prejudices that gripped the South after the traumatic conflict. In many ways they inherited these prejudices during the months they spent sitting in the presence of the grandfather they adored. In Kiffin's later writing it is difficult to determine his views on the societal issues prevalent in his day and beyond. It is not a stretch to assume that Paul and Kiffin often grew up hearing about African Americans in derogatory terms. To what extent Kiffin internalized such talk is difficult to say, since he did not specifically address the issue in the letters of his that survive.

And yet in a uniquely American way, these two boys who inherited this post–Civil War societal distress would later voluntarily choose to fight for their country in another war. And when their country decided to remain neutral, they offered their services to France instead. In a variety of ways, the First World War had a purifying effect on a United States still struggling with the aftermath of its brother-on-brother conflict. Once the U.S. entered the war, North and South joined together and fought valiantly to defend freedom in a foreign land. The purifying process would unfortunately take America over a century from the end of the Civil War—and in reality it still continues today—but for the men of the South, the First World War was the beginning of a redemptive story.

Paul and Kiffin surely did not sense these epic currents during their summers spent in South Carolina, but it is essential to understand this element of their story. The two boys who would later volunteer to fight in the First World War were not flawless and innocent young men enjoying lazy summer days. They carried scars and imperfections, but like many of the men and women in their families, they rose above their circumstances. Their story is the story of the South—one must understand the South to understand them.

2

Leaving Home

None of these burdensome topics weighed heavily on the young minds of Paul and Kiffin as they romped through their grandfather's fields. The coming war was in the distant future, and the Rockwell kids were able to just enjoy life as all children should. Yet during his childhood and teenage years, Kiffin's unique character began to solidify. He was a sharp boy with an insatiable drive to accomplish challenges and achieve difficult goals. As he grew older, his expectations broadened significantly, and he quickly realized that he was not cut out for a normal existence. The pursuit of justice and the desire to follow an endeavor with great purpose were powerful forces within his soul. Kiffin needed a cause and would not be satisfied until he found it.

In the meantime, the boys spent most of their time enjoying life outdoors. The region where Enoch Ayres's plantation was located had vast forests of timber including pine in the upland areas and cypress in the swampy lowlands. The boys chased deer, rabbits, squirrels, raccoons, foxes, and a great many other animals during those carefree summers. They even came across alligators in the Lumber and Pee Dee Rivers that were located only a few miles away. Kiffin was apparently the better shot, and he learned how to handle a gun before he was ten years old. He was also an excellent fisherman after learning the art of hooking trout and bass from his grandfather. Paul admitted that Kiffin did not care for his books, but that his brother did have a "keen and clever mind," enabling him to learn his lessons quickly. Young Kiffin seemed to be an all-around sportsman, excelling at swimming, horseback riding, and any other activity that he put his mind to. Paul remembers him as being "especially fond of mounting a wild and unruly Porto [sic] Rican pony we had at Newport."[1]

Loula Rockwell continued moving forward despite the sorrow of losing her husband. She poured herself into her three children while she simultaneously worked to provide for their needs. She worked with the town of Newport to open the Newport Grammar School and served there as a teacher for a few years. Loula Rockwell was selected as the school's first female principal and served in that capacity for two full school years. She was exceptionally well-educated for her day, and one hundred years would pass in Newport before another woman served as a principal at Newport Grammar School.[2] The Rockwell kids went to school there and continued their adventures outdoors as soon as they emerged from their lessons.

As is often the case in the transition to adulthood, the carefree days eventually came to an end. When Kiffin was still in grade school, Loula Rockwell moved her family to Asheville, North Carolina, in pursuit of better opportunities available to herself and the three kids. The schools in Asheville were much better than those in Newport, and the

2. Leaving Home

intriguing history of the area was enough to satisfy the rampant curiosity of the young Kiffin Rockwell. The first settlers in the area were men who had fought in the Battle of King's Mountain, a decisive American victory in North Carolina during the Revolutionary War. Furthermore, the Rockwells arrived in Asheville around the turn of the century, and the city was more than likely still talking about the majestic Biltmore mansion just down the road. George Vanderbilt opened his Biltmore Estate as a country retreat to family and friends on Christmas Eve of 1895, but he came to live year-round at the Biltmore in 1898 after his marriage to Edith Stuyvesant Dresser. It was no doubt an exciting time to live in Asheville.

Kiffin entered the Orange Street School in Asheville and quickly earned the admiration of a teacher named Mrs. Mary Walden Williamson. He remained somewhat impatient with schoolwork, yet clearly possessed a gifted mind. In fact, Mrs. Williamson documented her impression of Kiffin at the age of fifteen. She described him as "handsome, intelligent, chivalrous boy of fifteen, immaculate in person as in honor, impatient of the tedium of school routine, restive, though ever courteous under restraint; with serious deep-set, gray-blue eyes, aglow with enthusiasm over tales of daring adventure; breaking rarely into surprising light of merriment."[3] Mary Williamson's description of Kiffin could aptly describe him years after he left her classroom. He was always impatient with routines and lived for the day when he could chart his own adventure. Kiffin would always remain mostly serious, but in his life and in his later writings he retained a voracious drive to accomplish something great.

Kiffin's boyhood home in Asheville, North Carolina. His mother remained in the home for a number of years. It is still standing at 142 Hillside Street near a historical marker honoring Kiffin Rockwell (courtesy North Carolina State Historic Preservation Office).

For a boy filled with such passion and drive, grammar school and high school seemed more like prisons than opportunities to expand the mind. Kiffin also began to chafe more frequently under the burden of his mother's discipline. He could not fully empathize with her plight and never understood why she chose to be so strict. And yet this was also the time when Kiffin evidently began to realize the strength of his mother Loula. Her faith not only sustained her through the loss of her husband and the difficult years of raising children on her own, but she also managed to make quite a name for herself in the state of North Carolina. Before arriving in Asheville, Loula Rockwell received training in the medical practice of osteopathy and opened up a practice in 1903 with a man named Dr. William Banks Meacham. After finishing his degree as doctor of osteopathy from the Boston Institute of Osteopathy, Dr. Meacham and his wife arrived in Asheville just before he set up the practice with Loula Rockwell.

At the time, the practice of osteopathy was quite controversial. Dr. A.T. Still established the first school of osteopathy shortly after the Civil War and attempted to treat the whole person by emphasizing the relationship between musculoskeletal structure and organic function.[4] Many osteopathic physicians were convinced that traditional methods of medicating patients had a detrimental effect on their health and that many ailments could be cured through the manipulation of bones or muscles. The field had many benefits, including the focus on the whole body and natural remedies, but at times the pursuit of osteopathy seemed more like a social movement than a practice of medicine.

Dr. Meacham himself often acted more like a prophet than a physician. He later became the president of the National Osteopathic Association in 1916, and in one of his first addresses to the association he loudly sounded off against critics by proclaiming, "There is not force enough in the organization of the American Medical Association, there is not force enough in Congress, there is not force enough in the Central Powers and Allies combined to kill osteopathy, unless we murder it ourselves."[5] His zeal was clearly evident and apparently contagious. Dr. Meacham built a sanitarium (or health resort) in Asheville in 1912 that became an enormous success; adorned with Persian rugs, silk, draperies, and mahogany furniture, it eventually offered forty bedrooms where patients would come to stay from all over the country.[6] His enthusiasm certainly had some effect, for today the Ottari Sanitarium is on the National Registry of Historical Places.

Loula Rockwell's involvement in the burgeoning field was somewhat of an oddity to the people of Asheville, but she remained a respected member of the community. In fact, her belief in osteopathy is perhaps not surprising given the set of circumstances she had to deal with in her life. After losing her husband, she clung to her children and her faith. While the family was still living in Newport, Paul had serious ailments every year that terrified his mother. During the wintertime, he almost always contracted pneumonia, and the Newport doctors finally told Loula Rockwell that they did not believe her son would live beyond the age of fourteen. Despite this grim prognosis, Loula did not give up and pursued other options. She finally found a traveling osteopathic physician who Paul later claimed saved his life.[7] After Paul's healing from pneumonia, Loula Rockwell was a committed believer in the benefits of osteopathy, and she pursued her own career with gusto.

Much of the turmoil in Kiffin's relationship with his mother came from their divergent visions of what he should do with his life. She had forged her own successful path by embracing education, and she encouraged all of them to lead lives of scholarship. She described her thought process: "When my husband died, six years after our marriage, leaving me with three babies—for babies and books, he said, were all that preachers had in this world—my life became theirs. It was my purpose to train them for careers of scholarship, and my hope and inspiration in this task was that they would be my comfort and stay in old age."[8] Unfortunately, a life of scholarship was akin to being locked in prison for someone like Kiffin. A few years before, Paul had embraced the academic route and joined Wake Forest for a time before transferring to Washington and Lee University to study history and modern languages. Paul's departure was a blow to his younger brother since they had been constant companions for years. His sister Agnes departed soon after Paul to attend Wellesley College, and Kiffin was on his own at the Rockwell home until he graduated high school. After graduation, Kiffin was well aware that the carefree days of summers in South Carolina were gone, and he knew he could not bear the misery of normal college life by joining his brother at Washington and Lee. Instead of joining his siblings, Kiffin decided to strike out on his own. If a scholarly career was not his style, he figured the military life would suit him well. The tales of his grandfathers still thundered within him, and his chosen destination was none other than the storied Virginia Military Institute.

Loula Rockwell was never enthusiastic about her youngest child serving in the military, but she acquiesced because of Kiffin's obvious passion for the vocation. Loula had witnessed the aftermath of the Civil War and had personally experienced its lingering effects through the death of her husband and many other family members who had died over the years. Her discomfort with the idea of a soldier's life only became more pronounced as Kiffin grew older.

By all accounts, Kiffin Rockwell loved VMI and the challenges that it offered. The Virginia Military Institute was founded in 1839 as the nation's first state military college.[9] It was located in the beautiful Shenandoah Valley in the historic city of Lexington, Virginia—the same town where Paul was studying at Washington and Lee. Paul was happy to be near his younger brother again and remembered Kiffin enjoying the hallowed atmosphere of the school. His starry-eyed sibling would walk the halls and marvel at memories of Stonewall Jackson and other American military heroes. One of his favorite stories was undoubtedly the Battle of New Market, Virginia, where the VMI cadet corps fought under General John C. Breckinridge between a fork of the Shenandoah River and the Massanutten Mountain in May of 1864.

As a first year student, Kiffin was a "rat," and he endured the severe hazing that was common in those days. Paul claimed that the rats "were beaten regularly and religiously with bed-slats, tin dippers, flats of bayonets, broomsticks, or any thing that came to the hand of the masterful third-classmen."[10] Kiffin apparently did not let the hazing bother him because he would show off his bruises and stripes every Saturday when he met Paul for lunch at his fraternity. Washington and Lee University was only a few hundred yards away from the grounds of VMI, so Paul could keep an eye on his younger brother. Unfortunately, Paul could not control what happened to Kiffin during the week. He wrote, "I would fairly froth at the mouth with rage and indignation—I was never able to see him suffer, and even as a little boy would weep bitterly when Kiffin was punished for some mischief—but Kiffin would merely laugh in his dry way, and say that it was all in the game, and that the best way to make men of the 'rats' was to haze them."[11]

Kiffin certainly cemented his sense of honor during those months at the Virginia Military Institute. He always carried a profound desire for justice and wished to play a role in its enforcement, so VMI was a good place for him. Since its founding, the cadets at VMI lived by a code of honorable behavior, but interestingly enough they only established the cadet-run Honor Court in 1908—the year Kiffin attended the institute. The statement at the heart of VMI's honor code is *a cadet does not lie, cheat, steal, nor tolerate those who do*.[12] The code must have often been a subject of conversation during Kiffin's time at VMI, and it obviously left an indelible impression on him. Later in his service for France that started in the trenches of the Western Front, he would see this code routinely violated, and he always felt some measure of obligation to respond quickly and forcefully. But even at VMI, Kiffin began to long for something more, and in 1909 he pursued and received an appointment to the United States Naval Academy.

However, his prestigious appointment to the Naval Academy would not long satisfy Kiffin's thirst for a life of honor and adventure. At the time, he did not fully grasp what he was searching for, but he quickly realized that the Naval Academy was not for him. Kiffin entered the Werntz Preparatory School at Annapolis in September of 1909 to take a course for the Naval Academy entrance exams. By his own admission, he did not admire the boys he met at Werntz who would be his classmates, and this perception played into his dissatisfaction with his future at Annapolis. But his greatest concern was his prediction of the life that awaited him in the U.S. Navy. Paul writes that Kiffin "got the impression that it would be many a day before the United States Navy would see action, and caring nothing for naval or army life in time of peace, he wrote and asked me to try to influence our mother to let him resign his appointment...."[13] Loula Rockwell was comfortable with Kiffin's serving in the U.S. Navy during a time of peace, and she fought against her son's decision to give up his appointment to the Naval Academy. In the end she relented, and Kiffin decided to join Paul at Washington and Lee University. Paul still had one year remaining and happily convinced his fraternity brothers to accept Kiffin into the Virginia Epsilon chapter of the Sigma Phi Epsilon fraternity.

The university was founded in 1749 but was ultimately named after George Washington and Robert E. Lee. After the Revolutionary War, the Liberty Hall Academy in the town of Lexington was struggling, so George Washington gave the school its first major endowment and the trustees changed the name to Washington Academy. Washington responded to the honor by writing, "To promote the Literature in this rising Empire, and to encourage the Arts, have ever been amongst the warmest wishes of my heart."[14] Many years later, after the Civil War, General Robert E. Lee decided to accept the position of college president at Washington College in 1865. General Lee feared that he "might draw upon the College a feeling of hostility," but also added, "I think it the duty of every citizen in the present condition of the Country, to do all in his power to aid the restoration of peace and harmony."[15] By the time Paul and Kiffin studied there, the United States was well on its way to restoring peace and harmony in the nation.

Kiffin thoroughly enjoyed his time and his studies at Washington and Lee, and life was happy and carefree. He was able to spend more time with Paul and also majored in history—something Washington and Lee University had in abundance. Paul's description of his brother during his college years is an interesting one: "He was bright enough not to have to grind in order to learn his lesson, and had plenty of time to mix with the other students. A good judge of human nature, he did not quickly make friends with people and accept them into his intimacy; but he was never discourteous to anyone, and when he deemed someone worthy, he was a real and devoted friend. Therefore, he was very popular and well liked among his fellows. Tall and handsome, with clear blue eyes, a graceful dancer and of a pleasing manner, he was much sought after by the girls, but he was not of a sentimental nature, and was quite unspoiled."[16]

Kiffin remained restless and slightly impatient. He enjoyed the history of the school, his friendship with some of the students, and his time with Paul, but satisfaction always seemed to elude him. Paul wrote, "As I look back, it is clear to me that Kiffin was all this while only unconsciously marking time. He was in school more from family habit and tradition than from a real desire to follow classical studies. He usually had a far-away, dreamy look in his eyes, and often seemed to be living in another world from that surrounding him."[17] The young dreamer left Washington and Lee in 1912, and his family and friends could not keep him close. Kiffin was in pursuit of something, and what it was he still did not know. But he knew he wanted to see the world, and like many in his generation, and the generations before, his eyes turned to the West.

Kiffin set out on a grand adventure that took him from Virginia to the West Coast of the United States. What he did along the way is now lost in history, but he did travel through Western Canada once he made it to the Pacific coast. Kiffin eventually settled in San Francisco and nearly remained there for good. He enjoyed San Francisco a great deal, perceiving it as "more nearly like that of France than any other place he knew in America."[18] Indeed, San Francisco was an exciting and fascinating place to live in 1912. A man named Allan Dunn offered a captivating description of the city in that very year: "To pass the portals of the Golden Gate is to cross the threshold of Adventure. The great hearts that reared this metropolis ... from a huddled hamlet of the sand dunes are the light hearts who so cheerfully rebuilt their city on the ashes of a great disaster [i.e., the earthquake and fire of 1906], and, accomplishing it in record time, promptly forgot for all time there had ever been a fire at all and invited the world to a great exposition that celebrates the joining of two oceans, the hyphening of two continents, a romance of modern engineering intimately connected with the future of San Francisco."[19]

The city also teemed with people from all backgrounds and societies. The French occupied high society as bankers and high-class merchants, but also worked as chefs, bakers, and laundry folk. The Italians were bankers, merchants, wine culturists, fishermen and laborers. The Chinese and Japanese lived there in abundance, and every nationality seemed to have its own district within the city that the residents constructed to be identical to their native societies.

Kiffin Rockwell started an advertising agency in San Francisco and at one point had over twenty people working for him. He was tall and skinny, but even at the age of twenty Kiffin looked older than he really was. As a result, people afforded him a degree of respect that was unusual for someone his age. Kiffin's choice of entering the advertising profession is an interesting one, for at the time advertising was in the midst of a major transformation. Paul Terry Cherington described this transformation in 1916 when he wrote, "During the last ten years notable strides have been made in the advancement of business ethics.... From a more or less mysterious charlatanism advertising has gradually risen to the dignity of a profession, if not a science."[20] The advertising business was one that developed "from within itself exacting standards of ethics and morals," and leaders in the profession were "determined that advertising [was] to be as free from errors and waste as its friends [could] make it."[21] For someone who clearly believed moral and ethical behavior was essential, Kiffin chose a profession that at the time demanded very high moral and ethical standards.

Yet the West could not keep him for long. Something was drawing him back home, and he would soon find the destiny that had thus far eluded him. The urge to return to the South was strong within Kiffin, so in the fall of 1913 he made his way back to Asheville. Unfortunately, his reappearance only kindled the growing fire between him and his mother. Loula was not happy with the uncertain direction his life was headed, and she was especially displeased with his choice of acquaintances. One day Loula caught Kiffin lounging outside a pool hall with people of whom she disapproved, and she lost her temper. Loula marched up to her son brandishing a horsewhip and lashed him publicly in front of his friends. Kiffin was incensed and humiliated by the episode, and he wasted no time packing his bags. He left Asheville as soon as he could get a ticket out of town and headed south to reunite with his brother Paul. Kiffin never saw his mother Loula again.[22]

Paul was working in Atlanta, and Kiffin arrived during the day on the first of January 1914. He let himself into Paul's room, where he found his brother fast asleep. Paul wrote: "I shall never forget that morning when Kiffin arrived. I had been up late the evening before, properly ushering in the New Year, and was asleep at the Georgia Tech chapter house of our fraternity when I was awakened by the feeling that someone was watching me. I opened my eyes, and there stood Kiffin at the foot of my bed, with an amused expression on his face. I was amazed to see how tall he had grown; he was then a little over six feet two inches, having grown fully three inches since I had seen him."[23] Both of them immediately decided to never again part company. Paul was always very protective of Kiffin, and they made a great team. The two young men began to search for a suitable apartment where they could discover what life would bring them in the city of Atlanta. Little did the two of them know how drastically their lives would change in seven short months. Kiffin quickly put his split from his mother behind him and found a job in Atlanta's burgeoning advertising industry. He worked for Massengale Advertising Agency and achieved considerable success for the short time he was there.

In what would become a familiar refrain in his life, Kiffin's organization was no ordinary advertising business. The Massengale Advertising Agency was one of the best known and most far-reaching influences in the advertising world at the time. Its founder was a man named Elmo Massengale, who "was possessed of ideas which were deemed revolutionary by those who are always content to remain in the rut of mediocrity."[24]

Massengale was a major player in Atlanta's civic and commercial affairs, and he ran a tight ship. He employed "only the best writers, the most skilled artists and the ablest executives" with a "strict adherence to the highest commercial ethics."[25] Kiffin had inherited his father's gift of writing, so he was in good company among the other exceptional writers. He and Paul wrote a paper called "The Commerce of Greater Atlanta" that they intended to help boost the commercial activity in their adopted city.[26] But mostly they stayed busy in their jobs until the heat of the summer arrived.

As the hot, humid air stifled the city of Atlanta, a great storm started to rumble across the ocean. News from Europe was alarming as the month of July waned, and rumors of war were constantly on the minds of the two young men. The storm was brewing. The first thunderclap occurred at the end of July but was only heard within the Rockwell family.

Kiffin's beloved grandfather, Enoch Shaw Ayres, died on July 26, 1914. The one who had practically been a father to the boys was no more; it was now their time.

The memory of Enoch Ayres's exploits in battle must have loomed large as Paul and Kiffin met with two of their friends on the last Sunday of July. They all sat around the lunch table and talked about the coming war that most of them thought was inevitable. Kiffin and Paul talked about how interesting it would be to fight for France and how America needed to support the French cause. He and Kiffin were very well read in French history and fully sympathized with the side of France. However, their friends did not share their enthusiasm and seemed not to comprehend why they cared so much about a war across a vast ocean. Paul described how their two friends with "small imagination outside their business, agreed mildly that it would be a great thing to fight against the Germans, and turned the conversation to the hands they had held in their last poker game."[27]

Kiffin was not one to talk idly, however. He did things with passion or not at all. After their friends left, Kiffin cornered Paul and told him that his mind was made up. The two of them discussed the issue at length and ultimately decided to offer their services to France. Before the war had even been officially declared, Kiffin sat down and wrote the following letter:

> 136 Peachtree Street,
> Atlanta, Georgia
> August 3, 1914
>
> HIS HONOR THE FRENCH CONSUL,
>   New Orleans, Louisiana.
>
> DEAR SIR:
>   I desire to offer my services to the French Government in case of actual warfare between France and Germany, and wish to know whether I can report to you at New Orleans and go over with the French reservists who have been called out, or must I go to France before enlisting?
>   I am twenty-one years old, and have had military training at the Virginia Military Institute. I am very anxious to see military service, and had rather fight under the French flag than any other, as I greatly admire your nation.
>   If my services can be used by your country, I will bring my brother, who also desires to fight for the French flag.
>   Trusting to receive a favorable reply from you soon, I beg to remain
>
> Yours most sincerely,
> KIFFIN YATES ROCKWELL[28]

The die had been cast. The storm clouds in Europe were no longer just brewing—they erupted with a fury. The day after Kiffin sent his letter to the French consul, as the clock struck midnight on the night of August 4, the world was at war. Paul and Kiffin had vowed to never again leave one another. They would find their fate on the field of battle, just as their grandfathers had done two generations before. The battlefield waiting for them was in France, and they would soon discover how awful the war of their generation would be.

3

World War I Begins

When Kiffin penned his letter to the French consulate, he had no idea what he was getting into. To us, a century removed from the Europe of 1914, such a rash decision seems foolhardy and reckless. But the war we know now as the First World War was not the war that Paul and Kiffin went to fight. It was not the war that Britain, France, Germany, and Russia meant to fight either. In the minds of European leaders at the time, war was an essential tool among a variety of instruments available to achieve national objectives. War was certainly not intended to be a bloodbath with little chance to achieve anything of strategic value. Europe had been fighting wars for centuries—some worse than others—and this war was supposed to be yet another stanza in the cyclical song of European warfare. Unfortunately something went terribly wrong, and in 1914 the world hurtled toward an unforeseen disaster.

This war was also different in that American youth like Paul and Kiffin Rockwell were champing at the bit to participate and volunteered in droves. Young Americans had certainly fought in previous European conflicts, but this war drew Americans in far greater numbers and from a much higher social class than any previous European adventure. Why did so many American men flock to the conflict? And why did sons from wealthy families and graduates from elite schools like Harvard and Yale volunteer?

There were certainly a number of motivations driving American youth, but Kiffin's reasons for volunteering were similar to the vast majority of his future comrades. One of the main reasons behind their behavior was the nationalistic fervor present throughout the world at the time. The military historian John Keegan cheekily wrote, "It is commonplace to say that Europe in 1914 was a continent of naked nationalism: it was true all the same."[1] Nationalism certainly proved a potent motivation to the populations in Europe, but it also affected the transplanted Europeans across the Atlantic Ocean. Kiffin firmly believed it was his nationalistic duty to support France in her time of need. He wanted the United States to pay its debt to Rochambeau, Lafayette, and the other brave Frenchmen who helped America win its revolution. And if the United States chose to stay out of the war, then he would help pay the debt on his own.

Another reason related to the nationalistic motivation was France's self-proclaimed position at the center of Western civilization. Since the French Revolution, intellectuals in France had been trumpeting their country's universal mission to spread liberty, equality, and fraternity throughout Europe and beyond.[2] This idea resonated in the hearts of many Americans. Young men like Paul and Kiffin were certainly aware of this claim and believed in it to the extent that they were willing to fight for the democratic values that France claimed to hold so dear. Many of the elite young American men who volunteered to fight for France had also seen the country in person while traveling with their parents or living there in summer homes. France held a special place in the hearts of many Americans.

One final reason motivating a vast number of the American volunteers was simply the idea of adventure abroad. The war that was starting in 1914 would be their generation's great conflict and they did not want to miss out. The symbolic closing of the American frontier around the turn of the century had much to do with the spike in American volunteers in World War I when compared to previous European conflicts. Frederick Jackson Turner's hypothesis of the American frontier acting as an outlet for American democracy and character has merit when viewed through the lens of World War I. For hundreds of years, men and women seeking adventure in America turned their eyes to the lands in the west that were unknown to them. Kiffin saw this firsthand during his travels to San Francisco. He went west searching for adventure, found nothing truly appealing, and returned. Like many of the men in his generation, his eyes turned outward for the first time in American history. Adventure no longer resided between the boundaries of the Atlantic and the Pacific—adventure had to be sought on foreign shores. These were thoughts racing through the minds of Paul and Kiffin and the minds of many other young Americans, but they all had little idea of the horror that awaited them.

After decades of jockeying and posturing, the outbreak of war in 1914 was no major surprise. Whole books have been written on why World War I started, but a basic understanding of its causes is essential because it helps explain why Americans like Kiffin Rockwell marched off to war so willingly. Europe had always been plagued by the problem of having several powerful countries crammed into a relatively small area. Most of the nations in Europe were ambitious for greater power both regionally and globally, so they constantly maneuvered to gain an advantage over each other. The late nineteenth century was important because France had historically possessed the prominent position on the continent, but after the wars of 1866 and 1870, the German Empire supplanted French primacy over continental Europe.[3] The French greatly resented their turn of fortune, and the British eventually became alarmed with the growing power of the German Empire. The nations of Europe began to build a web of complex alliances to protect their respective positions within the European regional hierarchy. However, in order to fully safeguard their borders, they had to construct a number of mobilization plans to prevent their adversaries from rapidly conquering their territories. And once a mobilization plan commenced, it was very difficult to halt the process. Thus, the act of mobilization became tantamount to an act of war.

It was indeed an act of mobilization that finally tipped the tense situation in the summer of 1914 to outright warfare. The Austro-Hungarian Empire found itself in a precarious position when the newly independent Serbian state began to support a liberation movement for Serbs who lived in lands occupied by Austria-Hungary. Russia backed Serbia's rise, and the 1913 defeat of the Ottoman Empire at the hands of the Serbian-led Balkan League significantly alarmed the Hapsburg Empire. On June 28, 1914, a terrorist who had been trained by a Serbian-supported militant group assassinated Archduke Franz Ferdinand in Sarajevo.

But this was not just any archduke—Franz Ferdinand was heir to the historic and wealthy Hapsburg throne. His violent death ignited an already tense situation. Austria-Hungary reached out to Germany to request German assurances of support in the event of war. The imperial ambassador to Berlin, Count Szogyeny, met with the German chancellor and quickly wrote the following to the Foreign Minister in Vienna: "[W]hatever Austria's decision, she could count with certainty upon it that Germany will stand behind her as an ally.... If war must break out, better now than in one or two years' time when the Entente will be stronger."[4] With Germany's strong backing, Austria-Hungary declared war on Serbia on July 28—one month after Archduke Ferdinand's assassination. Suddenly the ball was in Russia's court. The Russians were obliged to support Serbia, but the British ambassador in St. Petersburg warned the Russian government that their mobilization would force Germany into a declaration of war.[5] Russia did not heed the warning and announced that July 30 would be the first day of its general mobilization, which "effectively shattered any prospect of averting a great European war."[6]

Germany quickly made its presence felt with an ultimatum to Russia demanding that the Russians suspend all war measures. Germany also warned France that French mobilization meant war. By this time, all of Europe began to mobilize, and war was all but inevitable. Germany commenced its mobilization on August 1 and then demanded free passage through Belgium to attack France on August 2. News of these events certainly appeared in the newspaper in Atlanta and was obviously the topic of conversation between Kiffin, Paul, and their friends during their Sunday afternoon lunch on the second of August. Germany finally declared war on France and Belgium about the time Kiffin wrote his letter to the French consul on August 3. Events were quickly spiraling out of control.

By the third of August, all eyes were on Great Britain. Germany had gambled on British neutrality, but Britain was not fooled. Sir Edward Grey, the British Foreign Secretary, stood before Parliament that day and told them that the British would not be able to reverse the situation if Germany managed to place all of Western Europe under its dominion. He argued that Britain was obligated by treaty to come to Belgium's aid and then presciently predicted, "The lamps are going out all over Europe; we shall not see them lit again in our lifetime."[7]

The lamps certainly were about to be extinguished in Europe, for all of the countries involved were ready to fight with unwavering resolve. The Field Regulations of the French Army at the time stated, "Defeat is inevitable as soon as the hope of conquering ceases to exist. Success comes not to him who has suffered the least but to him whose will is firmest and morale strongest."[8] The firm will and strong morale of both sides would cause millions of casualties. The fierce determination of the combatants in World War I was not a unique situation. The problem in 1914 was that every armed force now possessed weapons that could (and would) brutally punish blind acts of firm will and strong morale. Kiffin and Paul had no control over the forces that were about to collide at their desired destination.

Meanwhile, in the opening days of August 1914, the United States also had a major decision to make. Would it continue its long history of avoiding entanglement in European conflicts, or was this war unique? As is often the case, American policy had much to do with the opinions and beliefs of the man sitting in the White House. President Woodrow Wilson was an academic, a thinker, and one with a very different view of the world from that of his counterparts in Europe. By most accounts, President Wilson was shocked and deeply affected by the outbreak of World War I. He wrote a letter to his assistant Edward House in which he wrote, "I feel the burden of the thing almost intolerably from day to day."[9]

As the war spiraled out of control, many people around the globe probably shared Wilson's melancholy feelings about the war in Europe. And yet Wilson was absolutely opposed to American involvement in the war. He spoke in an exalted, religious tone about the United States. America was the nation chosen to mediate because it was the only nation that could truly remain neutral.[10] President Wilson also encouraged his own citizens to remain neutral. He made a public statement urging Americans to be "neutral in fact as well as in name and impartial in thought as well as in action."[11] Thus, as the conflict began to sweep through Europe, the United States government chose to continue its historical tradition of avoiding military entanglement in Europe. President Wilson wanted to occupy the moral high ground and shame the rest of Europe into a peaceful settlement. However, in 1914 Europe wanted nothing to do with Wilson's message of peace. The nations yearned for war, and war is what they got.

Kiffin Rockwell and his brother Paul ignored the official position of their own government and promptly booked a trip to France. Both of them were determined to fight for France whether the United States did or not. They were far from President Wilson's ideal of being neutral in fact and impartial in thought and were not convinced by his religious-sounding rhetoric. Kiffin certainly did not believe in the idea of neutrality. In his eyes, there was never any question that France was the victim and Germany the aggressor. His contempt for American neutrality was plainly evident in his letters, and he was not about to let government policy deter him. After sending the letter to the French consul on August 3 and then witnessing official declarations of war emerge from all the major parties involved, Kiffin and Paul did not wait for a response from the consul in New Orleans. They packed up their apartment in Atlanta, said goodbye to their friends, and took the Thursday express train from Atlanta to New York on the sixth of August.

Finding a ticket to Europe was a difficult task at the time. Britain immediately recalled many of its citizens from the United States to join in the war effort, so transatlantic tickets were hard to acquire. Paul and Kiffin managed to pull some strings and book passage on the SS *St. Paul*, departing from New York on the seventh of August. Both of them were filled with excitement at the opportunity awaiting them in France.

Kiffin felt guilty about his swift departure from Asheville and leaving the country without stopping to see his mother, so he wrote her a letter apologizing for their haste. In his note, he explained his reasoning to his mother for going off to war: "I don't want you to worry or feel bad. You have always told me that you wanted me to live my life without interference and this opportunity is one that only comes once in a lifetime.... You know how I have always been a great dreamer and I just couldn't keep myself from this trip, for I felt the call of opportunity. You have always said you had great faith in my future and now is the time for you to prove it, by not worrying about me ... my actions have often appeared as if I didn't care about you and the rest of the family, but it isn't that way. It is just that I must and will live my life as I think best even though I am often mistaken."[12] Opportunity beckoned and Kiffin answered. In hindsight, his decision may seem impulsive and irresponsible, but to a twenty-one-year-old the decision was plainly obvious and perfectly rational.

To Kiffin's mother, Loula Rockwell, his decision left her stunned. Her children were her life, and Kiffin had always conferred with her on anything of importance or interest to him. For him to leave so impulsively was shocking and devastating to her. And to add fuel to the fire, he had convinced her eldest son to join him in his martial pursuits. Years later she wrote, "I guess I was selfish … but I did not understand. I could not see where my two boys meant anything to France, whereas they meant something to me. Their life was mine."[13] It would take well over a year for Loula Rockwell to truly understand the decision of her sons.

The passengers on board the SS *St. Paul* were a fascinating assortment of people answering Britain's recall or pursuing their own opportunities like Paul and Kiffin. The Duchess of Marlborough was on board with two lords, several ladies, and a few knights. Several U.S. army officers, including two generals, had booked passage in order to evaluate the conflict and make recommendations to the general staff back in Washington, D.C. One of the army officers was a colonel named Samuel Reber, the chief of the aviation department for the U.S. Army. At the time, U.S. military aviation was in an abysmal state of affairs compared to some of the European nations. Colonel Reber would quickly discover how much the United States lagged behind the Europeans in terms of aircraft and trained pilots.

A reporter named Irvin S. Cobb also accompanied them on the ship. He was a famous writer who reported on the peace conference after the Russo-Japanese War and would cover World War I as a war correspondent for the *Saturday Evening Post*. Cobb was accompanied by another reporter named William Henry Irwin, who also made a name for himself as one of the leading war correspondents during World War I. Paul and Kiffin were entertained by a Brazilian count named De Besa, whom they believed to be a fake, and a multilingual Hungarian officer in the Red Cross, whom they suspected of being a spy. The ocean crossing was certainly an adventure with iceberg sightings, cold weather, and a major storm that lasted two days. But all passengers and crew members arrived safely in Britain on August 14, and the Rockwell brothers stopped in London to formally enlist at the French consulate.

Their eyes and minds quickly filled with amazement and awe at witnessing the great seat of British imperial power. As history enthusiasts, they had read all about the British Empire and the city of London, but seeing the sprawling metropolis in person made the stories come alive. Their time in London was short, but they set off to discover what they could. After exploring street after street, Kiffin wrote his mother that the British Museum was the most wonderful thing either of them had ever witnessed.[14] Kiffin described the people in London as very calm and proceeding with business as usual. He also noted that the war was popular in Britain and everyone was willing to fight it out despite the general expectation that it would last a long while. After staying in London for about ten days, Paul and Kiffin finally received their papers and left for Paris on the twenty-fifth of August.

Their arrival in the grand city of Paris must have been quite alarming since ominous news of German advances were arriving daily from the front. While Paul and Kiffin were crossing the Atlantic, the war on the Western Front had exploded. The French commenced their operations in accordance with their strategy of total offense. While they correctly predicted a massive German attack through Belgium, they concentrated their forces in the Alsace-Lorraine and attacked—a development correctly foreseen by Count Alfred von Schlieffen, the architect of Germany's original war plan.[15] The Schlieffen Plan called for a massive "right hook" intended to envelop the French Army and end the war in the west as quickly as possible. A quick French defeat would allow the Germans to focus their armies on the Russians in the east.

The French strategy crumbled rapidly as the Germans absorbed their attack in the Alsace-Lorraine and then defeated the French in the Battle of Ardennes. The French plan of relying on the offense by attacking in the Alsace left their flank vulnerable to attack, and Germany continued to advance. France quickly realized that pursuing their own offensives was useless if the German Army flowed around them and captured Paris. Their worst fears were confirmed when the German Army advanced through Belgium far more rapidly than anyone expected. General von Kluck commanded the German First Army, the main force of the German right wing, and on the twentieth of August his army swept through Brussels and attacked the British Expeditionary Force protecting Mons. The British had two corps occupying the lines at Mons, but they had rushed to their positions after mobilizing in the beginning of August and were unable to hold the line. The French were greatly alarmed by Germany's success and commenced a general withdrawal toward Paris.

By late August when Paul and Kiffin arrived in France, the French and British were rapidly retreating in the face of the German onslaught. France and Britain's ability to successfully repel the German advance was absolutely in question in the initial stages of the war. Britain joined the war in order to prevent Germany from conquering the entire European mainland, but in August of 1914 it appeared as if Germany would succeed despite Britain's support of France.

Paul and Kiffin entered Paris with even greater wonderment than they had experienced in London. The City of Light was the symbol of France and everything the country stood for. Seeing the broad avenues, iron balconies, and glass doors reminded them of why they had come. For two men from the Deep South, Paris seemed almost like a fantasy world. It was foreign beyond their comprehension but lovely and majestic at the same time. They shuffled slowly to their enlistment spot, gaping at the soaring Eiffel Tower as they walked through its narrow shadow. Their scenic walk through Paris continued until they rounded a final corner and found their destination—the Hôtel des Invalides.

This was no ordinary hotel. It was the project of King Louis XIV, of France who had wanted to improve the lives of the soldiers who fought for him. In the seventeenth century, veteran soldiers with debilitating wounds or diseases would often be thrown out on the streets to fend for themselves. Louis XIV built the hotel to house and care for these soldiers in order to make the military profession more appealing.[16] It was a sprawling complex with at least seven stories of multiple wings surrounding symmetrical courtyards. The façade and interior contained intricate carvings in stone and painted decorations throughout. The most prominent feature was the gilded dome that even today dominates the skyline east of the Eiffel Tower. Under the massive roof of the dome, surrounded by a vast pillared circle of marble bas-reliefs, lay the tomb of Napoleon himself.

Paul and Kiffin could only stare in amazement as they joined the French cause in the compound housing the final resting place of France's greatest military hero. From a statue in the wide main courtyard, Napoleon looked down on them with steely eyes and a characteristic hand between the buttons of his shirt. His stern expression warned them and the other recruits that the honor of France now rested on their shoulders. Her survival was in the hands of these new legionnaires and the men they would soon join.

Napoleon's scowl was a heavy burden to Paul, Kiffin, the soldiers, and the people of Paris. The people of the city now realized the full extent of the danger they faced. The Rockwell brothers stayed in the city from August 25 to August 28, a time of great trial for the Parisians. As the brothers awaited the start of their training, a sense of dread began to fall on the city. A war correspondent named Frederick Palmer described the scene: "And silence, only silence in Paris, the silence of old men and the women, and of children who had ceased to play and could not understand."[17] This clearly was not the reception that Paul and Kiffin had imagined when they left the United States. They had pictured their beloved France as a stalwart nation with a long history of military triumph. The fear that Germany would successfully conquer Paris was palpable in the city at the time, and the two brothers likely felt uneasy at not only France's prospects but also their own welfare.

Nevertheless, Paul and Kiffin bravely reported to the French military authorities at the Hôtel des Invalides and received the customary screening ritual for new recruits. French doctors gave them a thorough physical examination, customs personnel checked their passports, and military officials asked them several questions about their background. After enduring a few days of processing and answering questions, the two brothers finally received orders to a barracks training school in the town of Rouen. They left on the twenty-eighth of August as Paris began to prepare for the coming onslaught. Few in Paris, including the leaders of France, knew how the upcoming battle would end.

As Paul and Kiffin traveled to their training post, the French and British were in the midst of a two-week-long retreat. On September 1 the German army was only three days' march from the advanced line of trenches outside Paris. Soldiers under General Joseph Gallieni, the military commander of Paris, were frantically making preparations for the inevitable siege. They installed massive artillery batteries along a trench circuit of 110 miles around Paris, assured the flow of supplies to the men in the trenches by preparing railways, and assembled food and provisions for the four million inhabitants of Paris.[18]

All seemed to be going according to plan for the Germans when General von Kluck made a fateful error. Instead of continuing as ordered in a sweep around the west and south of Paris, in order to encircle the city, General von Kluck decided to maintain contact with the army of General von Bulow to his left. General von Kluck justified his decision to abandon the encirclement of Paris by describing the action as a "difficult and risky undertaking" that "would be scarcely possible in the circumstances to continue the offensive until the enemy was decisively defeated or partially annihilated."[19] The general also had unreliable communication to the rear, so he could not effectively coordinate with Supreme Command back in Germany. However, he must have known the gravity of his decision. If his army could not fulfill the encirclement of Paris and force the surrender of the French and British, then the Schlieffen Plan was lost. From this point forward, the Germans were forced to fight the two-front war that they desperately wanted to avoid.

At the time, the French and British had no way of knowing that General von Kluck's action had doomed Germany's initial strategy. The climax of the retreat towards Paris occurred on the fateful day of September 3. General Joseph Joffre, the French commander-in-chief, convinced Alexandre Millerand, the Minister of War, that Paris could only be defended by operations of the armies in the field, and "any unit diverted from this task, whether assigned to the defense of Paris or not, would be badly employed."[20] The government of France grudgingly agreed with General Joffre and decided to flee from the capital city because it could not guarantee that Paris would not fall to the enemy. That evening all the civil and military authorities signed a government proclamation: "For several weeks relentless battles have engaged our heroic troops and the army of the enemy.... This situation has compelled the President of the Republic and the Government to take a painful decision. In order to watch over the national welfare, it is the duty of the public powers to remove themselves temporarily from the city of Paris. Under the command of an eminent Chief, a French Army, full of courage and zeal, will defend the capital and its patriotic population against the invader. But the war must be carried on at the same time on the rest of its territory.... Endure and fight!"[21] After its dire proclamation, the French government left its capital city and hoped that its defenders had the strength to hold the line.

As government officials started to abandon the capital, the situation in the city of Paris became chaotic. A mass exodus of Parisians fled the capital city in whatever transportation they could procure. Lines of cabs, many filled with household goods, raced down the streets of Paris carrying passengers from their homes to the railway stations in the city. An Englishman named George Perris described the general feeling of the occupants of Paris at the time: "It is difficult now to recall the sense of impending calamity that then seemed so real, and lay hourly more heavily upon us.... We were, or appeared to be, nearly isolated. There might have been a great defeat. We did not know."[22] Thousands of people waited for trains at the railway stations, while trains from the north and east brought constant streams of wounded men into the city. All of the major embassies left except for the Spanish Embassy and the United States Embassy. The United States ironically demonstrated one of its first outward acts of neutrality when the American ambassador, Myron T. Herrick, took charge of the records of the British, the German, and the Austrian ambassadors.[23]

Yet the mass exodus from Paris did not deter many of its inhabitants. General Gallieni, the military commander of Paris, famously responded to the government's departure from Paris by proclaiming, "Army of Paris, Inhabitants of Paris, the members of the Government of the Republic have left Paris to give a fresh impulse to national defense. I have been entrusted with the task of defending Paris against the invader. That task I will fulfill to the end."[24]

On the fourth of September, as the French government rushed away from Paris, the German Emperor Kaiser Wilhelm II was beside himself with glee. He spoke to his delegation of ministers at his Luxembourg headquarters and gushed, "It is the thirty-fifth day. We are besieging Rheims, we are thirty miles from Paris."[25] The Kaiser's elation would not last long, however. General Joffre halted the French retreat on the banks of the Marne River, and the main German force advancing toward Paris turned to the southeast. General Gallieni and his staff decided that if the Germans would not come and fight them, then they would go to the Germans.[26] He coordinated with General Joffre, who had recognized a massive gap between the German First and Second Armies. General Joffre convinced British Field Marshal French to advance despite French's misgivings considering the losses he had already sustained. General Gallieni famously ferried his troops by rail and Parisian taxi cabs to strengthen France's Sixth Army that was on the verge of witnessing a German breakthrough.

The enormous counterattack at the First Battle of the Marne finally halted the German advance and alerted the German high command that their cherished Schlieffen Plan was officially dead. By September 9, it appeared as if the German First and Second Armies might be encircled, and the German chief of staff, Helmuth von Moltke, panicked. He ordered a massive retreat of the German army, and the tables appeared to turn for the French and British. General Joffre wrote a telegraph to the Minister of War on September

13 claiming, "The completeness of our victory becomes more and more apparent. Everywhere the enemy is in retreat. The Germans are abandoning prisoners, wounded, and material in all directions. After the heroic efforts displayed by our troops during this formidable battle, which has lasted from the 5th to the 12th of September, all our armies, exhilarated by success, are carrying out a pursuit which is without parallel in its extension."[27] Unfortunately, this was the First World War, and victory would prove frustratingly elusive.

The Germans knew their plan to avoid a two-front war was in shambles, but they certainly were not going to let the French and British erase all their recent gains. General von Moltke, having given the order to retreat, was quickly relieved of command on September 14. Just before his removal, Moltke ordered the troops to initiate trench warfare along the Aisne River. The German First and Second Armies reached the river first and began digging in. General Erich von Falkenhayn, the minister of war, replaced General von Moltke and supervised the construction of the entrenchments all along the Aisne River. The fortified German trenches on the Aisne effectively stopped the combined offensive of General Joffre and Field Marshal French. There were no more exuberant telegrams between Joffre and the minister of war. Fighting all along the Western Front had ground to a halt, and neither side could have predicted that the line where they stopped in September of 1914 would stay largely unchanged for the next two and a half years.

As the dust settled along the newly formed lines of trenches, both sides finally had a chance to take stock of their situation. The results after just over a month of fighting were horrific. The French had lost over 250,000 men, and the Germans had suffered nearly identical casualties. British casualties totaled around 13,000 men, but the island nation had yet to fully mobilize. These losses were utterly unprecedented and caused a great deal of soul-searching among commanders and politicians on all sides. In many ways the losses only strengthened the resolve of all the leaders—there was no going back. Paul and Kiffin Rockwell were proceeding to their training base with only bits and scraps of news from the Front. As word of the casualties began trickling in, their reception was likely a somber affair. A dark cloud had descended upon Europe, and it would be many years before the people would see daylight again.

4

Training in the French Foreign Legion

Kiffin Yates Rockwell did not start his service in World War I as a pilot. By the time he arrived in France, Kiffin had not even flown in an aircraft, and the idea of soaring over the battlefield was a thought that had not yet entered his ever-pondering mind. Kiffin started World War I in the trenches, that haunted and detestable place which now dwells in books as a euphemism for senseless slaughter. The popular notion of lordly pilots enjoying lavish lifestyles in between deadly aerial missions was a far cry from his initial experience in the war. Kiffin's first year in France was a trial of fire, one that tempered his character and opened his eyes to the awful consequences of armed combat. Like most combat veterans, he emerged from his ordeal a changed man, but his time in the trenches was not completely futile. He learned how to face danger, how to lead men, and how to cope with the impartial touch of death around him. But most significantly, Kiffin's time in the trenches forced his eyes skyward, and he quickly determined his future course.

Kiffin Rockwell's war on the ground also made him an eyewitness to the dark side of military organizations. While most famous units in military history are pictured as efficient, tightly run machines, this characterization is certainly not always the case. Many military outfits appear capable from the outside and can often achieve results, but on the inside they are dysfunctional and oppressive. Kiffin's first taste of military service was in the storied French Foreign Legion. Few military forces in the world have such a fascinating history, and the annals of World War I are littered with reports of the gallantry, sacrifice, and achievement of the Foreign Legion. And yet, in reality, life in the French Foreign Legion was a squalid existence. The men were paid almost nothing, given little in the way of nutrition, and forced to endure a daily routine that often bordered on anarchy due to the unique cultural features of the Legion. Kiffin learned little about the qualities of an orderly and highly disciplined force while serving in the Legion, but he certainly could comprehend the value of discipline after consistently observing its absence on a regular basis.

Life for Americans in the French Foreign Legion did have some benefits. Serving with like-minded countrymen was one of the prime advantages for fighting in the Legion at the time. Paul and Kiffin quickly found themselves among kindred spirits on the training grounds and on the battlefields of France. The caliber of young American men in the Foreign Legion was impressive. Students, professors, poets, businessmen, and warriors all flocked to the tricolor when their country decided to sit on the sidelines. It was a sight to behold. The *New York Times* described the merry band as recruits from all classes of society:

millionaires, writers, lawyers, engineers, former soldiers and sailors, boxers, butchers, explorers, and university students.[1] With such an extraordinary cast of characters, the question of individual motives naturally comes to the fore. Why would millionaires and lawyers—men with a great deal to lose—choose to fight for France? Paul Rockwell described their motivations fairly simply: "None came for money. Some came for the simple love of adventure, but I believe that the motive of most of them was an ideal."[2] Kiffin and Paul were in good company, for ideals certainly drove them to France. Adventure may have provided the initial spark, but their ideals turned thoughts into action. The belief that they were fighting for a worthy cause sustained them after the desire for adventure wore off. And sustainment would soon be required as they realized what kind of war they would be forced to fight.

The fact that most American volunteers eventually made their way into the French Foreign Legion was no accident. Since many of them were already living in Europe, several of the Americans in the Foreign Legion joined before Paul and Kiffin even set foot in France. As the story goes, several of them banded together and decided to visit the American ambassador in Paris about two days after war was declared. Some of them were concerned about the legalities of fighting for another country, so U.S. Ambassador Herrick consulted French and American laws regarding neutrality. After a brief review, he concluded that enlisting in the regular French Army would probably cost them their citizenship, but joining the Foreign Legion was likely a safe gamble. The ambassador then slammed his fist down on his desk and concluded, "That is the law, boys, but if I were young and in your shoes I know mighty well what I would do."[3]

All of them decided to take the risk and join the Foreign Legion, but they had to wait several days for their orders to arrive. In the meantime, they began to learn some of the basic military drills each morning in the garden at the Palais-Royal. A man named Charles Sweeny led the drills due to his previous experience. He was a tall, thirty-two-year-old adventurer who had enlisted in the U.S. Army at the age of sixteen.[4] Sweeny fought in the Spanish-American War and later entered the U.S. Military Academy at West Point, but did not graduate. He was married to a Belgian woman and living in France when the war broke out in 1914, so he was one of the first to visit Ambassador Herrick in order to gain approval to enlist with the French. Sweeny would go on to be a decorated officer in the Foreign Legion, a temporary brigadier general in the Polish army, and the co-founder of the American Eagle Squadron that fought for the British in the early days of World War II.[5] He was quite a talented man and quickly became one of the natural leaders among the Americans in the Foreign Legion.

After several days of drilling, the men finally received their orders on August 21. They attended a swearing-in ceremony in the courtyard of the Hôtel des Invalides, and on that day the French accepted forty-three Americans into the Foreign Legion. The Americans soon realized not to expect much compensation for their service. The French gave them a grand salary of thirty cents a month. The first group of Americans left for training on August 25, the day Paul and Kiffin arrived in country. They marched out in formation from the courtyard of the Hôtel des Invalides through a massive stone archway with Napoleon's statue gazing approvingly upon them from behind. The men passed through a wrought-iron gate flaked with gold leaf, surrounded on all sides by cheering Parisians blowing kisses and throwing flowers. As they marched to the train station, two of them took turns waving an American flag, which elicited cheers from the people crowding the streets and avenues to see the departure of the Legion recruits.[6]

Three days later, the volunteers arrived in Rouen, where they were housed with 1,600 other recruits. Their first impression of Legion training standards was depressing. One recruit described Rouen as an area "teeming with a marvelous, heterogeneous collection: wounded from the British army, stragglers from the Belgian army, refugees ... all wandering around the streets aimlessly, some terribly depressed, others hilarious and singing, and a good portion of them drunk."[7] They slept on thin beds of straw and did what they could to keep their spirits up.

Paul and Kiffin Rockwell joined them a couple of days after the first group arrived in Rouen. Kiffin seemed to enjoy his new life as a soldier despite its obvious discomforts. They all drilled about six hours a day with three hours of free time when they could do as they pleased. The young American trainees went to bed at eight every night, and the lights had to be extinguished by nine so they could wake up at five every morning. At this point, the Americans had only had a small glimpse of the Foreign Legion they had joined. According to Kiffin, the food was good, wholesome, and well-cooked, and the men were congenial and good-humored.[8]

The French even gave them an afternoon off, so the men could go visit the town. It was a beautiful city with a broad river and narrow streets filled with bakeries and all sorts of goods and crafts. Rouen's famous town cathedral was one of their first stops. Its ornate spires and stained-glass windows gave the place of worship a majestic appearance. Yet years earlier, Jeanne d'Arc (Joan of Arc) had been imprisoned under the base of the towering cathedral in a dungeon. Seeing the place where she was held before being burned at the stake was a major highlight.

Kiffin, with his interest in history, particularly appreciated the area. He called it "the most interesting city in France" and noted that Rouen was in Normandy, the place from which the Normans successfully invaded England.[9] Rouen was indeed the capital of historic Normandy, and Kiffin's comment indirectly alluded to the story behind his last name. The Rockwell family in England was of Norman origin, for the patriarch of the family was a man named Sir Ralph de Rocheville who settled in the county of York.[10] Sir Rocheville was one of the Norman knights who escorted Empress Matilda to England when she claimed the throne of that realm in 1141. Whether Kiffin knew he was standing in the land of his ancient roots is not entirely clear, but considering his interest in history it is likely he understood that Rouen was part of his ancestral homeland.

Their stay in Rouen did not last long, however. Only six days after the first Americans arrived, the Legion recruits received orders to transfer to the town of Toulouse, about 150 miles to the south. Rouen was northwest of Paris, and these were the early days of September in 1914. The French government had just evacuated the city of Paris, and the military clearly believed that Rouen's proximity to the German advance put it in jeopardy. None of the American recruits knew this at the time due to significant press censorship on the part of the French authorities. The officers escorted the Legionnaires to a train with small railway cars that reeked of manure, and they jammed fifty-six recruits into each small car.[11] They were given one large can of bully beef apiece and then the doors were shut. The sweltering heat of the waning summer days was palpable, and only half the men could sit at one time due to how tightly the officers had packed the train cars. It was a miserable trip.

To truly understand the hardship that the American recruits would suffer over the next several months, it is necessary to know a bit about the history of the French Foreign Legion. The French have a long tradition of employing foreign soldiers in their wars. The American historian John Elting describes this phenomenon: "The French, being a thrifty and practical people, have always been eager to let any available foreigners assist them in any necessary bleeding and dying for *la Patrie*.... From the Scots who rode with Joan of Arc to the Foreign Legion at Dien Bien Phu, the foreign soldier, idealistic volunteer or hard-case mercenary, is an integral part of the French military tradition."[12] The vast numbers of recruits who flocked to the Legion during World War I were only part of a larger story that continues to this day.

King Louis-Philippe created the French Foreign Legion in 1831 as an outlet for the political turmoil that was occurring in France at the time. Less than a year earlier, Louis-Philippe had ascended to the throne of France after the French Revolution of 1830 in July. Political uncertainty would plague King Louis-Philippe throughout his reign, so he was naturally inclined to contain events that could potentially increase the turmoil in his country. In 1831 the king had a number of foreign refugees residing in France whom he viewed as a conceivable threat to his throne. In the mind of an uncertain monarch, large numbers of idle foreigners was a recipe for disaster. So the king created a legion of the French Army that could employ immigrants who were not French citizens. The refugees would then have employment, and the army could keep them corralled so as to limit their involvement in nefarious political activities.

The French Foreign Legion quickly made its mark in the military folklore of France. A few years after the creation of the Legion, King Louis-Philippe sent General Thomas Bugeaud on a campaign to subjugate Algeria as a French colony. General Bugeaud successfully conquered Algeria and the king installed him as the governor-general in 1840. Unfortunately for the French, the Algerians mounted a potent insurgency under the command of Abd-el-Kader that caused significant problems for the French forces stationed in Algeria. The Algerian fighters obviously knew far more about the land than the French, and they could use the terrain and their mobile tactics to successfully evade the heavily laden French forces. General Bugeaud realized that he needed to make his Foreign Legion much more agile if he hoped to defeat the Algerian insurgents. He stripped down the equipment and rations of the Legionnaires and forced them to adopt mobile tactics that would enable them to exist for days on short rations.[13]

The French called their new tactic the *razzia*, and its success depended on some fairly brutal methods. Since much of the Arab population in Algeria was nomadic and their fighters rarely fought in large groups, the French could not defeat them using standard European military tactics. Rather than pursuing small bands of Algerian fighters all over the countryside, the French Legionnaires focused instead on the livelihood of the Algerians. One officer described the *razzia* as "a *coup de main*, which hurls a force upon a population with the rapidity of a bird of prey, stripping it of its riches, its herds, its grains—the Arab's only vulnerability."[14] The *razzia* tactics left an enduring mark on the record of the Foreign Legion for years to come. Furthermore, the long, forced marches of mobile warfare in Algeria became enshrined as hallmarks of the Legion. The Americans would soon get a taste of the Foreign Legion's trademark treks.

Over the next two decades, the French Foreign Legion saw action in the Crimean campaign, the Italian campaign, and even in Mexico. The Legion lost almost a third of its force in the lowlands of Mexico as it escorted convoys through areas infested with yellow fever. Along the way, however, the officers of the Legion gained a reputation for aggressiveness that formed one of the great strengths of the corps in Mexico.[15] Many of the officers in the French Foreign Legion were single men who joined in order to fight and gain glory. It was well known that if one wanted to see action then he ought to join the Legion. Naturally this legend attracted a certain type of man, especially among the officers, and it is no surprise that the men who answered the call were of an aggressive nature.

The legend of the French Foreign Legion expanded dramatically in the years between 1871 and the outbreak of World War I. After it played a role in the controversial massacre of twenty-five thousand members of the Paris Commune during the French civil war in 1871, the Legion fought in Indochina, Africa, Madagascar, and Morocco. These campaigns extended French colonial expansion, and Legion folklore grew to almost mythic proportions. In fact, two legends emerged that both served as effective recruitment tools for the French government. The first legend portrayed the Legion as a band of outlaws and an asylum of men on the run from the law, while the other legend depicted the Legion as a band of romantic, educated outcasts from good families who needed a place to bury their misfortunes.[16] These seemingly contradictory legends certainly increased the mystique of the Foreign Legion, since no one ever really knew where the truth stopped and the myth began. The Legion was thus perpetually shrouded in mystery—a fact encouraged by the French government, which enjoyed the steady flow of cheap recruits for its foreign adventures.

One of the perpetual problems in the Foreign Legion was the issue of language. With so many men from countries across the globe, it was very difficult to assimilate the recruits quickly. French was naturally the language of the Legion, but many of the men could not speak French when they joined the Legion. Over time their French-speaking ability would improve, but in the crucial days of initial training it was extremely challenging for the instructors to effectively communicate with their recruits. The issue of language also affected the leadership of the Legion. A foreign recruit might demonstrate remarkable leadership skills, but he was required to go through special classes and pass examinations in order to advance in the ranks. For someone with a weak grasp of French, promotion to noncommissioned officer (NCO) or officer was nearly impossible until he became fluent in the language. Consequently, a shortage of good NCOs was always a major weakness of the French Foreign Legion.[17]

Training and discipline in the Foreign Legion were historically brutal and often merciless. Instructors trained recruits to survive on the smallest rations while enduring maximum pain and discomfort. They marched recruits into the ground and did not tolerate those who quit or slowed the rest of the group. To many veteran Legionnaires, separation from the troops meant death because on campaign a man who dropped out of a march was disarmed and left to try his luck with the enemy.[18] Recruits quickly learned that falling out of a march was not tolerated. In order to enforce their harsh training requirements, officers and NCOs enforced disciplinary standards that seemed tyrannical to outsiders. Failure to perform commonly elicited punishments ranging from beatings and forfeiture of pay to deprivation and confinement. While these certainly seem like harsh measures, most soldiers did not mind spending time in prison at all. One officer wrote, "On the contrary, [the recruits] were rather proud of [going to prison] and it was proverbial that a man who had not been in prison often was not a good soldier."[19] Once the troops were on campaign, however, things became far more serious—gross violations of discipline could easily result in death. Life in the Foreign Legion was certainly a grueling affair, but those who emerged from training and survived a campaign were hardened fighters who could survive in impossible conditions.

By the eve of World War I, the French Foreign Legion had quite a reputation. The Legion was well known for its colonial exploits and its generally valiant actions on the battlefield. But at the same time, the people of France still viewed Legionnaires as little more than common criminals who could not find honest work in their own countries. Yet this was an image that the Legion actually embraced and promoted. By 1914, the Legion's self-image as a band of hardened but sentimental outcasts had become cast in concrete, and the Legion would seek to preserve this self-image throughout the twentieth century.[20]

The reason for the Legion's seemingly odd desire to promote itself as a band of outcasts is complex but has much to do with the performance of the Legionnaires themselves. One of the most infamous rules of the Legion meant officers had no legal way to dismiss bad troops until 1906. A poor-performing Legionnaire who spent a lot of time in prison actually served longer than a good troop because the days he spent in prison were not counted against his five-year enlistment![21] Thus, the bad apples tended to stay longer than those who avoided trouble. Interestingly, this phenomenon may have benefited the Legion in the long run. Many officers believed that the men who caused the most problems in garrison were the best fighters on campaign, so the Legion actually encouraged the image to a certain extent.[22] In the end, the French Foreign Legion was able to institutionalize the notion of "bad soldier but good fighter," so poor behavior in garrison became the foundation of the Legion's *esprit de corps* and combat effectiveness.[23]

The history of the French Foreign Legion, and its subsequent institutionalization of "bad soldier but good fighter," is absolutely essential to understanding Kiffin Rockwell's experience and that of his fellow Americans in the Legion. To an American, especially one immersed in the history of the U.S. Civil War as Kiffin was, the culture of the Foreign Legion was not only foreign, it was downright appalling. In Kiffin's eyes, war was meant to be fought by men who shared a belief in the cause, a love of country, and a desire for justice. These men would fight valiantly, and if they lost their lives in the process, than it was a noble and honorable sacrifice. Rockwell did not have a full understanding of the Legion's culture before joining the legendary unit, and the behavior of the hardened Legionnaires caught him totally off guard. Joining an organization full of men only a step above a common criminal was horrifying to him, and he often longed to join the regular French army. Yet over time, Kiffin would come to respect the Foreign Legion's fighting prowess, and he and the other Americans would participate in several battles where the glory and mystique of the French Foreign Legion increased all the more.

When Kiffin Rockwell and the rest of the American recruits arrived in Toulouse, they did not yet fully grasp the culture and history of the Foreign Legion they had joined. The excitement of their enlistment was still fresh, and it would still be several days before they joined the veteran Legionnaires. The trip to Toulouse had been characteristically miserable, though. They all ran out of water on the second day of the journey and practically climbed over each other to get water when the train arrived at a pumping station. Several of the Russians died on the trip because they hoarded some of the bully beef in their jackets and became violently ill after eating the meat, which had spoiled.[24] The journey by train lasted over fifty-five hours, and the recruits were overjoyed when they finally reached the station in Toulouse. Their officers made the men march in a parade through town, but none of them had been issued uniforms at that point. They were all still in the civilian clothes that they possessed when they joined, so most of the townspeople thought they were German prisoners and shouted and jeered at them instead! It was a rather depressing welcome for the weary recruits.

Life in Toulouse was difficult but bearable. The men awoke at four A.M. and typically worked about fourteen hours a day, but they only had two meals per day. Each morning around eleven, the recruits received a bowl of soup with bread and meat as well as a cup of coffee and a cup of cheap red wine. At five in the afternoon the men ate goulash, bread, and a cup of coffee and a cup of wine. The Legion officers and NCOs housed all the men in barracks with about thirty men per room. The beds had straw mattresses crawling with hidden insects that caused red welts to appear every morning. The men finally received their uniforms and equipment in Toulouse, which included a heavy blue greatcoat, coarse white duck fatigue uniforms, a red kepi, laced field shoes, wool shirts, a blue sash nine feet long, two blankets and a suit of long underwear.[25] They received 1868 Lebel rifles that weighed over nine pounds, and with a fixed bayonet the rifle was over six feet long! The days passed quickly and the men soon became accustomed to the schedule, the diet, and the training.

In 1914 when World War I started, there were two regiments in the Foreign Legion, consisting of about sixteen thousand men serving five-year enlistments. The First Foreign Regiment and the Second Foreign Regiment were serving in the French colonies when the war broke out in Europe, so the French needed to expand the Foreign Legion in order to absorb the new volunteers who were flocking to France. The French government created four new units called *régiments de marche*. The French added three marching regiments to the First Foreign Regiment and one marching regiment to the Second Foreign Regiment. Paul and Kiffin Rockwell started in the Second Marching Regiment of the larger Second Foreign Regiment. Their unit consisted of several hundred Russian Jews and Armenians along with foreigners from several other countries. The Russians and Armenians would quickly become a problem in the Second Marching Regiment. Paul remembered the Russians and Armenians as men "already afflicted with Bolshevist ideas and their presence and propaganda did much to sap the morale of the other volunteers, and to lessen their confidence in the fighting ability of their regiment."[26] These issues quickly surfaced as the recruits left Toulouse and marched to the Front.

Shortly after the new Legionnaires came to Toulouse, the volunteers all assembled to witness the arrival of a battalion of regular Legionnaires from the Second Foreign Regiment. These men were hardened veterans who had been serving in Algeria, and their skin had become dark from the desert sun. The veteran Legionnaires came to drill the new volunteers and to form a nucleus of qualified fighters in the new marching regiments. The French assigned the veterans to every section in order to balance the number of experienced soldiers and new recruits in each section. This decision, while prudent, caused substantial friction for the first year of the war. Paul Rockwell claimed, "There was considerable jealousy between the old Legionnaires of colonial service and the volunteers fresh from civilian life. The latter rather looked down upon the veterans as mercenary soldiers, while the old

Legionnaires quite justly considered the newcomers as inexperienced and raw."[27] This source of tension was bound to occur. It is natural for combat veterans to shun the inexperience of new recruits, but it is also not surprising that the mostly idealistic American volunteers would view these "mercenary soldiers" with contempt. Much of this friction would melt away as the new volunteers gained combat experience and the old hands realized that the trenches of World War I were not the deserts of Algeria.

There were a number of Americans among the early Legion recruits, but several of them were close companions and friends of the Rockwell brothers. The French placed most of the Americans in C Battalion of the Second Marching Regiment, and many of the tallest men in the battalion formed the *Neuvième Escouade* (Ninth Squad). Paul and Kiffin were both tall men, so they ended up in the Ninth Squad with other Americans such as Alan Seeger, Ferdinand Capdevielle, Dennis Dowd, William Thaw, Stewart Carstairs, and Frederick Zinn. There were also two British volunteers, one Norwegian, one Swede, a Serbian, and an old French Legionnaire named Pierre; the chief of the squad was a German from Saxony, Corporal Weidemann. The Americans of the Ninth Squad quickly became fast friends.

Many of these men became well known in their own right and had a great impact on the life of Kiffin Rockwell. One of Kiffin's closest friends was the aforementioned Alan Seeger, who is now known in literary circles as an accomplished poet. With the poetic achievements of Kiffin's father in mind, it is not surprising that Kiffin naturally connected with the young poet. By all accounts, Alan Seeger was a fascinating person. He was born in 1888 and spent a good part of his boyhood in Mexico, where his father had business interests. Seeger primarily grew up in New England and then studied at Hackley School to enter Harvard College. To the chagrin of his poet friends, he immersed himself in his studies at Harvard. Seeger later wrote, "I was a devotee of Learning for Learning's sake. My life during those years was intellectual to the exclusion of almost everything else.... I shut myself off completely from the life of the University, so full, nevertheless, of pleasures.... I felt no need of comradeship.... My books were my friends."[28] He wrote a great deal while at Harvard and published extensively in *Harvard Monthly*.

One of his friends at school, John Hall Wheelock, of the Harvard Class of 1908, wrote a fairly complete description of Alan Seeger years later: "Tall and rather sparely built, with a pale, but forceful and strangely immobile and mask-like face, straight black hair cut square across the forehead, and remote eyes, he sat through the entire evening in absolute silence.... At first this might have been attributed to either affectation or shyness, but a certain candor coupled with entire self-possession soon eliminated both solutions. On being questioned by a friend at the close of the discussions as to his extraordinary behavior, he announced with entire naturalness that the conversation had not appealed to him, and added that he was by nature not interested in trivial talk."[29] Seeger never sat in silence among the Americans in the Foreign Legion. This bookish man had ironically found his calling among the trenches in France, and the conversations they had in the midst of the war's terror were anything but "trivial talk."

Alan Seeger graduated from Harvard in 1910 but could not find satisfaction in a normal job. He drifted through life during those two years before finally deciding to travel to Paris in 1912. His friend John Wheelock recalls talking to Seeger in the summer just before his departure to France: "I recall the familiar fatalism that he then gave voice to, the fierce discontent and hunger of the man, as of one who seeks blindly for something greater than himself, whereby he may be liberated.... I recall then the sudden realization, new to me at the moment, that for some spirits the everyday pressure of life is not sufficient, the everyday demands of life not large nor heroic enough in their claim."[30]

Seeger spent two self-described hedonistic years in Paris searching for purpose and a publisher for his poems. He found neither, but when war came to France in 1914, Seeger volunteered immediately. He attributed his decision to his love for France and wrote of why he enlisted: "That memorable day in August came. Suddenly, the old haunts were desolate, the boon companions had gone. It was unthinkable to leave the danger to them and accept only the pleasures oneself, to go on enjoying the sweet things of life in defence of which they were perhaps even then shedding their blood in the north."[31] So Alan Seeger threw his name into the hat without another thought and found himself in Toulouse among other extraordinary men.

Ferdinand "Cap" Capdevielle was another of the young Americans who served in the Ninth Squad with Kiffin Rockwell. He was born in 1893 to a family with French roots and lived in New York City. He had a job as a clerk at a steamship company in New York, but his career had no allure to it after war broke out in France. Cap, who had just turned twenty-one, packed up his gear and sailed for his ancestral homeland. He must have boarded a ship directly to France because he managed to make it to Paris before the Rockwell brothers. Another New Yorker named Denis Dowd also showed up around the same time as Capdevielle. Dowd was raised in New York City and Long Island, but he graduated from Georgetown University in 1908. He later attended law school at Columbia University and was in Paris on legal business when World War I started. Cap and Dowd enlisted with Seeger and the rest of the boys on August 21 in Paris.

Another extraordinary man who fought in the Ninth Squad was a wealthy Pennsylvanian named William Thaw II. His grandfather, also William Thaw, started his business career as a clerk in his father's bank in Pittsburgh. In the mid–1800s, William Thaw and his brother-in-law owned a company of steam canal boats that controlled the Pennsylvania and Ohio canal lines. After trains emerged as the future of transportation, Thaw founded the Pennsylvania Company, which managed the interests of the Pennsylvania railroad in the west. Over the course of several years, William Thaw made a fortune in transportation and banking. He was enormously wealthy in his day and established scientific endowments at Harvard University and Princeton University as well as financing the construction of the Allegheny Observatory. Thaw had five children before his first wife passed away, and then had another five children after remarrying.

William Thaw II was the son of Benjamin Thaw from the first marriage of William Thaw, Sr. He was born in 1893 in Pittsburgh and had a lavish lifestyle due to his grandfather's fortune. The entire Thaw family had to endure a tragic moment in the spotlight when one of the Thaw clan was arrested and tried for murder. Harry Kendall Thaw was one of the sons from the second marriage of William Thaw, Sr. In a fit of rage in 1906, Harry Thaw murdered the famous architect Stanford White on the roof of Madison Square Garden. In a trial that was a front-page story in the era of sensational journalism, Harry Thaw was eventually found not guilty by reason of insanity and sentenced to incarceration for life in a state hospital for the criminally insane. The Thaw family managed to move on after the crisis, and William Thaw II attended Yale University, where he learned to fly in 1913. His father bought him a Curtiss Hydro flying boat, and he decided to quit his studies at Yale in order to fly his plane in the French Schneider Trophy races. Like many of the other Americans in the Legion who were residing in France when the war started, Thaw found the attraction to take up arms too much to handle. He enlisted in the Foreign Legion and would quickly become one of the most prominent Americans fighting for France.

James Stewart Carstairs was a noted artist who joined the Legion after spending years studying in a variety of interesting locations. He spent most of his primary years in American private schools before spending a year at Harvard. Carstairs went on to study at Oxford for a time and then ended up in Paris before the war. His paintings are very bright and beautiful pieces of art, featuring landscapes from locations around the world. Carstairs's father was an art patron, so he had an eye for detail—most of his work received solid reviews and sold well during his time. Yet he too decided to place his career aside and join the Legion when the war began.

Another American of the Ninth Squad was Frederick W. Zinn, a native of Galesburg, Michigan. Zinn graduated from the University of Michigan in 1914 and decided to tour Europe that summer. When the war started, he figured he could continue his European tour courtesy of the French Foreign Legion and joined with the rest of the Americans.

René Phélizot rounded out the crew of notable Americans who volunteered for France in August of 1914. He was a native of Chicago who ran away from home at the age of thirteen. Phélizot signed on as a cabin boy on a Mississippi River passenger boat, but he eventually followed his passion for adventure to lands across the ocean. After traveling a great deal, he ended in Africa on a big game shooting excursion. Phélizot's father was of French origin, so he chose Paris as a comfortable spot to rest after the long hunting expedition. Like many of the others, he could not bear the thought of Paris falling to German invaders, so he joined the Legion.

Many of these same men were responsible for the steady stream of Americans joining the French Foreign Legion in 1914. Phélizot, Thaw, and Carstairs had all been leading members of the American colony in Paris, and they sent the message of joining France out far and wide. At the beginning of the march to the train depot in Paris, before their departure to Rouen for training, a news photographer took a famous photo of the American volunteers crossing the courtyard outside the Place de l'Opera in Paris. Just prior to the picture, Charles Sweeny had finished calling the muster roll of American volunteers and blew his whistle to form the new recruits into lines for the march to the station. All of the men were still in their civilian clothes with different-styled hats and carrying their luggage. They marched awkwardly while Alan Seeger and René Phélizot each carried a large American flag at the front of the ranks. Frenchmen cheered them on and put flowers, cigarettes, chocolate, and bottles of wine into their arms as they marched past. One bystander said, "Those boys seem an unlikely lot for soldiers. Their lines were swaybacked and no one kept quite in step although Sweeny counted cadence until he was hoarse.... One thing I'll never forget was the pride in their eyes."[32] The pride remained evident in the bright eyes of the Americans as they prepared to leave Toulouse and march to the Front. The training would soon be over, and they would have their chance to personally fight in the defense of France.

Toward the end of September, the Americans in the Foreign Legion finally received word that they would join the mass of men already at the Front. The men reacted with a mix of nervousness and excitement. They had heard some news of the staggering casualties in the opening act of the war. They had also witnessed the carnage firsthand when they saw the dead and wounded being transported back from the Front. Their thoughts often wandered to loved ones back in the United States or wherever their family members might reside.

A day before the American Legionnaires left for the Front, Kiffin Rockwell wrote his mother a letter exhibiting some of the emotions that the men felt during this time. Kiffin knew the danger that he faced, but he was more worried about his mother's apparent displeasure than the perils that lay before him. He was troubled that he and Paul had only received one letter from her, and he believed that she was upset with his decision to fight for France. Kiffin's internal struggle between guilt for causing his mother significant anxiety and his desire to prove himself was plainly evident in his letter: "You would not wish my life to be a failure in my own mind, even if by doing so I should live many years and always be with you. If I should be killed in this war I will at least die as a man should and would not consider myself a complete failure. I know you must think me selfish and inconsiderate of your feelings, but I am not. You expect great things of me and I want to do great things, and can see a great future before me. If I am killed in the attempt to attain that future, I have at least done my best; that is all any of us can do."[33] Kiffin's character was clearly on display in this letter to his mother. He was a man who was very much in touch with his own emotions and the thoughts of those around him. He was not oblivious to his mother's plight as a purely selfish son might be. He also knew that it was critical to address the issue instead of allowing it to fester. Kiffin never parsed his words or attempted to avoid uncomfortable conversations. He always tackled a crisis with an attitude of thoughtful aggressiveness. His mother was suffering greatly from the consequences of his seemingly rash decision, but Kiffin was unwilling to apologize for an action that he unwaveringly believed was right. He loved his mother dearly, explained his actions to her in the best way possible, and then he acted. This was Kiffin Rockwell.

Loula almost certainly knew this was the response she would receive because this was the boy she raised. She later wrote, "Perhaps I was a silly mother … but I made every possible effort to have my boys taken out of the army and returned to this country. During the months following their departure, I was almost frantic with grief, for I felt that I should never see them again."[34] Her efforts were all for naught. And Kiffin would not take the easy road; such an idea was absolutely foreign to him. At the end of his letter to his mother, he wrote, "It is going to be a life of hardships but I am willing to go through them, and actually enjoy them."[35] Kiffin's friends in the Legion quickly discovered the quality of the man with whom they were serving, and they followed his lead along the dark road ahead of them.

For now the Americans began to make preparations for their imminent departure. They received word on Sunday, September 27, that they would be leaving the next day or the day after. Alan Seeger was in fine spirits as he whimsically looked forward to the upcoming march. One would never know the young poet was on the verge of facing the enemy for the first time after reading his diary entry that day. Seeger simply wrote, "The arbor of a little inn on the highroad running east of Toulouse. Beautiful sunny afternoon. Peace. The stir of leaves; noise of poultry in the yards near by; distant church bells, warm southern sunlight flooding the wide corn-fields and vineyards." It is difficult to juxtapose this quaintly peaceful scene with the terror that lay before them, but it is hard to fault Seeger for soaking up the serene tranquility before he headed off into the unknown.

The next day the men were still in Toulouse waiting for orders to march. The Americans were impatient as they waited for word, and many of them grumbled about the delay. Each of them was equipped with three days' rations and 120 rounds of cartridges. The wagons were all loaded, and the horses were ready to begin the journey. The French had compressed two years of training into about five weeks due to the unending demand for soldiers to fill the lines at the Front. The men had grown accustomed to the tiring twelve-hour days, but all of them hoped to eventually earn more than one penny per day for their efforts. Such a salary seems almost criminal today, but these were desperate times.

The Americans continued to train while they waited for their departure. They woke up as the sun was rising every day and marched to the end of the ridge that lay behind their barracks. In a large open field surrounded by cornfields, vineyards, and harvest-fields the men practiced battle drills, marching, and close-quarter fighting. Even on the training field, Seeger lost himself in the world around him—an episode that occurred often. He described the scene: "[P]oplars, little hamlets and church-towers, and far away to the south the blue line of the Pyrenees, the high peaks capped with snow. It makes one in love with life, it is all so peaceful and beautiful. But Nature to me is not only hills and blue skies and flowers, but the Universe, the totality of things, reality as it most obviously presents itself to us...."[36] Even though Alan Seeger tended to immerse himself more in life's natural vistas, his mind worked in much the same way as Kiffin's mind. His thoughts rarely settled on his own life for long. As he prepared to leave, Seeger also thought of his mother back at home. His words echoed those of his friend Kiffin: "I hope you see the thing as I do and think that I have done well, being without responsibilities and with no one to suffer materially by my decision, in taking upon my shoulders, too, the burden that so much of humanity is suffering under and, rather than stand ingloriously aside when the opportunity was given me, doing my share for the side that I think right."[37]

All of these American men were members of a unique group. Most of them joined for the same reasons that Kiffin Rockwell and Alan Seeger expressed in their letters, and all of them willingly and courageously faced the dreadful conflict that lay before them. Their thoughts more than likely mirrored those of Rockwell and Seeger, but these two men were in many ways the spokesmen of the group. Kiffin provided the blunt, black-and-white analysis of the situation, while Seeger beautifully described their surroundings, their emotions, and their hopes. All of these men marched into danger with their heads held high and minds convinced that they were symbolically fulfilling the duty of their native country. They had answered the call that few in the United States were even willing to contemplate, and they were proud of this fact. The order to march finally came two days later, and the men advanced into the darkness that had engulfed Europe.

5

At the Front

The arrival of the French Foreign Legion at the Front sparked a chain of events that would culminate with the creation of the Lafayette Escadrille. In many respects, the baptism of fire that the young American recruits would soon endure was also the proving grounds for the fledgling aerial unit that would arise out of the Legion. The Foreign Legion did not create the Lafayette Escadrille, but over half of the squadron's original members came from its ranks. As the Lafayette Escadrille earned its spurs in the skies over France, dozens of additional American men would leave the Foreign Legion to join the famous American squadron. Kiffin Rockwell and the others who served in the Foreign Legion before flying for France would get their first taste of combat in the mud-filled and bloodstained trenches outlining the front lines. In light of this significant connection, the story of the Lafayette Escadrille must begin with the story of the Foreign Legion.

The men who would later become masters of the air started as slaves to the rattling machine guns and the whistling shells. In the trenches, one had little control over living or dying. When death came, it snatched up its victims with sudden and permanent force—there was little any of them could do about it. In the air, they would regain some authority over life or death that they had lost in the trenches, but they would never forget their days among the valiant men on the ground. Looking down from the sky on their brethren swarming like ants along the ground, memories of their former lives would rush to their minds and open the wounds that lay festering within them. The men of the Lafayette Escadrille later fought with abandon in the air because they were free from the prison and hopelessness of the trenches.

The metaphor of breaking free from some unseen force is what defines pilots around the world. Those who fly, no matter what country they are from, are typically characterized as flamboyant, independent, and undaunted by traditional rules and customs. This is no accident. When humans first took to the air, they broke one of the most fundamental rules in all of human history—they defeated the laws of gravity. Gravity no longer confined them—they burst forth from its tenacious grip and never looked back. The character of pilots around the world quickly followed suit.

Among American combat pilots the breaking-free metaphor is especially strong because of the trenches in World War I. It seems uncanny, but the earthen lines of France shaped the soul of American combat flying as much as any other important factor in the development of American air power. The Lafayette Escadrille was the genesis of air combat in America. The Americans in the squadron learned their craft and then bequeathed it to the United States Air Service in 1917 and 1918. But the most influential men in the Lafayette Escadrille—the men who shaped and steered the squadron from its inception—started in the trenches. On the ground among the maze of mud, wood, and stone, these men felt trapped like rats in a cage. When they finally took to flight, they not only broke free of gravity's firm grip, but they also slipped away from the bitterness of the trenches. They fought like devils because they were finally free of a world that none of them would ever forget. And they left a legacy that defines an Air Force today.

Of course at the time, the Americans had barely heard of a trench and certainly did not know that the war they had joined was already hopelessly stalemated. When the Kaiser replaced General von Moltke in mid–September, the American recruits were in the middle of their training period in Toulouse. Erich von Falkenhayn took command and immediately

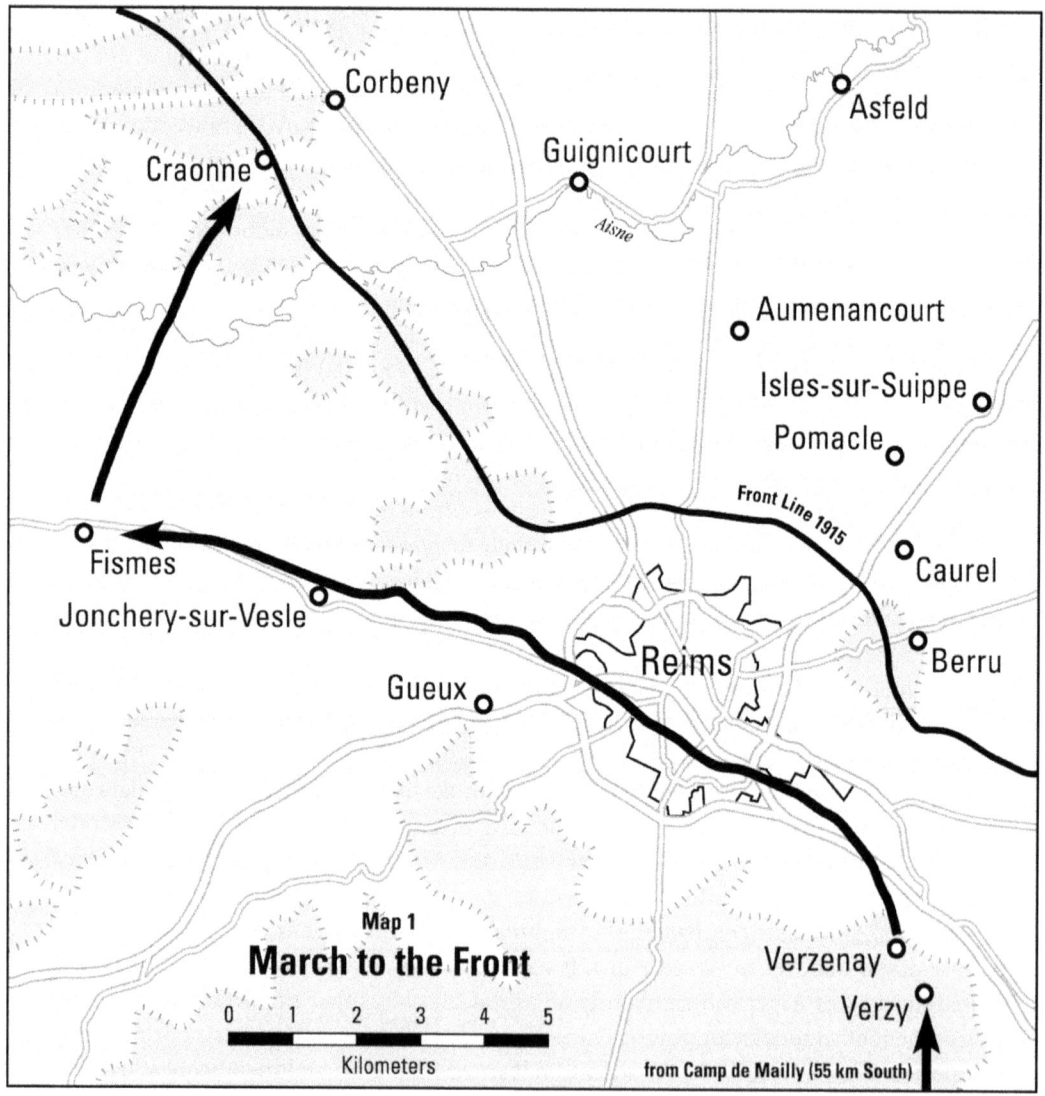

Kiffin's march to the Front in the fall of 1914 with his brother Paul and fellow soldiers of the Foreign Legion. The grueling march ended with several steep climbs in earshot of the terrifying wail and blasts of artillery fire (map by Eureka Cartography, Berkeley, CA).

sought to outflank the French to the north in order to regain the advantage for the German Army. General Joffre countered Falkenhayn's maneuvers while the British attempted to link up with the Belgians along the coast, and the famous "Race to the Sea" began.

As the Americans started their march to the Front, the Germans attacked Antwerp in Belgium in order to protect their supply lines. The city fell on October 10, and the flanking maneuvers continued to move north toward the sea. The British Expeditionary Force (BEF) attempted to advance against the Germans at Menin on October 19 but failed, and for a short time it appeared as if the German Army might overwhelm the Belgians right along the coast near the city of Nieuport. King Albert desperately ordered the sea locks at Nieuport to be opened, and the resultant floods erased any possibility of a German breakthrough along the coast. Falkenhayn then focused his efforts on the city of Ypres, where the First Battle of Ypres began on October 21. The Germans correctly assumed that this would be their last chance for a decisive breakthrough, so they threw a massive force of about four corps against the British lines that consisted of nearly the entire British regular army. The results were devastating as the British defenders mowed down German soldiers, some of whom were young, relatively untrained students. The engagement became known in Germany as the "Massacre of the Innocents," and Falkenhayn slowly realized that his desired advance was sputtering to a halt. The British line held, and the Germans ceased their attacks after November 11, 1914.

Kiffin Rockwell and the new recruits of the French Foreign Legion left Toulouse on September 30 to help shore up the line near the city of Reims, where the Battle of the Aisne had occurred about two weeks prior. Their first march ended quickly at the train station, where they boarded a train without knowing the final destination. It was a long journey, but after sixty hours they arrived at Camp de Mailly, about eighty-five miles east of Paris. When they arrived, the Americans found out that Mailly was about the furthest point that the Germans reached before the Battle of the Marne forced them to retreat.[1] This fact and the marks of destruction around them definitely convinced the recruits that they were nearing their desired place among the troops in battle. Alan Seeger noticed damaged buildings in villages and other structures that had been completely destroyed.[2] The commanders in the Foreign Legion quickly resumed training and drilling while they waited for their first trip to the front lines. The rumbling of siege guns to the east sounded like low thunder to the soldiers training in the field and trying to comprehend what lay ahead of them. On the night of October 3, some of the sentries found two Germans hiding in the woods near the camp. One had already died from hunger and exposure and the other was near death. Neither of them had surrendered because their officers had told them that the French would shoot them on sight if they turned themselves in. The German must have been relieved when the French did not shoot him because he admitted that there were probably thirty or forty others still hiding in the area.

On October 10, the Americans finally received the legendary initiation into the Foreign Legion—a long and grueling forced march. They marched for seven long hours from Mailly to a high field where they set up tents and prepared to spend the night. Just as the men were sure they would receive a break, the merciless officers ordered them to break camp and start marching back to Mailly. The men obeyed and began the long trek back through battlefields strewn with exploded and unexploded shells and abandoned equipment. About this time they learned that the fortress of Antwerp had fallen to the Germans in Belgium.

After hearing the news, Seeger seemed to have recognized the futile situation they faced: "This is the most important event of the war to date. It means the entire subjugation of Belgium. The Germans, as far as I can see, occupy all the territory they have coveted and all that they would keep in the event of their ultimate victory. It is my idea that they will now wage a defensive war entirely, limiting themselves to holding what they have…. On the whole, their situation seems good and the task of the French and English in driving them back a desperately hard one."[3] Seeger was not far off the mark.

The next several days involved training tailored to what they might encounter in a skirmish on the front lines. The maneuvering grounds were five miles away, which required forced marches to and from any training event they received. The men would drill for a few hours and then go on a scouting expedition through the brush and forests in the hills. The officers would always split the recruits into two elements, and one element would attempt to oppose the troops on the scouting expedition. They learned how to gain the advantage and attack, but the thick brush and uneven hills provided a great deal of amusement to the officers, who casually watched the struggling troops from on top of their horses.[4] After hours of pushing through the scraggly hills with no food, the men would quit for the day and begin the long march home.

During these maneuvers, the men learned to fight with their *comrade de combat*, a concept still followed in many modern armies. All the men had one combat comrade, and the pair was required to stay together at all costs during any engagement. Bert Hall, one of the Americans in the Legion, had a combat comrade by the name of Conti who hailed from Italy. Conti had been a bicycle thief prior to joining the Legion and claimed to have been out of jail only nine days during the previous eight years. Whether this claim was true or not is irrelevant at this point, but Conti lived up to his claim in the Legion. Even though he and Hall became great friends, Conti used to steal Hall's knife an average of twice a week. On one particular day, Hall received a box of chocolates from a lady in Switzerland and promptly hid his treasure in his knapsack. When Hall returned later in the day, his chocolates were gone and he immediately suspected Conti, who was sleeping peacefully nearby. Hall crept up on his comrade, put his oft-stolen knife up to Conti's neck, and ordered him to give up the chocolates. Hall's assessment perhaps sums up this aspect of their experience in the Legion: "He produced [the chocolates]. Stealing was second nature with most of these men."[5] Stealing was indeed rife within the Legion, but the Americans quickly learned to deal with this reality.

About eight days after the start of maneuver training, the Foreign Legion decided the new recruits were ready to travel the rest of the way to the front lines on foot. After all the days of additional drills and road marches, the Americans felt as if they were prepared for the long journey. Many of them became excited as they realized their day had finally arrived. The battle was near, the order had come, and the march would only be a mild inconvenience as they traveled to their final destination. Seeger was in high spirits as he wrote, "I go into action with the lightest of light hearts…. I am happy and full of excitement over the wonderful days that are ahead."[6] He told his mother that he would most likely see her the next summer, after the war was over. Unfortunately he could not have known that the war would be far from over in the summer of 1915.

The Legion set out in grand fashion on October 18. The entire Second Regiment of four battalions marched from Camp Mailly on the road heading north to the lines. Four thousand men filled the ranks of the Second Regiment, so the American contingent was but a tiny fraction of the mass of troops leaving the camp. Kiffin's mood at this time was far more serious than that of his friend Seeger. He told his mother that France expected a long, hard war and that news had been bad since the moment they arrived. His confidence was far from shaken, though. He confidently told his mother, "Eventually, the Allies will win, but I fear it will take a long time."[7] Kiffin's intuition was accurate, but it did not make the march any easier.

The march from Mailly to Reims was more than fifty miles, and the Legion commanders characteristically believed this could be done in only a few days. With seventy-pound packs on their backs, the men marched fifteen miles to Fere-Champenoise on the first day, and the Americans were overjoyed that none of them fell out. Vertus was the destination for the second leg, and the men saw growing evidence of the massive battle that marked the outbreak of World War I. They marched through areas that had witnessed the panicked withdrawal of the French army in the first month of the war and the subsequent German retreat to the current line. Whole villages were in ruins, fields had been shredded by artillery fire, and fresh graves marked the resting place of soldiers recently buried. The following day they toiled through the vineyards of Champagne while the fog descended upon them and obscured the beautiful landscape around them. As they climbed the steep hills so prevalent throughout the landscape, the men began to feel the pain of the forced march. Their feet were on fire and William "Bill" Thaw seemed to have one of the worst cases. Hall explains, "Bill Thaw suffered most. His feet were swollen like Zeppelins, and they were not like Cinderella's feet at the beginning either. But he stuck it out, game old Bill."[8] Thaw and another man named King collapsed on the ground next to the column of marching men to ease the searing pain of the blisters on their feet. This was not acceptable behavior in the proud Foreign Legion, however. A French officer rode up, pointed his pistol at the two men, and forced them back into the line of trudging men.

On the night of October 20, the men received a small reprieve from the brutal journey. A quaint village overlooked the last hilltop they climbed, and the Americans stayed in the barn of a rustic chateau just behind an old church. As they sprawled out on the straw, the men gingerly took their boots off to survey the damage to their fiery feet. Corporal Weidemann walked among the troops inspecting their feet. He was the leader of Ninth Squad and a seventeen-year veteran of the Foreign Legion who also used to be an NCO in the Prussian Guards. Any veteran who stayed in the Foreign Legion as long as Weidemann was bound to be a bit crazy, and the men would later find this to be a true statement in the case of their corporal. On this particular night, they were glad for his experience. Weidemann showed all of them how to drain their blisters by passing a needle with heavy thread through each blister and then smearing tallow over the inflamed area and around the inside of the shoe.[9] Sleep that night came quickly to the weary men who collapsed among the hay in the barn loft.

The Americans may have thought their march was over, but the worst was yet to come. They woke up early the next morning with the first leg of a crushing nineteen-mile march. Over the course of the day, a large number of recruits fell out from utter fatigue. Most men wondered if they could make it to their destination. The Second Regiment was bound for Verzenay (about ten miles southeast of Reims) that evening, from where two battalions would immediately leave for the trenches upon arrival. The Americans would receive a slight reprieve in Verzenay, but the men had no idea as they toiled on that day. As twilight approached, the town of Verzy appeared in the distance, nestled in the side of a steep hill with forests above it and vineyards below. The men hoped to stop there, but the trek continued.

The last part of the march from Verzy to Verzenay was brutal for the fatigued legionnaires. They climbed stiffly up the final ridge, one foot after another, urging every muscle within them to continue. The road sauntered its way through patchy champagne vineyards clinging to the war-torn hills. In some areas, the grapes rotted on the vine amidst occasional shell holes and leftover equipment from clashing armies. In other areas, some enterprising farmers had managed to harvest the grapes in the middle of the onslaught. Rockwell and Seeger sank heavily to the ground with a sigh and surveyed the area below them. Verzenay was perched near the crest of a ridge overlooking the city of Reims and a wide valley torn by conflict where the two young men finally got their first look at the German war machine. Cut rudely through the landscape below them, they could see a mass of menacing lines snaking their way along the ground. Ruins were evident in the city of Reims and the environs outside of it. The land closest to the front lines was stripped bare of trees and grass—a lifeless vista surrounded by barbed wire, concrete, and wooden trench works. It was a depressing scene.

The Germans fired salvos of shells twice a day at Verzenay, and shrapnel would rain down on the village and the troops scattered within it. The French would of course return fire, causing a duel of pounding concussions across the valley. The two comrades stared in amazement at the war tapestry unfurled before them. After several minutes of taking in their coming fate, Rockwell and Seeger retired to their shelters. The awful carnage of the scene they had witnessed did not fully register with the two of them. Their excitement at finally being so close to the battle overshadowed the reality ahead. Seeger's poor mother had to endure the following words from her son, "I am feeling fine, in my element, for I have always thirsted for this kind of thing, to be present always where the pulsations are liveliest. Every minute here is worth weeks of ordinary experience."[10] The war seemed to have injected life into Seeger in a peculiar way.

The men only stayed in Verzenay for a couple of days, and then the Legion received orders to move once again. Most of the Americans were irritated by this point because they had not made their first trip to the trenches yet. When the time came to move out, their joy at the sight of a large number of troop-carrying busses rapidly evaporated when they discovered that the Ninth Squad would not get a spot in the convoy. Instead, the Americans had the distinct pleasure of marching behind the wagons carrying ammunition and rations for the battalion. Some of the Americans blamed their predicament on Corporal Weidemann, who had a toxic relationship with Sergeant Teresien, the section leader who doled out unpleasant tasks.[11] Regardless of who was to blame, the Americans in the Ninth Squad initially felt good because the Legion allowed them to place their heavy packs on the wagon. Such uncharacteristic kindness in the Foreign Legion should have alerted them that something sinister was afoot. In the Legion, soldiers marching without packs meant that soldiers could march far greater distances. The officers had no problem forcing them to march nearly uninterrupted from 6:30 in the morning until 10:30 at night—a distance Seeger estimated as 55 kilometers! As if to add insult to injury, they received no food on the journey, and the men nearly passed out when the order to halt finally came.

Seeger was one of the unlucky ones picked for sentry duty as soon as they arrived. He stayed in front of the wagons fighting heavy eyelids until midnight. The only thing that kept him awake was an attack that started along the front lines a few kilometers from his position. He could hear rifle and machine gun fire along with the heavy retorts of the mas-

Kiffin Rockwell (center) aiming his rifle from an entrenched position. Before he became a pilot, Kiffin served over a year in the trenches with the French Foreign Legion. He believed endless sheltering in earthen works was an awful and inglorious existence for a trained soldier (Virginia Military Institute Archives).

sive siege guns. Bright magnesium light pierced the darkness around him every time the men in the trenches fired looping flares to illuminate the ghostly field between the lines. A soldier just a few hours prior had told Seeger about how his regiment had made a mighty charge near the very spot where he stood. The Germans had nearly wiped out the unit, leaving 700 men dead on the ground. Perhaps it is not surprising that Seeger's light demeanor soon soured. After the brutal march all day and sentry duty until midnight, Seeger only slept until three in the morning, at which point the officers forced all of them to march again. His words adequately reveal the mood the men were in when they arrived: "[W]e got up again and continued the march ten or twelve kilometers to this wretched village, where we are lodged for the day in a dirty stable."[12]

The Americans had finally received their wish—they were at the Front. The Second Regiment was attached to the 36th Division, holding the line in a strategic position about twenty miles from Reims and in the hinge of the Aisne-Champagne fronts—a juncture known as the cornerstone of the defense of Paris.[13] From here, their lives alternated between the hellish front-line trenches and the backbreaking reserve trenches. The men were only supposed to spend a few days at the Front, followed by a respite in the reserve trenches, where they could avoid most of the terrifying artillery shells. Reality was much different, however. The Americans sometimes spent days on the front lines under constant stress, threat of attack, and deadly shelling. The few days they would spend in the reserve trenches were full of digging more trenches, hauling supplies, dragging logs, and performing endless additional physical labor. It was utterly exhausting work.

Life in the trenches was far worse. The trenches were deep, narrow, and meandering to prevent unnecessary casualties. The depth allowed the men to keep their bodies obscured from the enemy, but the army also wanted them narrow in order to reduce the target footprint for enemy artillery attacks. Trench engineers designed them in a zigzag pattern in order to minimize casualties if attacking forces penetrated the lines.[14] In a letter to the *New York Sun*, Alan Seeger provided a fairly complete depiction of what the trenches looked like:

> The typical trench dugout resembles catacombs more than anything else. A long gallery is cut in the ground with pick and shovel. Its dimensions are about those of the cages which Louis XI devised for those of his prisoners he wished especially to torture, that is, the height is not great enough to permit a man to stand up and the breadth does not allow him to stretch out.... The roof of the dugout is built by laying long trees across the top of the excavation; felling trees for these coverings occupies a large part of our rest intervals. On the completeness with which these beams are covered with earth depends the comfort and safety of the trench. Wicker screens are often made and laid across the logs, sods are fitted over the screens so as to make a tight covering and then loose earth is thrown back on tops. This is an effective protection against all but the heaviest shells.[15]

Inside the trenches, the wet winter weather wreaked havoc on the lives of the poor souls dwelling in the ground. An American in the Foreign Legion described the mud as one of the real horrors of war: "Liquid mud, full of treacherous roots. Mud like chewing gum. Mud with a stench obscene and putrid."[16] Their soaked feet even gave birth to a new medical condition accurately described as trench foot. After days of exposure to the mud and water in the trenches, the men's feet would begin to go numb and the skin on their feet would decay. Trench foot would often involve open sores and fungal infection, while serious cases even involved gangrene. Some of the men would go for a month without even taking their shoes off, which exponentially aggravated the medical condition. Bert Hall claimed that from mid–October to mid–December he never washed his face or hands, never had his shoes off, and had no change of clothing.[17] The appalling lack of hygiene naturally contributed to the high rate of illness among the men. Nevertheless, they at least learned that keeping their feet warm and dry prevented the onset of trench foot, but their new methods of avoiding trench foot could not alleviate the worst suffering.

The daily shelling of the front lines was by far the most horrific aspect of life in the trenches. Artillery pounded the soldiers' precarious positions, and the whistle of falling shells kept men constantly on edge. When a shell landed in the trenches, the results were devastating, and those who were not wounded or killed were left to pick up the pieces. Peeking out above the top of the trenches was a death wish as machine gunners or soldiers on both sides were ready to fire at any foolhardy soul willing to expose himself. Any soldier who successfully dealt with all of these challenges also had to realize that orders may come down for a new offensive in his sector. And every man knew that all bets were off once he advanced forward from his trench. The odds of surviving several assaults on fortified trench lines were slim indeed. Thus, coping with falling shells, precisely aimed bullets, ringing ears, and the fear of an assault order was enough for strong men to eventually break down.

The Americans in the Foreign Legion received their initiation to the trenches in the final week of October 1914. As the cutting wind and cold air descended upon France, they took up positions along a forest line near the village of Craonnelle, where they spent a day building shelters along the lines that could withstand some of the German shelling. Gazing through the trees, Kiffin, Paul, and the others could see the village below them partially hidden by a small knoll with the remains of the church steeple peeking out above it. Beyond the village on a length of high hills, the Germans faced their position. No sooner had the men completed their shelters than the Germans shifted their artillery fire to their sector where the shrapnel burst in the woods all around them. They spent all day hunkered down in the trenches until nightfall came.

The Americans quickly realized that sleep was hard to come by on the front lines. At that time, barbed wire had not come into general use as a defensive measure, so the Legion sent patrols out each night to maintain the integrity of the line.[18] The shout that would always wake them from their slumber was the cry of *"Aux armes, aux tranchees!"* The men would scramble to their positions while bullets snapped overhead, but the call to arms rarely resulted in an engagement with the enemy. Since most nights allowed for little rest, the Americans would try to sleep during the day oblivious to the whistle of passing shells and the chatter of machine gun fire. After four days and four nights in the trenches on the front line, the Americans of Ninth Squad earned a reprieve. Their company lost two killed and nine wounded, including a man named Van der Veldt who was killed by a large piece of shrapnel only fifteen or twenty yards from their position.

Kiffin and Paul soon began to grow accustomed to the brutal routine. Five days in the trenches was usually followed by one day of rest, after which the soldiers were forced to dig outer lines of trenches. They usually had two days of digging before returning exhausted to the front line trenches after only three days away. The Americans spent most of their time reading, talking, and sleeping while in the trenches or enjoying a rare day of rest. They could not play cards because there was no money to gamble with, and most of the men felt that playing cards without money was a waste of time. They did talk a great deal, and Hall wrote, "We used to talk mostly about eating. That sure was our most popular subject. As soon as you mentioned something good to eat, someone would tell you to shut up, not to talk about such things as we would never eat again, and we did almost get out of the habit."[19]

One day a German shell entered the hayloft where the Americans usually slept. They were in the trenches at the time, so the shell found other victims, killing five and wounding thirteen. Week after week, Kiffin and the others plodded through the trench-rest-dig-trench routine. By December 10, the routine began to take its toll on the men. Kiffin wrote his mother telling her that only fifteen of the American bunch were left—noting that only one had been wounded; the rest were either sick in the hospitals or found easier jobs.[20] He talked of spending twenty-one out of the last twenty-four days in the trenches, while enduring brutally cold nights before they were finally allowed to make fires in structures that masked the smoke. Life for the American Legionnaires was far from pretty.

Many of the men suffered from their shattered expectations of armed combat. They had read of glorious charges, and before they signed up they probably pictured themselves advancing shoulder to shoulder with the Frenchmen they came to support. Instead of glorious advances, the idealistic Americans were hidden in dark trenches, forced to hide from their enemies. Instead of marching side by side with regulars in the French Army, they shared a unit with some men they considered only a step above criminals.[21] Alan Seeger, the man who left Toulouse with a light heart and a smile on his face, was far from amused by this point. He lamented about the inglorious conditions in a long letter he wrote to the *New York Sun*:

> This style of warfare is extremely modern and for the artillerymen is doubtless very interesting, but for the poor common soldier it is anything but romantic. His role is simply to dig himself a hole in the ground and to keep hidden in it as tightly as possible. Continually under the fire of the opposing batteries, he is yet never allowed to get a glimpse of the enemy. Exposed to all the dangers of war, but with none of its enthusiasms or splendid *élan*, he is condemned to sit like an animal in its burrow and hear the shells whistle over his head and take their little daily toll from his comrades. The winter morning dawns with gray skies and the hoar frost on the fields. His feet are numb, his canteen frozen, but he is not allowed to make a fire. The winter night falls, with its prospect of sentry duty and the continual apprehension of the hurried call to arms; he is not even permitted to light a candle, but must fold himself in his blanket and lie down cramped in the dirty straw to sleep as best he may. How different from the popular notion of the evening campfire, the songs and good cheer.[22]

Seeger's disgust at the type of warfare that characterized World War I is unambiguous in his words to the editors in New York. Glory and triumph were nothing more than a fleeting mist or whimsical dream on the fields of France in 1914.

As Christmas approached, the thoughts of the Americans inevitably turned toward home. Seeger thought the pine boughs above the trenches that served as a screen against shrapnel reminded him of Christmas trees decorated for the holiday celebrations. Kiffin talked at length in his letters about the wonderful packages they received from home to supplement their typically meager diet. Every day the men would receive a half a loaf of bread, half a box of sardines, a cup of coffee, a small piece of cheese, a bar of chocolate, and a cup of soup.[23] Every evening, the Americans eagerly awaited mail call, when they would tear open boxes to see what goodies lay inside. Christmas Day was a good day because an American doctor in the Legion brought a Virginia ham to share with the Americans. They also had candy, nuts, jam, and cheese to celebrate the holy day. Kiffin was even overjoyed with the simple pleasure of receiving an orange from a British soldier who had received it in the mail.[24] It was a good day for the men who had grown accustomed to only violence, sickness, and death.

Christmas also allowed the Americans to reflect on their current situation. Kiffin had a nasty cold, but his thoughts continually drifted to his brother and some unfortunate fellow countrymen. Several Americans had been wounded or invalided out with illness, but the worst blow to Kiffin was the departure of his brother. Paul, who had gone along with Kiffin's crazy plan to volunteer, had been injured while out on a patrol. Paul's patrol was out between the lines near the village of Craonelle, and the men were suddenly attacked by blistering machine gun fire and artillery rounds. A shell exploded close enough to Paul to launch him into a nearby communications trench. Shrapnel from the blast wounded him, and he broke his collarbone as he landed in the trench. His injuries were not life-threatening, but at some point during his transfer to the hospital he developed inflammatory rheumatism. After a long stay in convalescent care in Paris, Paul found that the effects from his wound and subsequent illness would not allow him to serve in the Legion again. He bitterly resigned himself to his new fate and lamented the fact that he could no longer provide his characteristic protective cover for his younger brother. From this point on, Kiffin had to endure the trials of combat without his faithful brother by his side.

Kiffin's thoughts also strayed to three other Americans who received the ultimate ticket out of the Foreign Legion. Bill Thaw, Bert Hall, and James Bach all received orders to leave the Legion and transfer to the French Air Service. The thought of being stuck in a blind trench was abysmal to a man like Thaw, who had felt the thrill of soaring above the earth. Thaw tried to enlist as a pilot when he first joined the French, but French officials insisted that he must first join the Legion. After living the life of an infantryman for a few months, the wealthy heir began to pursue his dream of military aviation once again. Bach and Hall were immediately interested in the idea, and the three of them talked for hours in the trenches about transferring to the air service. Somehow, the three men were granted permission to visit the aerodrome of Escadrille D.6, a squadron of two-seat monoplanes known as Deperdussins. They enlisted the help of a Lieutenant Brocard, who promised them that he would do what he could to help them.

Much to Thaw's dismay, the first orders to arrive were transfer orders for James Bach. In November, Bach bid farewell to his comrades and headed to Saint-Cyr for training. Bach was one of the Americans who enlisted in the Legion at the start of the war. When he received his orders and started training at Saint-Cyr, Bach gained the distinction of being the first member of the Lafayette Flying Corps.[25] Unfortunately, about a year later he also gained the distinction of becoming the first American captured by Germany as a prisoner of war.

Bill Thaw was not one to be deterred, however. A few days after Bach left the Front, Thaw went back to Escadrille D.6, hiking the entire thirty-two kilometers on his own. His friends saw this personal march as an act of commitment to his cause: "That he actually walked this distance is, to those who know Thaw's love of less exhausting modes of travel, sufficient comment on his determination to become a military aviator."[26] After his initiation to trench warfare, one can hardly blame the man for his intense desire to break away from the prison shackles of the trenches. Lieutenant Brocard assured him that his orders would arrive, and both Thaw and Hall received their transfers in December of 1914. Bert Hall, the Missouri native and one who already had gained a reputation as a fabricator of stories, and

William Thaw, the heir to a family fortune, set off for a new life and all the hope that came with it.

For the Americans left behind, the Christmas celebrations were somewhat muted. Several Americans still remained in the Legion, and they all bonded together to face whatever dangers or hardships lay ahead of them. On New Year's Eve, they received orders to march back to a small village named Cuiry, where the men spent four days in a much-needed state of relative relaxation. The Legion officers marched the men ten kilometers on New Year's Day to a bathhouse where they were able to take a hot shower for the first time in three months. Unfortunately, they also received typhoid vaccinations, which made some of them feverish during the final two days of rest. At midnight on January 4, 1915, the men started off for the front lines once again. The night was dark and rainy, which caused the men to trip and slide for three hours before finally arriving in a small village. Kiffin told his sister, "This is a village that I should say probably had five thousand inhabitants before the war and it has been fought over quite a bit, the Germans having lost two thousand in a night attack on it in the early part of the war. There is now not a building that has not been demolished by shells."[27] Walking down the gutted streets on a stormy night was a sobering reminder of the war's dreadful cost.

The remaining Americans in the Foreign Legion grew accustomed to their miserable existence in the trenches along the front line. As the months passed by, they grew increasingly disillusioned with the style of warfare necessitated by the great stalemate. All of them longed to fight the enemy openly instead of cowering in the dark and dirty caverns cut into the earth. To them, a massive offensive was preferable to the daily grind of the trenches, even if it carried enormous risks. The glorious advance that the Americans hoped for would come soon enough.

6

The Battle of Artois

In January of 1915, Kiffin's battalion moved up to the line in an area near their former location, and his section occupied a fantastic old château on a hill south of Craonelle. The château was in ruins from the constant shelling; the entire top floor had disintegrated and its outside was pockmarked with holes, blast marks, and burns. The basement of the château remained intact, however. Sixty men could comfortably dwell within its confines, so most of Kiffin's section moved into the once magnificent structure. The men rushed into their new abode with relief; they were thankful to be out of the cold rain and done with the frustrating night march.

Unfortunately, the Legionnaires had no idea how precarious their position was. In typical fashion, the sergeant called the Ninth Squad to *petit post* (sentry duty), which gave Kiffin the opportunity to scout out their new position along the front line. When he discovered the layout of their post, Kiffin was appalled. The château was part of a large wooded park overlooking Craonelle in the narrow valley below. An eight-foot wall ran around the whole park (about two miles in circumference), and the château was only about one hundred yards away from the wall. Kiffin and three others took up their post along the wall, which he described as a wall from a castle in medieval times. Five other men from his section and their corporal occupied different stations along the wall. Kiffin's station covered a large shell hole in the wall that had a door in the middle and narrow openings on either side to observe the enemy. He climbed a nearby ladder to see the enemy lines and finally realized the danger they faced. The ground was flat for about one hundred yards beyond the wall and then dropped off toward the valley and the village of Craonnelle. The area around the château was lightly wooded, and French trench lines snaked their way through the woods and connected to the château compound on both sides. Looking north through the woods and the narrow Craonnelle valley, Kiffin saw a line of hills towering much higher than their small hill where the château was perched. The Germans were dug in all along the opposing hillside with a perfect view of the entire wooded park. They were completely exposed!

When the sun rose the next morning, the Americans quickly found themselves under merciless gunfire. Corporal Weidemann sent Kiffin and another guard to the château for breakfast, and on their way back the Germans began to fire. They tossed the food aside and sprinted for the wall as bullets whizzed by them from what appeared to be three directions. Both of them realized how close the German trenches were now that it was light enough to see. They made it back to their position and dove into small dugouts that provided some protection from enemy fire. Kiffin could barely contain his rage in a letter to his sister Agnes: "All that day we crouched in little dug-outs and cursed our officers for putting us in such a death-trap without more men and without telling us the real situation."[1] Little did they know that the following night would be even worse.

The Ninth Squad continued to maintain their position along the northern wall, but the tyrannical Sergeant Teresien only delegated six men for the job. The six Legionnaires had to watch a wall about a half mile long, while one communication sentinel and the corporal shuttled back and forth between the wall and the château. The sentries would rotate at their positions two hours on and two hours off until six the next morning. The officers and NCOs issued dire warnings concerning sentries dozing off because the four men were protecting hundreds of additional troops in the rear scattered in and around the château. It was not a well-conceived plan.

At ten-thirty that night, Kiffin stood at the same small door along the wall as the previous night. Alan Seeger was the communication sentinel that night, and after one of his runs to the château, he came up to check on Kiffin about that time. As the young poet walked up, something fell at Kiffin's feet, sputtered a little and then went out. Both of them were confused, and Kiffin casually said, "What's that?" He reached down and picked it up as Seeger yelled, "Good God! It's a hand grenade!" Horrified, Kiffin threw it away and sent Seeger to run and get Corporal Weidemann. A few minutes later, Seeger and the corporal sprinted back to the position just as another grenade came soaring over the wall. Not wanting to press his luck a second time, Kiffin dove over the ladder toward Weidemann as the grenade exploded. They both shouted "*Aux armes*" to alert the rest of the camp. After checking for injuries, they heard a noise and looked back to the hole in the wall. Their worst fears were confirmed when they saw the door cave in and Germans streaming in through the gap. Corporal Weidemann and Kiffin were completely exposed, so they turned and ran for cover. Seeger had already moved to the line of woods after the grenade came over the wall, so they ran as fast as they could towards his position. After running ten feet, a rifle flashed and Kiffin dropped to the ground. He heard the corporal fall heavily beside him and realized that Weidemann was probably dead.

With no one returning fire, Kiffin had no choice but to continue to run for the cover of the woods. As he ran, the bullets snapped by him, but he successfully made it to the woods. The five other sentries jumped up on a platform along the wall to return fire, but the Germans in the trenches and the Germans inside the wall quickly directed their fire at the raised platform. The sentries all fell off the platform into the mud below. "Cap" Capdevielle had a bullet clip his ear; Fred Zinn had one pass between his fingers, skinning them; and Buchanan, an Englishman, had his rifle shattered. The sentries lay in the mud and did not return fire because they were now pointing back towards friendly lines and did not want to hit their own soldiers. From the wood line, Kiffin furiously tried to clear a jam from his gun as he watched the scene unfold before him. The Germans cut off all of Weidemann's equipment, took his gun, and repeatedly pounded his body with the butts of their rifles. The young Rockwell was purple with rage at his inability to stop his enemies. Before he could find another rifle, the Germans escaped out of the door without a shot being fired from any of the Legionnaires. Seeger joined Kiffin and when Sergeant Teresien arrived with two others, they all advanced to the door and secured the position. It was a profoundly sad day for the Ninth Squad.

The episode at the wall affected Kiffin on multiple levels. First and foremost, he was disgraced at his performance and the mistakes he had made. He was also upset that none

6. *The Battle of Artois* 59

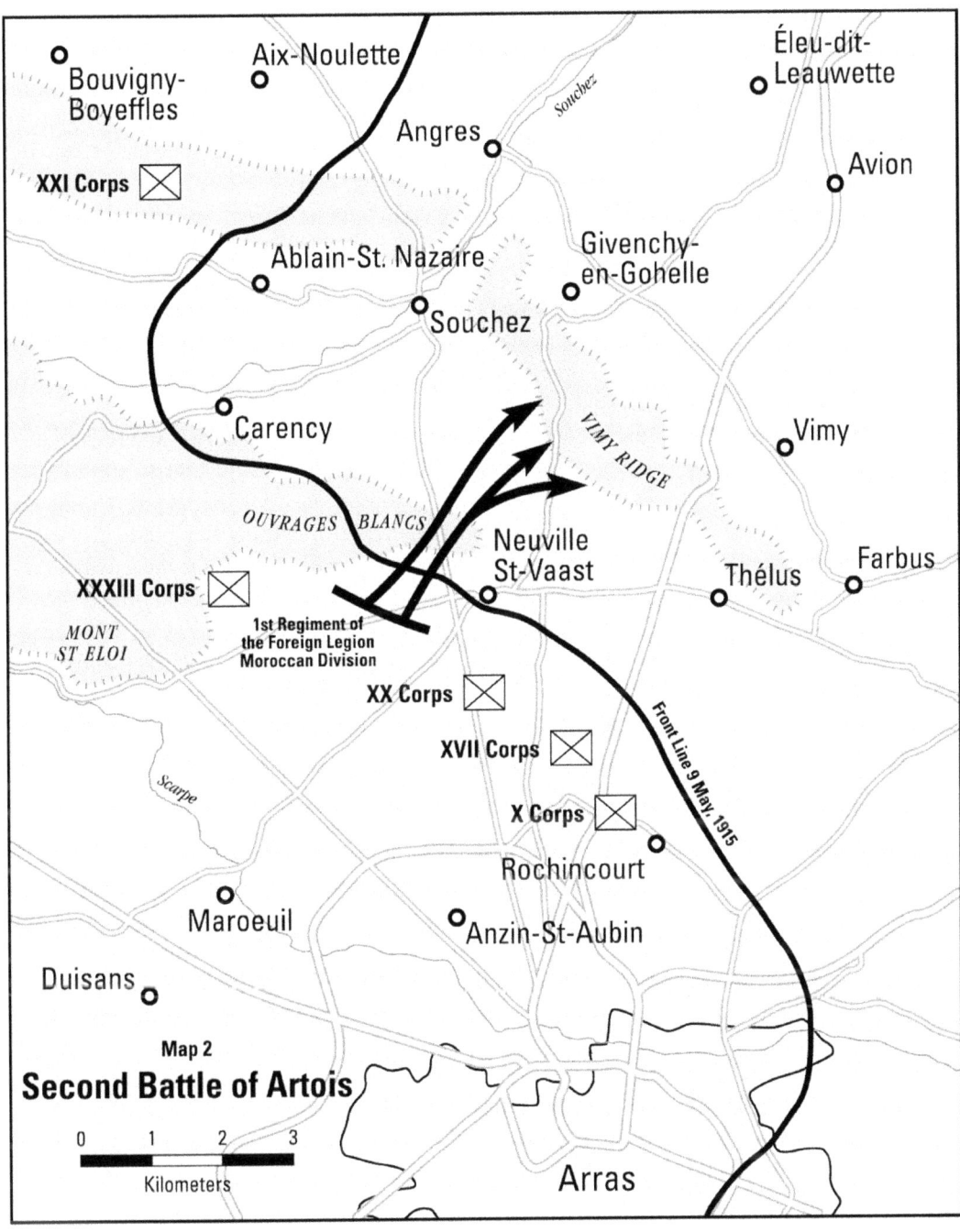

Kiffin's first experience beyond the front line occurred during an infantry charge near the city of Arras in the Second Battle of Artois. The Foreign Legion was given the task of seizing Vimy Ridge, which towered over their position about three kilometers to the northeast. Portions of the Legion made it to Vimy Ridge after braving murderous fire from the town of Neuville St.-Vaast, but they were ultimately forced to withdraw. Kiffin was wounded in the battle and retreated to a barn west of Neuville St.-Vaast (map by Eureka Cartography, Berkeley, CA).

of them returned fire when the enemy troops successfully breached the wall. Kiffin was furious at the German method of fighting. He wrote to his sister, "The whole thing impressed all of us more like a murder than warfare. The Germans had no military point to gain by doing what they did. It was done as an act of individualism with a desire to kill." He could not get over senseless killing with no real objective. The episode also affected Kiffin's nerves. After Sergeant Teresien and some reinforcements arrived, they had Kiffin resume his post by the wall. He crouched in the dark, once again by himself, and covered the same terrifying hole. Furthermore, the other men had left Corporal Weidemann's shattered body right by the hole, so Kiffin had the awful result of his failure to protect the line sprawled out in front of him. When the Red Cross men finally came and retrieved the body, Kiffin called the acting chief of the squad and "told him he would have to relieve me as my nerves had gone all to pieces."[2] As he trudged back to the rear, he felt the events of that night weighing heavily on his soul.

However, one more thing occurred that night that repaired his nerves and fueled the fire in his heart forever. The thoughtful Legion officers gave him a whole thirty minutes to restore his splintered nerves and then sent him to another post for the rest of the night! About two hours after he took up his new post, he heard something that made his body quiver with outrage. He wrote, "[T]here came from the German trenches the most diabolical yell of derision I ever heard. It was mocking Weidemann's last words, his call 'Aux armes,' and it practically froze the blood to hear it. Up until that minute I had never felt a real desire to kill a German. Since then I have had nothing but murder in my heart, and now no matter what happens I am going through this war as long as I can."[3] The episode at the breach in the wall would stay with Kiffin in the years to come. He was committed now—there was no going back.

The next several weeks were miserable for Kiffin. He could not sleep the day after Corporal Weidemann was killed, and the next night he had sentry duty once again. The following day he was just drifting off to sleep when someone called a false alarm of "Aux armes," and he had another sleepless day followed by sentry duty at night. Early the next morning, the Legion mercifully relieved Kiffin's section and sent them five kilometers to the rear. Kiffin lamented, "Nothing could be worse than those four days and nights. The uncertainty of it all—lying in the rain and mud, eternally watching and listening, knowing that everywhere men were prowling, trying to slip up on one another in the dark and kill."[4] Unfortunately, his time in the château was not yet complete. The Ninth Squad made two additional trips out to what Kiffin termed "the village death-trap": one eight-day stint followed by a short rest and then another four days. During the last four day stay, Kiffin only had a total of five hours of sleep. One night he had to crouch by the wall for fourteen hours in the sleet and snow with four others. They were all under orders that if they moved from their post, they would all be court-martialed. About fifteen minutes after leaving their post for the last time, their replacements were shot up and several were killed.

The Americans who were left in the Ninth Squad were nearing their breaking point. Kiffin wrote Paul and asked him, "If you can get me into a French regiment, get busy, for I want to get out of the Legion. This regiment is no good; the officers are no good. It is just luck I am not dead, owing to their ignorance and neglect."[5] Kiffin spent the rest of January trying to convince Paul not to come back to the Legion: "In regard to your coming back to this regiment, I will say for the last time, don't be a fool. At least one third of the men who left Camp de Mailly have gotten out of the Regiment.... I told the boys you were trying to come back and not a one of them but said that they thought you had more sense."[6] By February there were only four Americans left in the Ninth Squad—Kiffin, Seeger, Cap, and Dowd. In another section of the regiment, an American and 1908 Harvard graduate named Edward Mandell Stone died on February 27, 1915, after succumbing to an earlier wound from a piece of shrapnel that had penetrated his lung.[7] The Englishmen had been transferred to the British Army, and Kiffin was given the option of going with them, but he declined. He decided that, despite his misgivings, since he started with the French he would stick with them. Seeger and the others who remained felt the same.

By this point, Kiffin began to vocally express the ignoble position of the infantry that Seeger had articulated a few months earlier. He viewed the war as an artillery war and thought it possible to go through the entire war without ever fighting in the way he and Paul had imagined they would when they left the United States. For a man willing to fight for a cause he believed in, the inaction drove him crazy. Kiffin wrote about an engagement on January 29: "[A] battle was raging on every side of us, and we were in a very advanced position. Our artillery near us did the most damage of any. It simply raked the valley, yet we didn't fire a shot. We sat with our rifles in our hands underground, ready to go out any minute and fight, but that was all."[8] The frustration of sitting underground wore on them day after day. When they were not on the front lines, their workload increased as a result of the drastically reduced number of troops in the company. The remaining men still had to accomplish the tasks assigned to a full-strength company, so the work was exhausting and never-ending.

In the middle of February, Kiffin's section finally began to receive replacements. The Ninth Squad received six husky Alsatian rookies whom the veterans planned to put to work immediately. The American contingent now included Cap, Zinn, Dowd, Kiffin, Seeger, Trinkard, King, Phélizot, and Chatkoff. An American named Edward Morlae also returned after studying for a few weeks in a corporals' school. The Legion promoted him to sergeant, and he ruled over Kiffin's section with a lordly air. Morlae constantly insulted the Americans to curry favor with the officers, and the rest of the Americans began to view him as little better than a traitor. Kiffin instructed his brother to keep his letter in case he did not make it back, so Paul could counter Morlae if he tried to return to the U.S. and gain a lot of cheap notoriety.[9]

At the end of February, the men returned from a six-day trip to the lines, where they served in an open trench close enough to hear the Germans talking! Seeger was nearly killed there when he exposed himself for about two seconds in a shallow section of the trench. A German sniper fired, and the bullet tore through the sleeve of Seeger's capote, grazing his arm and raising a lump on the skin. Seeger was very grateful to be alive after the incident and also thankful that his wound was not serious enough to make him leave the ranks.[10] A few days after Seeger's near-death experience, Fred Zinn was evacuated to a hospital in the rear. He had been sick for months, which caused him to fall asleep on guard. The Legion officers punished him with short stints in prison and extra work but finally realized that he was too sick to continue. The ranks of the Americans who had started the war were now very thin.

When March arrived, the Americans were desperate for a change of sectors. They had heard rumors of a great offensive, and they knew that their valley with its menacing German positions would be the last place the French would decide to attack. All of them worried that they would miss the coming charge while stuck in their familiar trenches. Kiffin was especially frustrated because their current line of trenches near the château was only about seven hundred meters from the first trenches they occupied back in October of 1914. He wrote to a friend in Paris, "I have always been a great roamer and to have to stay in the same place is my greatest trial."[11] Thus, the monotony and inactivity of their lives in the trenches was compounded by the thought that they might miss the glorious advance that they had imagined for so long.

On March 11, the morale of the Americans stooped to its lowest level yet. Kiffin wrote to Paul and informed him, "[W]e are practically under arrest now. That is, we can't go out in the streets because it would mean a war."[12] The "we" in Kiffin's letter were the remainder of the American contingent, who had gotten into quite a scrap a few days prior. During a break from the front lines, Herman Chatkoff strolled up to the coffee wagon in the courtyard and asked for a cup of coffee. The Moroccan cook sneered at Chatkoff and told him he was a cheat and a liar like all the Americans. Rene Phélizot, the dashing young American who had brandished the United States flag with Seeger on the march through Paris in August 1914, walked up to support his fellow countryman. Phélizot laughed at the remark and challenged the cook. When the cook backed down, an Arab man from the machine gun section began fighting with Phélizot. A ring of men circled around the fight, and Phélizot was clearly besting the Arab man when another man of Arabic descent pushed through the men into the circle. The incoming man had a canteen full of wine at the end of a leather strap, which he swung toward Phélizot and knocked him unconscious.

The man's treacherous act sparked a huge brawl between the Americans and the machine gun section that left five additional Americans and six other Legionnaires unconscious as well. It reportedly took three men to pull Chatkoff away from the Arab man who had felled Phélizot.[13] When Phélizot finally came to his senses, he knew there was something terribly wrong with his head. He asked to be relieved of duty, but the doctors did not clear him and forced him to go on the march the next day. Phélizot collapsed on the march and a lieutenant found him paralyzed with lockjaw setting in. He died two days later after suffering terribly, but just before he died, he lifted an American flag and cried, "I am an American."[14]

When Phélizot's section heard the news, they were enraged, and the fight resumed with a fury. The Americans and other internationals in Phélizot's section descended upon the machine gun section, which placed the whole camp in a state of mass confusion. The Legion officers and NCOs had to break up the fight with the points of their bayonets and found that the Arab man who had killed Phélizot had been kicked to death. Not knowing who was ultimately responsible, the officers arrested the entire group of Americans. The men later found out that the Legion arrested them in order to protect them from future acts of retribution.[15] No one ever discovered the man responsible for killing the Arab man who had murdered Phélizot. It was certainly an unfortunate episode and it marked the breaking point for Kiffin. He could no longer serve in a unit that had killed his friend Rene Phélizot.

On March 18, 1915, Kiffin Rockwell received a transfer to the First Regiment of the Foreign Legion. He had completely lost faith in the leadership of his former unit, and some of the other Legionnaires had created a toxic environment due to their radical thinking.

According to Paul Rockwell, the Second Regiment (the unit Kiffin left) had several hundred Russian Jews and Armenians who were afflicted with Bolshevist ideas. He wrote that "their presence and propaganda did much to sap the morale of the other volunteers, and to lessen their confidence in the fighting ability of their regiment."[16] Shortly after Kiffin's transfer, the Russian Jews mutinied and several were shot or banished—some eventually traveling back at the end of the war to hold important posts in the new Bolshevist regime in Russia.

When Kiffin received news of his transfer to the new unit, he was relatively happy for the first time in a long while. It hurt having to leave good friends like Seeger and Cap, but he had lost faith in the leadership and makeup of the Second Regiment. On the day he left his old unit, he toiled with the other Americans digging ditches in the lines to the rear. When Kiffin returned, he found orders transferring him to the First Regiment of the Foreign Legion. He hurriedly packed his bag and left two hours later on a wagon to a town in the rear. The trip restored his spirits from the very beginning because he was finally on the move. The next morning he briefed a general at the Army Corps headquarters and then grabbed a ride with a captain to another corps headquarters. A different captain took him the remainder of the way, regaling him with tales of shells and bullets flying around his vehicle as he ran the gauntlet every day. Kiffin and the captain drove through Reims, which was in terrible condition from the constant bombardment it had endured over the last seven months. When he finally arrived, he wrote, "My trip here was the most pleasant thing I have experienced since leaving the States."[17] His joy only increased after meeting the Americans in his new section.

The American men who fought in the First Regiment of the Foreign Legion were just as intriguing as those Kiffin had served with in the Second Regiment. Kenneth Weeks was older than Kiffin by about four years, but they quickly became fast friends. He was a hardened veteran like Kiffin by March of 1915 and had a young face masked behind a dashing moustache that extended with a slight flare about an inch on either side. Weeks was born in the Boston suburb of Chestnut Hill and went to school at the Massachusetts Institute of Technology before he moved in 1910 to Paris with his mother, Alice Weeks. He planned to make architecture a career but spent most of his time writing books before the fateful summer of 1914. Kenneth followed many other Americans into the ranks of the Foreign Legion that August.

Kiffin was thrilled to meet Russell Kelly because Kelly had attended the Virginia Military Institute in 1910. They swapped stories of their days as "rats" while daydreaming about their homes back in America. Kelly was the son of a New York City lawyer who left New York on November 3 on a voyage to France with two other American volunteers named Laurence Scanlon and John Smith. Scanlon was from Long Island and had been studying electrical engineering before he decided to quit school and head to France. Smith was an adventurer with many careers under his belt by the time he shipped off for France. His real name was John Earl Fisk, and he had been a gold prospector in Alaska, a mercenary in the Mexican and Chilean revolutions, and a U.S. soldier during the Spanish-American War. All three of them joined the Foreign Legion upon their arrival in France.

Paul Pavelka rounded out the group. He went by the name Skipper and was a true wanderer at heart. He was relatively short with a sly smile and an eternal spark in his eye. Skipper had been a cowboy in the American West, had hiked across the Andes in South America, and had crossed the Pacific to the South Seas as a sailor. When the war started he was lounging at a sailor's home in New York with no real plan for his life. Kiffin described him as one who "never had any ambition, otherwise [he] could have made a success as he has quite a lot of genius in several ways."[18] Kiffin bonded quickly with all of them, and they were soon an inseparable band of tough Legionnaires.

Kiffin was impressed with life in the First Regiment. The officers were excellent and the soldiers were effective—in many ways a completely different experience from his first outfit. He spent twenty-two days in the trenches upon arrival, but the French had turned trench design into quite an art form by that point. During the winter, the regiment built a system of trenches much like an underground city. Kiffin described their architecture: "They are about eight feet deep and three feet wide and wind around in every direction so that you can walk for hours, all of them leading into the front combat trench, which is especially well made, having loopholes every two feet and a little place to stand in when shooting."[19]

Spring was in the air, so the men enjoyed the weather when they were not in the trenches. Russell Kelly wrote about an impromptu baseball game that the Americans put on for the rest of the soldiers. Skipper Pavelka had just returned from a stay in the hospital, and since he was quite a handyman, he volunteered to make a baseball for them. The game had the rapt attention of the whole company until "home-run Scanlon, the heavy hitter" drove the ball into the canal and lost it.[20] The men were clearly disappointed but resolved to make a new ball so they could play again. But there would be no more baseball. As the spring matured, dark clouds began to gather once again. A storm was coming, and the First Regiment would be in the center of the action.

By the spring of 1915, the French were beginning to feel desperate—the war was not going well. The Germans had taken a significant chunk of strategically critical territory in 1914, and the French counterattack had stalled at the Aisne River. Both sides lost several hundred thousand men during the opening months of the war. These were staggering numbers, and the nations involved had no time to recover from the horrific losses. As spring approached, Germany was confident that it would achieve victory in 1915—so much so that German leaders drafted the September Programme, which included the peace terms they intended to impose on their defeated enemies.[21] However, the Germans drastically underestimated the determination of the French and the British. France clearly had the most to lose at this point, and French national pride and national economic necessity demanded that they go on the offensive in 1915.[22] Britain finally managed to muster a force large enough to make a difference along the Front, and the British government was united in the stand against Prussian militarism after seeing what had happened to Belgium.[23] The stage was set for a fight to the death. And death came quickly to the three nations as they nearly destroyed themselves over the course of the next year and a half.

The French and British decided to launch a massive offensive in several sectors during the spring of 1915. The British and French would conduct combined operations in Flanders and Artois while the French attacked independently in Champagne. General Foch submitted a detailed plan of operation to General Joffre on March 24, about a week after Kiffin arrived at his new unit. General Joffre described the plan: "An attack by three Army Corps, with the Vimy ridge as objective.... Two flank attacks.... A note issued to Armies on April 19, 1915, laid down the methods to be employed in the preparation and execution of the attacks. It was pointed out in this Note that the object of an offensive action was not confined to seizing a line of hostile trenches, but included driving the enemy from the whole of his position, and defeating him before he had time to take up a fresh one."[24] Unfortunately, no one seemed overly concerned that the Germans held the high ground all along Vimy Ridge and were well prepared to absorb a major attack. Joffre's plan had all the trappings of another mass slaughter.

The camp was buzzing with excitement on April 21 when the Americans packed up to leave. All the men seemed to realize that a major offensive was in the works, and they were overjoyed with the thought that they might participate in the attack. Their departure was delayed, but the men were heartened by the news that Italy had declared war on Austria.[25] Joy soon gave way to a sense of dread when news trickled in about the German gas attacks on April 22 during the Second Battle of Ypres. The German offensive had little strategic purpose other than to test a new weapon, chlorine poison gas. While the chemical attacks were not a game-changer, the possibility of dealing with poison gas only increased the anxiety of the Legionnaires as they prepared for battle. The men finally left on April 24 with rumors that they were going either to Lyons for repose or the Dardanelles to fight on another front.[26] Instead, the troop train went through Paris and then turned north for Artois.

General Joffre set the date as May 7 for the opening volley of his spring campaign. When the Americans arrived in the Artois sector, they began to prepare for the coming offensive. Kiffin noted that the French people seemed to have cheered considerably compared to the hysterical and excitable demeanors he had seen earlier in 1914.[27] But it was news from home that really occupied Kiffin's mind on the eve of battle. He received several letters from friends and family at home that irked him greatly: "Others have written me, and all of you write and act as if you thought I came over here for notoriety and to try to be a hero. It has hurt me and made me mad also to think how few people there are who give me credit for any strength of character. Maybe the restless life I have led justifies all in their opinions. However, I am sorry that such is the case and it means to me that I will never try to live in the South."[28] These were strong words for a young man with such deep Southern roots, but it shows how sensitive Kiffin was about the subject of fighting for notoriety. He had seen his fair share of men who fought for fame and took the first boat home to cash in on their new celebrity. To be compared to these men was deeply insulting to Kiffin and only served to strengthen his will to fight.

In his last letter before the battle, Kiffin spoke of the general feeling in camp and the preparations they were making. The men actually received several special meals and all the wine they could drink in the first week of May. They had a party each day and performed very little work when they were not in the trenches. But the sector was heating up quickly. Kiffin lost one of his Italian friends to a well-aimed bullet on the same night when one of the battalions had four killed and fifteen wounded. The night before the Italian was killed, fifteen men in his battalion lost their lives. Kiffin wrote Paul: "I hate to think of what is going to happen soon, for we are all going into hard action. A big battle is going to commence soon, and we have already received instructions as to what our position will be in it and what we have got to do. It is no rumor this time. I have seen the troops, artillery, etc., enough to convince me. So in the meantime we are making the best of things and getting the most out of life possible."[29]

On the seventh of May, the Americans received word that the attack was imminent.

They were scheduled to go to the rear, but instead received news that the French offensive would begin at midnight that night. Their battalion would lead the regiment, so the men spent all day preparing cartridges, gathering food, and building an embankment right in front of the German barbed wire. When they were all ready, they sat and waited for the artillery bombardment to commence, but the night was silent. Looking up at Vimy Ridge was daunting. The men were located on a flat plain to the west of the ridge, facing German lines on the flat lands ahead of them and all the way up the ridge behind the closest lines. They saw the barbed wire barricading the closest German positions as well as all the crossing fields of fire below and on the heights above. It was somewhat terrifying to all of them when they contemplated that they would probably be running that gauntlet fairly soon. The weather did not cooperate, however, so the Americans marched twelve kilometers to the rear after standing guard that night and hearing that the attack had been postponed. The next night the officers awoke the men at one in the morning, and they silently marched back up to the Front, arriving at daybreak on May 9.

The attack began with a fury just after Kiffin's battalion set up its position along the line. Kiffin wrote, "In a few minutes it began to sound as if all hell had broken loose, when our artillery all along the line opened up on the Germans."[30] The men could see nothing but smoke and debris after the French guns pounded the German-occupied ridge for hours. Kiffin's moment had come. Today there would be no hiding underground—the men were going to fight for France. At ten in the morning, the first line of men received the order to advance. Kiffin described the organized chaos as the men rushed out of the trenches: "I saw the finest sight I have ever seen.... There was not a sign of hesitation. They were falling fast, but as fast as men fell, it seemed as if new men sprang up out of the ground to take their places. One second it looked as if an entire section had fallen by one sweep of a machine-gun. In a few moments, a second line of men crawled out of our trenches; and at seven minutes past ten, our captain called '*En avant*,' and we went dashing down the trenches with the German artillery giving us hell as we went."[31]

Kiffin's section quickly scampered to the first-line trenches where a shell burst near his captain. The captain wiped his hand across the face, said it was nothing, and ordered the men to keep moving. The machine-gun fire and pounding of artillery shells was deafening and lethal. The men would run forward about twenty-five or fifty meters and then drop when the enemy fire was too much to handle. They would lie behind their packs until they could breathe again and then would jump up and continue moving forward. It was an exhausting but apparently exhilarating experience: "To think of fear or the horror of the thing was impossible. All I could think of was what a wonderful advance it was, and how everyone was going against that stream of lead as if he loved it. I kept that up for five hours. By then we had advanced three or four kilometers, but were badly cut up and also mixed up with men from other regiments.... Most of our officers had fallen, including the Colonel and three commandants. (I understand that there only remain now four officers out of the whole regiment.) We had taken most of a village and were taking the rest of it."[32]

Despite the tremendous German counter-fire, the Legionnaires continued their advance toward the objective of Vimy Ridge. Kiffin's unit was slightly to the left of the Neuville-Saint-Vaast, the village he described, and they were receiving murderous fire from the front and from the rear of the village. He and Skipper Pavelka were lying next to their second lieutenant when a messenger ran up and told the lieutenant that he was in command of the company—all the other officers had fallen. The lieutenant soberly accepted the news and told Kiffin and Skipper to follow him one at a time. The lieutenant bounded off and Kiffin followed with Skipper behind him. About twenty meters into his sprint, Kiffin felt as if his leg had been cut out from under him. He went down hard and finally realized that a German bullet had incapacitated him. The young man from Asheville, North Carolina, was wounded and had no idea if he would make it off the contested battlefield alive.

As Kiffin started to stem the flow of blood out of the hole in his leg, his superiors at every level took stock of the situation. General Joffre, the man ultimately responsible for the Allied forces in France, received a number of messages describing the battle. Some of the notes indicated that the morning was a great success. Frenchmen were advancing in droves, and the Germans were on the run. Yet the old, experienced general knew better than to believe the initial reports. He quickly realized that his forces could not capitalize on the advance. Joffre wrote that good progress was made on May 9 with the Moroccan Division reaching Hill 140 about 11 a.m., but the division used up all its reserves in its extraordinary rapid advance.[33] Kiffin's regiment was part of the Moroccan Division, but his unit's advance had nearly reached its climax when he fell. The lack of reserve forces kept the French from exploiting their hard-fought gains. They maintained their progress but could not capture Souchez or Neuville-Saint-Vaast, two of their primary objectives. General Joffre lamented: "In trench warfare of this description, bitterly contested as it was on both sides, there were but fleeting opportunities of snatching a fruitful victory.... As early as the evening of May 9th, I felt that a brilliant success had just eluded us. Nevertheless, I decided to continue the offensive without a pause ... although I fully realized the strain entailed on the troops."[34]

The strain on the troops caused by Joffre's continued offensive was considerable. The fighting continued through mid–June, but the combined French and British offensive only captured 6,500 yards of trenches to a depth of 3,000 and 4,500 yards. They also captured nearly 7,500 German prisoners during the advance. But what was the cost for these paltry gains? The British lost 28,267 killed, wounded or missing, while the Germans lost 49,446 men. The French in their glorious charge lost 102,533 men![35] These numbers are absolutely astounding, but this was the reality of the First World War. The fighting would only continue as the world watched humanity destroy itself on the fields of France.

7

Kiffin's Recovery and New Hope

When Kiffin Rockwell fell, he knew nothing of the drastic turn his life was about to take. He learned right away that he was extremely lucky to be alive, but it would take some time to reflect on what he had experienced over the last nine months. During his long recovery, Kiffin had time to ponder life in general, the life of an infantryman, the hard realities of the Foreign Legion, and his desired role in the conflict that had engulfed Europe. After weeks of deliberation and a brief return to the front lines, Kiffin realized he could not go back to the kind of warfare that emerged from the stagnant trenches in France. Never again would he choose to fight the way he had in the Foreign Legion.

It was not ground combat that irked Kiffin and his colleagues, but the peculiar brand of ground combat during World War I. In his opinion, the life of a soldier in the trenches was deplorable because it destroyed the drive and the intensity of a man trained to fight. There was no heroism in hiding underground away from the enemy like scared rabbits. The trenches denuded them of passion and made them automatons that occasionally attacked the enemy lines in suicidal frontal assaults. In 1915, if a man wanted to fight with passion and freedom to maneuver against the enemy, he did not have to look far. With a slight glance upward, the men of the trenches could see a life remarkably different from their own. A new world was unfolding above their heads, and the men with idealistic fervor in their hearts were forcefully drawn toward it. And once a man's eyes shifted to the air, there was no going back.

When Kiffin crumpled on the 9th of March, he was not yet thinking of life after the trenches—his first task was to survive the ordeal. Fortunately for him, the bullet that struck had gone clean through the fleshy part of his thigh and missed the bone. When Skipper saw his friend collapse, he skidded to a halt beside Kiffin and prepared to assist. Kiffin yelled at Skipper to continue, while he dragged himself into a hole to bandage his wounds. One of his comrades from the regiment was lying nearby with a bullet through both hips and a shell fragment in his stomach. He gasped for water, but all the men had used up their water earlier in the day. Kiffin stayed by his side until he died.

Kiffin spent a great deal of time huddled in his hole trying to survive the horrendous shelling. His regiment had not advanced far from him, so the Germans were furiously shelling the entire area. Three times a shell landed within ten meters of him and convinced him that he was about to die. He would hear the shell falling and when the whine was deafening, Kiffin knew it would land on him. All three times he said to himself, "Well, it is over," shut his eyes and waited for certain death.[1] But every time, the shells would explode with a terrific roar, and Kiffin would find himself covered with dirt but alive. At one point during a lull in the shelling, Kiffin wriggled up to the front line to be with the men in his regiment. When he arrived, his friends told him to crawl to the rear because if the Germans counterattacked he would surely be captured. Kiffin reluctantly agreed with their assessment and dragged himself about a kilometer to a haystack where other wounded men had congregated. His marathon crawl had been excruciating and the bandage had torn away from his leg requiring him to reapply it on his wound. By the time he arrived at the haystack it was dark, and a Red Cross man informed the wounded soldiers that they would have to wait for evacuation until the following day. Kiffin did not want to wait, so he found a stick and hobbled two or three kilometers to a farm, where he slept the rest of the night.

Kiffin spent the next day trying to make it to a place with medical care. He hobbled some more, hitched a ride on an artillery cart, and then finally received an evacuation card with a spot on a train headed to the rear. The train left at midnight, and Kiffin could barely move his leg from that point on. After a miserable ride all day, including a stop in Paris where none of the wounded men were allowed off the train, Kiffin disembarked and asked an Army officer for a train to a hospital in Paris. The officer obliged but accidentally put him on a train to Rennes. By the time he arrived in the wrong location, the hospital personnel decided it was too risky to send him to Paris. It had taken Kiffin four days to reach a hospital, and his wound was starting to fester, which concerned the staff. Military Hospital 101 in Rennes took great care of their American patient, however. They put him in the officers' ward and quickly cleaned his wound before any further damage could be done. When he finally fell asleep in the comfortable hospital bed, Kiffin noted that he was lying between two clean sheets for the first time in nine months.

In his first few days of reflection, Kiffin could think of nothing but praise for his regiment in the Foreign Legion. He was proud of the new group of men that he had served with, even for a short time, in the First Regiment. He described his comrades to his friend the Vicomte du Peloux in Paris: "They were more serious about the war, and the volunteers were men who engaged out of love and admiration for France, and because they knew they were *right*. They were men who had the courage of their convictions and were willing to die, if necessary, to prove it. So the day we were called upon to attack, every man went into it willingly with the determination to do his best, and humming the Marseillaise. As to the officers—no officers ever led their men better than ours led us. Practically every one of them fell, but they fell at the head of their men, urging them onward."[2] The description of his unit's glorious advance must have struck a chord in his heart, for he was soon apologizing. Kiffin realized that his friend might think he was glossing over the deaths of men in his unit, so he continued: "I don't want you to think that I am cold-blooded, without feeling, but the horror of it all is overshadowed by the feeling of pride and admiration I have for them all. This life does not hold such great value in my eyes as it does in some people's, and I feel that those men who died that day, died having made a success of their lives in their own little way, doing something for the world, for posterity, and that their characters are their souls which will forever live and be passed down from generation to generation."[3]

In fact, Kiffin's battalion, Battalion B of the First Regiment, had fought valiantly the day he fell and throughout the rest of the battle. Kiffin's friend Russell Kelly described their advance after two of the other battalions had already charged and had many men cut down.

They left the trenches under heavy rifle and machine-gun fire, crossing the fields "well strewn with dead and dying of Battalions C and A."[4] Kelly's description matches Kiffin's version of the battle. It was a series of advances, followed by halts after heavy gunfire, and then further advances as the artillery narrowed in on their static positions. After Kiffin fell wounded, the men finally took the crest of the hill and dug themselves in as night began to fall. Kelly wrote, "It is a nightmare: during the entire night the cries of the wounded rang out. Grand, grand indeed is this butchery they call war!"[5] The next day the men withstood a tremendous German counterattack in which artillery shells cut down Legionnaires without mercy. Amazingly, the new line occupied by the Legion held against the German onslaught, but the men were exhausted and stretched thin. They ran out of water and had to suffer through almost a full day and a night without a sip of water. The wait was excruciating, but eventually a reserve unit moved forward and relieved the shattered remains of the First Regiment. As Russell Kelly trudged fitfully back to the rear, he surveyed the utter destruction around him and remarked, "I laugh when I try to think of civilization. But with all we must admit it is a great world and I do not regret that I am here."[6]

For some time, Kiffin temporarily overlooked his previous frustrations with the life of a soldier in the trenches. He had no idea about the fate of his colleagues until news of the battle and letters from his fellow Americans came trickling in as he lay in bed at the hospital. He learned that the initial French assault had gone as well as could be expected. Before he was wounded, the French managed to advance three miles in just over ninety minutes. They reached Vimy Ridge and could overlook the plains below, but reserve forces were too far behind them. The French tried repeatedly to capture the towns of Souchez and Neuville-Saint-Vaast (where Kiffin fell), but the German positions were too strong. The Foreign Legion played a major role in the offensive, but after all the suffering, the French captured only about 10,000 yards of enemy territory and gained absolutely nothing of value.

After the Battle of Artois in May 1915, General Joffre knew his chances of winning a decisive victory were fading fast, but he still tried to view the battle in a positive light. He wrote, "This battle marked a distinct improvement in our methods of attack and in the power of our materiel. We had captured 6,500 yards of trenches … while the enemy had been forced to bring up all his available reserves.… Severe losses were inflicted on him.…"[7] General Joffre's positive spin seems paltry when compared to the loss of 100,000 men for no strategic gain—it would become a sorrowful refrain throughout the war.

Kiffin finally heard of his friends' fate a few days after arriving at the hospital. His thoughts naturally centered on the advance of the Foreign Legion's First Regiment, and he remembered how all of the Americans had been waiting for months to participate in a grand attack. As the terrifying minutes of the assault flashed through his brain, the months of hiding in underground tombs faded into the back recesses of his mind. The advance of the First Regiment had resulted in catastrophic numbers of casualties, but the thousands of deaths did not incapacitate Kiffin with grief because he believed the men died an honorable death for a worthy cause. It certainly helped that the other Americans had also been extremely fortunate. Russell Kelly, Skipper Pavelka, Laurence Scanlon, John Earl Fisk, and Kenneth Weeks had all survived despite the terrible losses. The rest of the squad and the battalion were not so fortunate. Of the fourteen men in Kiffin's squad, only the five Americans and one corporal had survived. The Legion lost so many officers and men that the corporal became the company commander on the second day of the battle, and the whole First Regiment of four thousand soldiers was reduced to about seventeen hundred men.

The hospital in Rennes was ideal for a man recovering from a war wound and many chilling memories. It had been a large school for boys before the war and had a nice garden where he could enjoy the fresh spring air. He shared a room with a second lieutenant and a young artilleryman who both spoke English and treated him kindly. Kiffin's brother Paul had started work as a war correspondent for the *Chicago Daily News* and temporarily moved to Rennes to help take care of his brother. He came every day from twelve until five bearing more magazines, books, and newspapers than Kiffin had time to read. Many of the nurses spoke English, and English-speaking residents of Rennes came to visit Kiffin from time to time. Kiffin seemed particularly attracted to a blonde nurse from Alsace who came to see him nearly every afternoon. He enjoyed their long talks together, especially after Paul left in early June to go back to Paris. During these peaceful moments, Kiffin often felt as if the whole war had been a horrible nightmare, but then his thoughts eventually wandered back to his friends who were still toiling in the trenches. The guilt would set in and he wrote, "[I]t doesn't take me long to disillusion myself. The hospital has so many pitiful examples of the effects of the war—men crippled and terribly disfigured for life."[8]

After Kiffin heard that he would have to stay at the hospital in Rennes for at least eight weeks, he slowly began to lose patience. The first target of his displeasure was his own

Convalescent soldiers, nurses, and helpers at the Hôpital de la Mothe in 1915. Kiffin's brother, Paul Rockwell, is the tall man in the doorway, and his fiancée, Jeanne Leygues, is the lady with a dark shawl three people to the right. The chateau is currently owned by Jeanne's great-niece, Céline Raphael-Leygues (from the archives of Loula Rockwell Brown, courtesy W. Vance Brown II).

country. He could not understand why the United States refused to support France—it was unfathomable to him. Kiffin complained, "We are all watching the U.S. now. If she wants to keep up her name and be respected by other nations, I don't see how she will keep from fighting." Still, he held out hope that President Wilson would come to his senses and not disappoint him.[9] It was, in hindsight, a futile hope, since President Wilson would remain adamantly opposed to the war for another two years.

His mother constantly worried about her son and sent letters to nearly every American in Paris asking them to release Kiffin from the Foreign Legion. She also wrote Kiffin giving him advice about what he should do if he became a prisoner of war. Kiffin quickly responded that if he had followed her advice, "I would have been immediately put up against a tree and shot."[10] It was all too much for Kiffin, who felt that his mother did not understand him at all—although it is worth noting that he did not fully empathize with her plight either. His attempts to explain himself often made the situation worse. After being in the hospital for over a month, Kiffin wrote to his mother and told her: "When you write of the chances of my being killed I can see that you have a great horror of it. But I don't see anything so terrible in death.... So if I should be killed I think you ought to be proud in knowing that your son tried to be a *man* and was not afraid to die, and that he gave his life for a greater cause than most people do—the cause of all humanity."[11] Kiffin's words, in many ways, summarized his entire journey from Atlanta in 1914 to the Battle of Artois in 1915. It was classic Kiffin Rockwell prose. His cause, the cause of France, was more than that of just a single country. It was the cause of all mankind. His choice of words, "the cause of all humanity," became his trademark, the phrase that hundreds of men and women eventually associated with Kiffin Rockwell.

While this hardly would have comforted a worried mother, it was ironically this letter that brought Loula Rockwell to her senses and marked a turning point in Loula's relationship with her son. She suddenly realized why Paul and Kiffin had left and why they chose to fight. Kiffin's mother wrote: "I shall never forget that day. I was on my way to see a patient one morning when his letter was handed to me. I sat alone in my little car and there read his letter for the first time without shedding a tear. I saw then, for the first time, what compelled them to go to France, and saw it in the light that they saw it.... It was this letter ... that brought me to myself. I realized that my sons were no longer boys to be dictated to, but men, and I felt the seriousness of their purpose. I was proud of their forefathers' fighting spirit that I saw in them, and I honored them for the vision of justice and right that they had caught. Realizing that my sons were warriors, I steeled my heart for any fate."[12]

Kiffin's words clearly indicate how he viewed the war and his purpose in fighting for France. Kiffin firmly believed that the war going on in Europe was not just another typical European balance-of-power conflict. To Kiffin, Germany's actions threatened all of humanity. He never really elaborated on why he believed Germany's attack was an attack against mankind itself. It is likely that he believed Germany's philosophy at the time was diametrically opposed to the liberty that he believed characterized France, Britain, and the United States. He spoke of defending America and France often and proclaimed his willingness to fight to the death in the process. He also spoke of paying the debt of Rochambeau. Since the French general came to America in order to help the American revolutionaries win their independence, it is almost certain that Kiffin volunteered to help France defend her freedom. But without knowing his exact thought process, it is impossible to know with complete certainty why Kiffin had such strong views on the war. What is crystal clear is his belief that he was fighting for all of humanity—a belief that would eventually propel him to even greater heights.

By the middle of June 1915, Kiffin desperately wanted to be back with the soldiers of the Legion. He received a letter from Skipper Pavelka that described the drastically reduced ranks in the regiment. Their company only had thirty-five men when it previously had close to one hundred men. The sharp reductions convinced the Army to withdraw the First Regiment from the front lines until it could replace some of the fallen men. Kiffin also heard that his old unit, the Second Regiment with Alan Seeger and the others, had missed the Battle of Artois. They were currently shifting sectors but had not endured the kind of losses that the First Regiment suffered. The news from the Front was making Kiffin impatient with his slow recovery. However, a few days after receiving Skipper's letter, a new influx of wounded men brought some foreboding news with them.

Kiffin's battalion had endured another massacre in the same cursed spot where he had been wounded and many others had fallen dead. The flood of wounded men continued, and Kiffin managed to find a pair of second lieutenants who had served in his battalion. One of them said that there were only six men left in the company when they left the battlefield. The officer told him about how they breached the German lines, and the cavalry charged through the huge hole to further the advance. Unfortunately, the infantry reserves did not follow the cavalry as intended, so the cavalry and the advance infantry suffered significant losses. When Kiffin heard the news, he became anxious about his American friends who had survived the first assault. He sent letters to Weeks and Skipper, and wrote Paul to ask him to scour the Paris hospitals for them, but he feared the worst.

A few days later, Kiffin received a letter from Skipper. His friend was lying in a hospital recovering from a bayonet wound. Skipper had charged the enemy trenches with the other men, and he was pierced with a bayonet as he prepared to jump on a German soldier. Kiffin was relieved that his good friend had survived, but he worried about Skipper's convalescent period after the hospital. He wanted Skipper taken care of, so he wrote to Paul: "Skipper's family didn't amount to anything and he never had any education to speak of, and he has been on his own lookout ever since a child, rambling about the world, but he has the sentiments of a gentleman. He did not have to enlist for France, he could have gotten a boat away from Europe and continued as a sailor. But he is a good lad and brave. He has no way of getting money from home and no friends in France.... You and I can keep him in spending money, and his wants are simple and few."[13]

The rest of the Americans were not so fortunate. On the eve of the battle, Kiffin's American friends learned that their battalion, Battalion B, would be the first to leave its sector. They knew what this order meant because they had seen what happened to Battalion A and C when they were the first to advance on May 9. They all remembered jumping over and scampering around the bodies of the first battalions to advance, so they understood what awaited them on the following day. Nevertheless, on the morning of June 16, Battalion B valiantly rushed out of the trenches in the face of withering fire from machine guns, rifles, and shrapnel. Many of them fell before reaching the first line of German trenches, but those still on their feet continued to advance toward the second line of trenches. Paul Pavelka received his bayonet wound as he jumped into the second line of trenches, and Lawrence Scanlon was hit in the leg and foot by rifle fire, leaving him severely wounded.

He and Skipper lay wounded and watched the three remaining Americans advance. Russell Kelly received a wound to the shoulder that did not seem serious to one of his companions, but he and John Earl Fisk were never seen again.[14] Kenneth Weeks was last seen on the 17th of June, running towards the third line of German trenches, his right arm extended and facing the enemy. On November 25, 1915, the French found his body and buried him in a military cemetery near Mont St. Eloi.

The battles of May and June were a catastrophe for the First Regiment of the Foreign Legion. Every officer in the regiment was killed during the last battle in June, but the French only gained about two miles in depth over a front of two miles.[15] Kelly, Weeks, and Fisk were all missing and presumed dead. Skipper and Scanlon finally had stretcher-bearers retrieve them and bring them back to the rear. Skipper healed relatively quickly, but it took Lawrence Scanlon months to fully recover from his wounds. When the fighting finally ended, the First Regiment marched back to the rear again. The horrendous losses forced the French to reorganize the Legion. The First Regiment had four thousand men on its roster when it went into battle in the beginning of May. After returning to the rear in June, the Foreign Legion held a roll call for the First Regiment and only 700 men answered.[16] The Foreign Legion had been thoroughly baptized by the raging inferno of the First World War.

Kiffin finally received his long-awaited discharge from the hospital as he learned of all the devastating news. He left the hospital on the 24th of June and moved to a convalescent ward until he received the paperwork for his convalescence leave. While he waited impatiently, he received another letter from his mother that apparently questioned why he continued to serve France instead of his own country. (His mother had sent this letter before she received his letter that finally changed her focus.) In characteristic fashion, Kiffin shifted the focus back to the cause: "In regard to what I have done for France—I had rather be fighting for France than doing anything else right now. If one is going to fight, I don't see why the *country* should have as great an influence as the *principle*. I am just following out my old theory that we are part of this whole scheme of affairs and that we can't successfully confine ourselves to one small district."[17] It was vintage Kiffin Rockwell. He loved the United States dearly, but he also believed in fighting for what was right. In his mind, the principle of defending France superseded any comfortable life he could have in the U.S. at the time. The war was his chance to show what he believed and with whom he would stand.

But as he started his convalescent leave, a thought began to twist Kiffin's heart into knots. He was still committed to the cause with all his being, but the Americans he had served with had all fallen. The memory of the trenches came rushing back into his mind like a relentless flood. The thought of languishing in the trenches waiting to fight the enemy started to haunt him. He could not bear to be shackled and hidden in the mud and tunnels again. Leaving the Legion had become inevitable, but what was his alternative?

8

Pilot Training

The alternative to life in the trenches resided among the puffy white clouds casting shadows on the battered French countryside, but it took Kiffin a few months to fully realize it. Compared to the mud, the darkness, and the deadlines of the battlefields below, the air above the trenches appeared pure, fresh, and glowing with life. After his convalescence, Kiffin would have to return to the front line because no other options came to fruition before he was called back to the Foreign Legion. He would soon find that many people were helping him behind the scenes and that a much different future awaited him. The call of flight, and the freedom that it contained, started to beckon him, and Kiffin quickly responded. His days as a soldier in the trenches were numbered. The young man who had never soared above the earth would find his calling in the cold, crisp sky above France.

For the time being, Kiffin focused on enjoying his convalescent leave in Paris with his brother Paul and their growing circle of friends. He arrived in Paris in early July and relished the opportunity to spend time with people unaffected by the horrors of the trenches. Paul was working for the Information Section of the French Army General Headquarters where he helped them produce propaganda. In his spare time, he continued his war correspondence work with the *Chicago Daily News* and enjoyed his budding relationship with a woman named Jeanne Leygues. Paul first met Jeanne when she nursed him to health at her mother's château after his shrapnel injury. The two had been inseparable ever since.

Paul proposed to Jeanne before Kiffin arrived in Paris, so his younger brother was anxious to meet his future sister-in-law. Jeanne's father, Georges Leygues, was a longtime politician who was elected to the Chamber of Deputies at the age of twenty-five and entered into the Cabinet of Republican Defense with Alexandre Millerand in 1899. He later became prime minister of France after Alexandre Millerand was elected president of France in September of 1920. Georges Leygues was also extremely wealthy. A Parisian merchant named M. Chauchard, who owned a Paris department store called Magasins du Louvre, was so pleased when he received the grand cordon of the Legion of Honor that he bequeathed a fortune to Georges Leygues.[1] When Paul eventually married Jeanne over a year later, the *New York Times* described her as one of the wealthiest heiresses in France.[2]

Kiffin was happy that his brother had found a new and meaningful life in Paris. He told his mother that Paul had found a fine woman and described Jeanne and her mother in glowing terms. Kiffin also finally met Paul's friends, the Vicomte and Vicomtesse du Peloux. The du Peloux family was a well-known and aristocratic family that had been involved in many of France's most historical events over the years. Kiffin had been corresponding with the Vicomte from the Front, and the couple acted as if the Rockwell brothers were their own children. Paul and Kiffin dined with them often and thoroughly enjoyed their company, but Kiffin noticed that a solemn pallor had fallen on the people of Paris. The reality of the war had struck with all its fury, and sadness reigned in the streets of Paris and in the hearts of its people. He told his mother that everyone desperately wanted the war to end, but there was very little hope of a rapid conclusion since "the only peace that would be any good is a peace of complete victory, which will take time, for the Germans are still strong."[3]

The month of convalescent leave passed quickly for Kiffin, but the thought of his fellow Americans weighed heavily upon him. Kelly, Weeks, and Fisk were still officially listed as missing, so the Rockwell brothers and the rest of the American community in Paris held out hope that they might have been captured by the Germans. He and Paul made numerous friends across Paris, including Mrs. Alice Weeks, the mother of Ken Weeks. Alice Weeks moved back to Paris in January of 1915 to be close to her son Ken as he served in the Legion. After her son disappeared during the Battle of Artois, she opened her home to the men who had served with her son, including Paul and Kiffin Rockwell. The idea of supporting American soldiers in France came to her gradually: "Soldiers came; they came again, bringing others. Letters came from the Front and were answered. Almost without realizing the process, Mrs. Weeks suddenly found herself with the responsibilities [of those] who needed assistance of one sort or another."[4] Alice Weeks became a mother figure to many of the Americans who were far from home. She eventually started an organization called the Home Service, which was funded and supported by a committee of American businessmen.

Kiffin playing pool at the Hotel Pomme d'Or with James McConnell (left) and Victor Chapman (center) while the hotel proprietor watches. Kiffin's mother had chased her son away from a pool table years earlier due to her displeasure with his pool buddies. He apparently did not give up the hobby (Virginia Military Institute Archives).

Kiffin's desire to fight for France was as strong as it was before, but the desire to fly started to stir in his soul. He reached out to Bill Thaw and some of the others already in the French Air Service in order to seek out the possibilities of joining the aviation branch. By the end of July, he had not received an order to transfer, so he prepared to make the lonely trip back to the Front. It was at this point that Kiffin found out what his mother had been doing behind the scenes before her heart changed after receiving his letter. While he was in the hospital, she had pleaded with the U.S. Ambassador in Paris and asked him to intervene by blocking Kiffin from rejoining the French Foreign Legion. Kiffin wrote his mother about her secretive work: "I had a long talk with our Ambassador this week. He told me that owing to the letter he received from you he went to the War Department and tried to get Paul and me released. I was awfully sorry to hear that he had done that; but he offered to do anything possible for me. So I asked him to go back to those people and explain things, and tell them I regret that such a request had ever been made. I hope to get a few favors from the War Department now, so I want to fix things with them."[5] Kiffin knew his mother was only trying to protect him, but a release from service was not what he had in mind. He had formally requested a transfer to aviation from the War Department, so the last thing he wanted was for them to think he was responsible for the release from service request. It is hard to blame Loula Rockwell for trying to protect her beloved son, but Kiffin was idealistic and headstrong, and it was impossible to sway him from the path he had chosen.

Kiffin's return to the Front was not a happy affair. He arrived at a staging area in Lyon on the first of August 1915, and told Paul that conditions were not good. The place was filthy and the food rotten. His leg also bothered him a great deal, and he inquired about a new electric massage treatment that was available. The Foreign Legion was so drained of men that the French reorganized the two drastically depleted regiments into one regiment. Whenever Kiffin inquired about anyone he knew, they would always say "dead," so he stopped asking. He wrote Alice Weeks and told her that the train ride back to the Front was the saddest night in his life: "I was not sad because I was going back to the war, but it was from thinking of the ones who stay behind. I was in a second-class coach and very comfortable but I could not sleep. I just thought and thought all night long and could not keep the tears out of my eyes. I want to live now more than I ever did in my life, but not from the selfish standpoint. This war has taught me many things, and now I want to live to do whatever good is possible. But if I am killed at any time during the war I will not be afraid to die, and you may know that I will die like a man should, feeling that it is the greatest death that a man can die. I will always take the greatest care of myself and not do foolish things, but will always try to do my duty to the upmost for what we are fighting for."[6]

Life in Lyon did not get any better after Kiffin settled into a routine. His leg had not yet healed enough to return to the front lines. The muscles surrounding the wound were still very weak, and he could only handle walking on it for eight hours at a time. For an active man like Kiffin, the waiting and inactivity were driving him crazy. All of his friends had been killed, had left the Foreign Legion, or were assigned to other units. He told Paul he was totally demoralized and said, "Every single nationality that is engaged in this war is being released…. The ones that will be left will be a rotten bunch. If by any chance I am not transferred to the aviation, they ought to at least put me in a French regiment."[7] When given an opportunity to travel with a detachment to a nearby camp, Kiffin agreed immediately. He arrived in La Valbonne on August 8 and was pleased to find Skipper already there with another American veteran Legionnaire named Trinkard. La Valbonne was much more pleasant than Lyon, with fresh air, trees, and grass providing a pleasant scene for the arriving soldiers. Kiffin also noted that the town had several cafés where the men could all go to relax and get a drink. He was easing back into the Foreign Legion, but Kiffin's heart lay elsewhere. The desire to fly was now a powerful force within him.

On August 11, Kiffin received a message that sent his spirit soaring. The officers called both him and Skipper to the personnel bureau, where they found an order transferring them both to aviation. Kiffin and Skipper were so excited and overwhelmed that they called several of the men together for a large celebration. The next day they signed papers all morning at the bureau and passed a medical examination. After formally signing the transfer orders, the two friends began to wait for the order to move. Their eyes shined with anticipation as they tried to imagine what it would feel like to climb into a flying machine for the first time. Unfortunately, their happiness and eagerness began to fade as the wait turned into days and then weeks. The orders still did not come, and the Legion began to train the new recruits on the intricacies of trench life. Kiffin, Skipper, and Trinkard wanted to share their ideas of how to survive in the trenches, but the inexperienced officers taught the new recruits while the veterans dug trenches for twenty-four hours. It was backbreaking work and did nothing to improve the morale of two men who were only biding time until they received orders to move.

By the end of August, Kiffin believed that the movement order would never come and decided to volunteer for the Legion unit fighting in the Dardanelles. His regiment in La Valbonne was a small patchwork of veterans from the old regiments supplemented by new recruits who had very little idea of what the future held. Kiffin thought the new officers and recruits were unprepared and unorganized for the deadly trials that awaited them. He told Paul, "[I]t is such a disgrace to France for such things to happen that I wish something could be done to stop it. My idea is that the Legion should be broken up...."[8] These were strong words from a young man who had served the Legion proudly and believed that it had performed gloriously two months prior. But the Legion he knew had been decimated and dismantled after the spring offensives. The one that remained only reminded him of the senseless actions that seemed to characterize the First World War. He had reached his lowest point. Volunteering to make the long trip to the Dardanelles, with a stop in Algeria, seemed far preferable to the monotony of trench training and the certainty of returning to a futile life on the front lines. But just as his misery began to peak, Kiffin received the news he was convinced would never come. A blessed telegram arrived instructing him to leave for Lyons within the hour.

When Kiffin Rockwell permanently left the Foreign Legion to pursue his new calling, he left a small group of Americans behind in the Foreign Legion. Most of the surviving American Legionnaires had either transferred to aviation, joined regular French Army units, or resigned from army life altogether. Additional Americans were arriving every month to serve in the Foreign Legion, but there were only a select few who had started with the Legion and would finish—or die—with the Legion.

Alan Seeger was the most famous individual of the men who decided to stick with the Legion for the duration of the war. Despite pleas from fellow Americans to join aviation and pleas from his family to leave France, Seeger continued to fight. In a final stroke of poetic irony, the young, idealistic composer fell dead on Independence Day, July 4, 1916. He was cut down by a hail of bullets after cheering on his fellow soldiers to charge a position bristling with machine guns. His most enduring words come from his poem "Rendezvous," which eventually became one of President John F. Kennedy's favorite poems.[9] Seeger's words are a haunting description of life (and death) in the darkness of the trenches along the front lines:

> I have a rendezvous with Death
> At some disputed barricade,
> When Spring comes back with rustling shade
> And apple-blossoms fill the air—
> I have a rendezvous with Death
> When Spring brings back blue days and fair.
>
> It may be he shall take my hand
> And lead me into his dark land
> And close my eyes and quench my breath—
> It may be I shall pass him still.
> I have a rendezvous with Death
> On some scarred slope of battered hill,
> When Spring comes round again this year
> And the first meadow-flowers appear.
>
> God knows 'twere better to be deep
> Pillowed in silk and scented down,
> Where love throbs out in blissful sleep,
> Pulse nigh to pulse, and breath to breath,
> Where hushed awakenings are dear...
> But I've a rendezvous with Death
> At midnight in some flaming town,
> When Spring trips north again this year,
> And I to my pledged word am true,
> I shall not fail that rendezvous.[10]

Many of the other men suffered fates similar to that of Alan Seeger. Dennis Dowd was wounded in Champagne on October 19, 1915. He joined the Lafayette Flying Corps after recovering but was killed in an airplane accident in flight training on August 11, 1916. "Cap" Capdevielle changed to the 170th Regiment of the French Army, where he eventually became a sergeant. He was decorated for gallantry at the famous Battle of Verdun, but when the United States finally joined the war, Cap decided to continue to fight for France. Just weeks before the Armistice, he was killed on October 3, 1918, when a bullet struck him as he led his men in an attack. Charles Sweeny was wounded in 1915, but went on to be a major in the American Army. Lawrence Scanlon followed Skipper and Kiffin into aviation after he recovered from the wounds he suffered during the battle on June 16, 1915. Fred Zinn was wounded on February 1, 1916, became a gunner in a bomber unit, and later served in the American Air Service. In all, these men served honorably for France. It is a testament to their spirit and their sense of duty that they were willing to give their service (and in some cases their lives) for the defense of France.

The Americans who preceded Kiffin Rockwell in French aviation paved the way for the flood of Americans who would follow. When William Thaw, Bert Hall, and James Bach left for flight training at the end of 1914, they knew the French would be closely observing their performance. Only Thaw had previous aviation experience, but Bert Hall was not the type of person to let another overshadow him. Instead of confessing his total inexperience, Hall convinced the French that he was already a seasoned pilot, so they put him into an aircraft right away. He climbed alone into the machine and took a deep breath—it was the first time he had ever seen an aircraft up close! The instructors showed him how to start the aircraft and then stood back to observe his first flight. Hall's lie had forced him into an awful situation, but he was also not one to readily confess his misdeeds. Rather than telling the instructors that he had embellished his record, Hall decided to take the chance and find out if he could figure out how to fly on his own. He somehow motored the aircraft to the field, opened the throttle, and began hurtling away from the observers. After he went "zigzagging [around the field] like a drunken duck … [he] crashed headlong into the wall of a hangar."[11] The knowledge necessary to pilot his aircraft did not come to him in those fleeting seconds, and he crashed the plane at the far end of the field. Amazingly, aside from his wounded pride, Bert Hall was unhurt; even more astonishing is the fact that the French did not immediately throw him out of the Air Service. They were desperate for pilots, but they also liked his brashness, so they sent him off to pilot training. Unfortunately, Bert Hall's exaggerations continued and would follow him well into the future.

On the other hand, Bill Thaw immediately impressed the French authorities with his flying skills. At first the French had tagged him as a *soldat-mitrailleur* (machine-gunner), which at the time meant flying in the back seat of an aircraft and crudely firing carbines or automatic pistols.[12] Thaw had no intention of being a gunner confined to the back seat, so he convinced the French that he could pilot any kind of machine, and they sent him to Saint-Cyr west of Versailles. Saint-Cyr was a famous military academy started by Napoleon in 1802 and is still the foremost French military academy. During World War I, the French also had a flight school where pilots learned to fly the Caudron G.2. Thaw flew solo in the G.2 on the first day even though he had never seen the aircraft before. He quickly mastered the machine and began flying at the Front with Squadron C.42 in March of 1915.

James Bach successfully completed pilot training without harming himself as well. At the time, the accident rate among flight students was treacherously high, so this was no easy feat. He transferred to the Front as a pilot in a French squadron of Morane Saulniers, which were primarily designed for reconnaissance. Not long after Kiffin started pilot training, the French chose Bach and a French aviator named Mangeot to fly on a secret mission behind enemy lines. Bach and Mangeot took off in separate machines on September 23, 1915, each with one French soldier stowed in the rear seat. The soldiers were trained saboteurs who carried a large quantity of explosives "with which they were to destroy a section of the railway line between Mezieres and Hirson."[13] The pilots would land behind enemy lines, let the soldiers out, and then fly back to France. Meanwhile, the hapless saboteurs would blow up the railroad, gather information about the disposition of enemy troops, and somehow make their way back across the lines. It was quite a daring mission! Unfortunately, the saboteurs chose the landing site due to their knowledge of the countryside, "but being soldiers of earth, they had selected a field not at all suitable from the airmen's point of view."[14] The field was covered with bushes and small trees, but somehow Bach and Mangeot managed to land without smashing their machines.

The soldiers bid adieu and proceeded on their mission, while the two pilots prayed that they could successfully take off without hitting a tree. Bach's prayers were answered, but Mangeot turned his machine over on takeoff. Concerned for his fellow aviator, Bach successfully landed a second time on the ill-suited field, but his luck had finally run out. After retrieving Mangeot and taking off the second time, his wing hit the limb of a tree and the aircraft crashed. The two pilots were justifiably concerned at this point because they knew that if the Germans caught the saboteurs, they would suspect the pilots of infiltrating the soldiers. The penalty for such subversion was death. Bach and Mangeot tried to make their way back to France, but the Germans captured them and tried to court-martial them twice for espionage. After a brilliant defense by a German lawyer, the two men were found not guilty and were designated as prisoners of war.[15] Bach spent the rest of the war as a P.O.W. and tried to escape several times, but he was never successful. After the Armistice, he was released and was reunited with his comrades who survived the war.

Thaw, Hall, and Bach had certainly paved the way for subsequent Americans to fly in the French Air Service, but learning to fly aircraft in those days was a dangerous business. None of the countries fighting in World War I had anywhere close to the kind of flying safety standards that are present in modern air forces. Students had to glean as much knowledge as possible from their instructors, or they would quickly experience a violent death. Training was swift and insufficient for building the necessary experience to survive in combat. Most countries could build aircraft far more quickly than they could train pilots, so the demand for pilots drove the training timeline. The machines of the day contributed to the casualty rate because the wings were made of fabric and the internal structure was made of wood. Inexperienced students would often find themselves in situations that stressed the aircraft beyond its design capabilities—few men survived these incidents.

Most student pilots ignored the dangers because the thrill of flying overshadowed all else. The vast majority of men chosen to enter the French Air Service had no previous flight experience. Looking at a flying machine, running their hands along its wings, and watching the aircraft fly above were novelties—entering a cockpit and piloting a machine was like a dream! The desire to fly was strong among the men, and once they were given the opportunity to fulfill their dreams, they put a great deal of pressure on themselves. Their entire vocation was only about a decade old in the early days of World War I, so the pilots were learning as they went. Those who learned quickly tended to survive; those who learned slowly were either released from service or were killed. It was a tough existence.

A large number of student pilots learned to fly pursuit aircraft. Pursuit machines were small, fast, and capable of fighting other aircraft. The French called the machines *avion de chasses*, and successful pursuit pilots quickly gained a reputation. Compared to the horrific destruction wrought by artillery shells and machine guns on the ground, the pursuit aviator seemed like the men of legends from the past. A stalemate did not exist in the air above the front lines. Pilots could fly over enemy territory and return if they avoided being shot down by anti-aircraft guns. When a battle occurred in the air, there was often a definite victor. One pilot would shoot down the other and claim a victory for the day. Compared to the terrible losses that typically characterized a "victory" in a battle on the ground, the aerial triumphs seemed like a different world. The men who quickly learned their profession and successfully racked up victories became known as aces and knights of the air. For a soldier jaded by months or years in the trenches, the life of a pursuit pilot was indescribably rich.

Teaching a pursuit pilot to fly was a difficult task because many training machines did not have dual controls. In a dangerous situation, an instructor could not seize control of the aircraft to prevent an accident. In fact, most men were alone the first time they ever left the earth's surface.[16] The instructors had to instill enough knowledge into the students on the ground, or a student's first sortie might also be his last. Before ever setting foot in an aircraft, student pilots learned all the essential movements necessary to pilot an aircraft. One had to master every phase quickly because, as one of Kiffin's fellow aviators remarked, "In this preparatory training a great deal of weeding out is effected, for a man's aptitude for the work shows up, and unless he is by nature especially well fitted he is transferred to the division which teaches one how to fly the larger and safer machines."[17] A student started on a roller, which was a machine with stubby wings and little power. Because it was impossible to get the roller to fly, the machine aptly earned the nickname Penguin. The primary purpose of the Penguin was to teach the students how to steer an aircraft on the ground. The students learned how to use foot pedals to steer a rudder at different speeds. Once a student mastered ground steering, he was ready for the class that taught him how to leave the ground.

Taking off and landing were the two most dangerous aspects of pilot training during the First World War. The French put their students in a low-powered Bleriot aircraft that could leave the ground but could only fly a few feet in the air. If a student did not ease forward on the controls to let the aircraft settle back down on the ground, the machine would dive and crash. After a student mastered the "hop-skip-and-jump" flights, he moved on to another class where he learned the rudiments of landing. A few days later, he would fly to sixty feet, maintain a course for five minutes, and then come back to land. After several incrementally short stages designed to perfect takeoffs and landings, a student finally graduated to real flying machines. During this phase students learned how to land their machines with a failed engine, how to spiral down to a specific spot, and how to make short trips in the area. When the phase ended, the student pilots were finally ready to earn the coveted military brevet.

In France a military brevet certified a man as a pilot, so earning a brevet was the ultimate goal of any green aviator. Some men earned it fairly quickly due to great skill or great fortune. Many skillful pilots waited months for their brevet because of seasonally rainy weather or maintenance problems that limited the number of available aircraft. The pressure on the men increased enormously when they started the tests for the military brevet. In this final phase, the students had to accomplish three different flights. The first two flights consisted of flying to certain towns approximately one hour away and then returning safely. The final flight was in the shape of a triangle: the students had to land at one point and fly directly over the other two points. Usually, a student's nervousness quickly melted away and was replaced with excitement at his first opportunity to fly a great distance. For our modern minds this seems rather mundane, but for men who had never traveled from one place to another in the air it was a thrilling experience beyond their wildest imaginations. At the end of the third flight, the military brevet awaited the triumphant aviator, and "the student becomes officially a *pilote-aviateur*, and he can wear two little gold-woven wings on his collar to designate his capacity, and carry a winged propeller emblem on his arm…."[18]

The military brevet did not mark the end of training, however. Newly brevetted pilots immediately transferred to schools called *écoles de perfectionnement* where they learned how to fly the modern pursuit machines. In 1915, the French put the new pilots into Morane monoplanes that performed similar to the Nieuports in use at the Front. The pilots learned all the basics of flying the Morane and then took a gunnery course focused on familiarizing them with the different machine guns they might use. Three weeks later they attended combat school where they learned battle tactics, how to fly solo and in formation, and how to escape from a perilous situation. The pilots also learned aerobatics and participated in mock aerial battles against more experienced aviators. By the time the new pilots finished combat school, the French Air Service considered them sufficiently trained to join the reserves, where a pilot continued flying while waiting for his call to the Front.

When Kiffin Rockwell received orders in early September directing him to leave at once for aviation, he left in a hurry. Kiffin was overjoyed beyond comprehension at his new fortune. He told Paul, "This is such a relief to be out of the Legion that I can hardly believe it. I think that if I had to stay at La Valbonne for a month or so longer I would have gone completely 'nutty.'"[19] Kiffin reported to a base in Camp d'Avord about two hundred kilometers south of Paris and to the east of Bourges. He quickly checked in with the captain in charge of the school and waited for his chance to fly. Kiffin must have been glowing when he wrote his mother: "I have at last gotten what I have been trying to get these past two months. I am transferred to the aviation as a student-pilot. That is a jump from the lowest branch of the military service to the highest. It is the most interesting thing I have ever done, and is the life of a gentleman.... I am perfectly satisfied here and everyone treats me royally."[20]

Kiffin had found the outlet for his passion that he had been waiting for all his life. He threw himself into the study of his new vocation with unparalleled energy. At Camp d'Avord, the students started on a 1913 model Maurice Farman and then graduated to the 1914 version. These aircraft actually had a rear seat where an instructor could coach the student in the different phases of flight. A typical day consisted of waking up at four-thirty in the morning, moving machines out of hangars, checking the condition of the machines, and then taking turns flying with an instructor. Breakfast was at seven, followed by a lecture on flying, and then free time until nine-thirty. The men usually took a quick nap after lunch and then continued their flying exercises until dark. Dinner was served at eight, and then the men went to bed with little foolishness since they were all intent on learning to fly as quickly as possible.[21] The men apparently had to purchase their own uniforms since Kiffin wrote of going to Bourges twice in one week to order his uniform. He described his uniform as all black with broad red artillery stripes down the legs of the trousers and a black kepi (hat) with red stripes. He planned to wear the uniform during his tests for the military brevet, which he estimated as only a couple weeks away.

Kiffin soon learned the fundamental rule of flying—never underestimate the weather. His guess of two weeks quickly changed into six weeks. Like any pilot, he grew impatient with the low clouds and often wondered if he would ever complete the tasks required to earn his brevet. Camp d'Avord also had its share of broken machines and delays in returning them to full operation. On one day the students smashed nine different machines. Kiffin's aircraft was one of the nine. He had missed flying for two days, and on the third day he went into the hangar to inquire about his aircraft. The mechanics said the wheels were not good and the motor did not work well, but they said he could try it if he wished. Kiffin foolishly agreed, and when he started down the field to take off, the wheels caused the machine to veer and the motor did not have enough power. His machine literally came apart around him. Kiffin emerged unharmed, but his pride was bruised and a smashed plane meant several more days of waiting.

Life at Camp d'Avord lacked the shells and machine-gun fire of the Front, but Kiffin's new vocation was full of constant hazards and untimely deaths. On one day three men were killed and one badly injured at the airfield. Kiffin's description of one of the incidents gives a chilling reminder of how quickly death could strike in the new aerial contraptions: "Two of the deaths were very horrible. It was one of the instructors on a Morane aeroplane and a mechanic. They started out to the end of the field to an accident. On the way a puff of wind caught the aeroplane and almost upset it, then something went wrong and it shot straight up in the air, then fell. The instructor and the mechanic were imprisoned in the wreckage and there was an explosion and the whole mess went up in flames, and they were burned alive with all the men watching but unable to do a thing."[22]

At the end of September, just after his twenty-third birthday, Kiffin Rockwell met a fellow student-pilot who became a dear friend and fellow warrior. Victor Chapman was cut from the same cloth as Kiffin and the two shared a unique idealistic fervor. He was born in New York, went to St. Paul's School in Concord for several years, lived abroad in France and Germany for a year, and then spent a year at the Stone School in Boston. He attended Harvard like many of the young men running around France in those days and graduated in 1913. Victor's unique personality and character mostly came from his mother, who was quite an extraordinary woman. His mother's name was Minna, and she had grown up in Milan, Italy, as the daughter of a rich American father and an Italian mother. For several years, Minna lived a life of luxury among the high society of Italy. But when her father died, she left to live with an aunt in the United States and eventually married Victor's father, John Jay Chapman. Mr. Chapman was the great-great-grandson of Chief Justice John Jay and an incredibly talented writer. Chapman loved his wife dearly and knew she was a unique woman. He wrote that Minna was "the author of the heroic atmosphere, a sort of poetic aloofness that hung about [Victor] and suggested early death in some heroic form."[23]

Victor had no world outside of his mother's presence until her untimely death. He was still young, but his mother's death completely rocked his young world. His father described the experience: "When Victor was six years old his mother died suddenly in child-birth, and Victor, who had lived in her as an egg lives in its shell, who had scarcely ever been out of her sight or hearing—for she dragged him about as a lioness drags her cub—was left suspended in an unknown universe, with his grief and his visions."[24] Victor brooded for many years after his mother's death but sought solace in the company of his brother, who was two years younger. Unfortunately, Victor's tragic life continued. When he was twelve his younger brother drowned before his eyes in a rapidly flowing river after Victor had left him alone for a moment. He blamed himself for a long time afterwards until the years buried some of his grief.

As the product of his mother's early nurture and a tragic childhood, Victor Chapman, like Kiffin, was unique even among the extraordinary men who became America's first fighter pilots. He is probably best described as a fervently religious daredevil. His mother had been an extremely religious woman, and she bequeathed this trait to her eldest son. Victor's father described his son's religious fervor: "He continued … to make the sign of the cross in saying the same prayers that she had taught him—which ended with the phrase—'and make me a big soldier of Jesus Christ who is the Lord and Light of the world.' He folded his hands like a crusader as he said them. He was a part of the middle ages in this piety."[25] But it was Victor's love of danger that, oddly enough, seemed to complement his religiosity. Again, his father's description is the best: "Victor never really felt that he was alive except when he was in danger. Nothing else aroused his faculties. This was not conscious, but natal—a quality of the brain. As some people need oxygen, so Victor needed danger."[26] Victor, his father, and his stepmother were all in Europe when the war broke out, and he pleaded with his father to let him enlist. John Jay Chapman would have none of it and unintentionally insulted his son in his response. Victor relented and morosely left the room. When he was gone, Victor's stepmother told his father, "He has submitted through his humility and through his reverence for you. But I had rather see him lying on the battlefield than see that look on his face."[27] His father relented, and within a week Victor was in France ready to enlist in the army.

Victor's peculiar mix of piety and intrepidness made him a perfect candidate for the new field of pursuit flying. He started in the Foreign Legion as a machine-gunner but served the whole time in static trenches with no opportunities to advance on the enemy. The constant sniper bullets and shells strained his nerves, and he was even more jaded from trench life than Kiffin when he joined aviation. But the thrill of flying blew away the bad memories like a strong wind. He viewed his aviation orders as a knighthood, and the experience totally transformed him. Victor Chapman, like Kiffin Rockwell, had finally found his calling.

Victor and Kiffin quickly swapped stories of life in the trenches and in the Foreign Legion. The two budding pilots rapidly grew inseparable as they spent more time with each other. Victor was especially impressed that Kiffin had been part of the May 9 charge that had become nearly mythical in the Foreign Legion by that time. The two of them had plenty of time to talk in early October because a thick mist enveloped the aerodrome every morning and prevented them from flying. When the weather was good, maintenance problems continued to plague the men. Everyone, including the mechanics, was pushing to finish as quickly as possible, and the rush began to take its toll on the pilots. After the fifth death in a short period of time, Kiffin decided to go a little slower because he viewed any death during training as an unnecessary tragedy. Victor updated Kiffin on the plans for an all-American flying squadron. Several influential Americans were lobbying the French government about the idea, and Victor had met several of them just before he started pilot training. The two talked excitedly about the chances of serving in an American unit and what it would mean.

During the down time, Victor and Kiffin both heard news of the latest battle on the Front. The French and British decided to launch a combined offensive near the city of Loos, close to the Belgian border, while the French attacked alone in the Champagne sector. The Legion participated in the Champagne assault, which was designed to seize the railroad linking German operations in western and eastern France. Both sectors had planned four-day preliminary bombardments followed by massive infantry assaults. General Joffre put half a million men just in Champagne to ensure overwhelming odds.[28] The results were sickeningly typical. The British lost 61,693 men and the French lost 48,230 men in the combined sector, while the French lost an additional 143,567 men in the Champagne sector. Joffre's half-million-man assault force did not even make it halfway to their railroad objective.

Skipper Pavelka was still stuck in the Foreign Legion, and the Legion had been selected to participate in the Champagne offensive. Kiffin had heard from his friend Skipper just before the operation on September 23 and feared the worst after hearing no further news. He wrote to his friends the Vicomte and Vicomtesse saying that he believed "the Legion is done for.... It has evidently been a glorious advance but I know what those things mean and I feel rather sorry that they tried it unless they continue to advance; and the last two days' reports appear as if they have stopped, like we did."[29] Kiffin's skepticism concerning the strategic value of such uselessly bloody offensives was well-founded. Observers of the war were finally coming to grips with the fact that an easy offensive solution to end the stalemate did not exist. Both assaults withered away without attaining their objectives, and the winter months finally put an end to any further attempts.

By mid–October Kiffin was ready for the tests required to earn his brevet. He completed the spiral dive flight and told Paul that he was deaf for an hour afterward because the spiral was hard on the eardrums. Kiffin also received a quick note from Skipper that he was alive but headed back to the trenches. Victor Chapman received news of the death of his friend Henry Farnsworth, another Harvard graduate and member of the Foreign Legion. Several Americans died during the Champagne offensive, so Victor and Kiffin were in somber moods during the month of October at Camp d'Avord.

Not long after receiving the sobering news from the Front, Kiffin finally started the three final flights before receiving his brevet. He wrote Paul on October 16 describing his incredible foolishness during his first flight. He had to fly from Camp d'Avord to another field at Chateauroux and back, but the weather was cloudy and a little foggy that day. Kiffin could not stay under the clouds, so rather than turning back he recklessly flew up through the clouds and then above them. He used a clock and a compass to determine where Chateauroux was located, and when he thought he was near the aerodrome, he descended back through the clouds with no instruments to guide him. Twice he ran into heavy fog and became hopelessly lost until he found a town where he could land nearby and inquire about his location. He continued to try to blindly find Châteauroux when darkness fell and alarm set in. Kiffin finally spotted the lights of a town and wisely decided to land instead of continuing to fly. Without a lantern to light the field, he miraculously managed to land nearby without breaking anything, "something that would not happen one time out of a hundred under similar circumstances."[30]

Kiffin was exceedingly fortunate to be alive after flying in awful weather conditions with such a primitive aircraft. The townspeople unknowingly rewarded his foolishness by showering him with food, wine, and flowers. He told Paul that about two hundred people followed him everywhere he went, and they fiercely guarded his machine. Kiffin discovered that he had landed next to the town of Vierzon with a population of about 40,000 people. Seeing a plane and pilot up close was a first for many of the townspeople, so they treated Kiffin like a king. The fog continued and he remained stuck there for three days until the weather finally cleared. When he came back to his machine, it was covered with messages from admiring women. He thanked his gracious hosts and then hurried back to Camp d'Avord. When he arrived, the chief pilot laughed and told him he was lucky that he did not break his neck. Kiffin felt sheepish but wrote, "It was very foolish but at the same time it has given me much confidence, and confidence is the greatest asset in this game."[31]

Confidence was indeed the greatest asset to any pilot. Kiffin finished his flights a few days later and received his *brevet militaire* on October 23, 1915. He was brimming with confidence as he put on the shiny gold wings marking his entry into a new fraternity of warriors. The soldiers who became pilots had a new dimension in which to fight, but they brought the same spirit required of an infantryman to their new profession. Over time they adapted their fighting spirits to the unique rigors of air combat. And in the midst of this process they created something incredibly special that stood the test of time.

9

The Creation of the Lafayette Escadrille

The significance of the time period that Kiffin Rockwell and Victor Chapman were about to enter is vastly underappreciated today. American air power was born here—in France—over a few months at the end of 1915 and the beginning of 1916. A number of influential Americans meticulously assembled the political support necessary to create an all-American squadron of pursuit pilots which eventually became known as the Lafayette Escadrille. But the men who primarily shaped and forged the character of the Lafayette Escadrille all came from the Foreign Legion. Students of American air power cannot truly understand their subject without first understanding the impact of these former Legionnaires. The most influential American pilots who first flew in combat, almost to a man, came from the Foreign Legion. Understanding American air power requires an understanding of the Foreign Legion. But first it is necessary to dispel a myth.

It is absolutely false and historically negligent to trace the roots of the United States Air Service back to the U.S. Army Signal Corps. Unfortunately, almost every official history or historical analysis of the United States Air Force, the U.S. Army-Air Corps, or the U.S. Air Service gives the impression or states outright that these organizations started with the Aviation Section of the Signal Corps. These accounts occasionally mention the Americans who fought for France, but none of them truly establishes the significance of the link between the Lafayette Escadrille and the Air Service. The administrative roots of the Air Service may have come from the Signal Corps, but the character, spirit, and soul of the Air Service came from the Lafayette Escadrille. Understanding the administrative origins of the Air Service may have some importance, but it pales in comparison to a grasp of the origins of the Air Service's character and spirit. The superiority of modern American air power does not stem from administrative origins—it comes from a deep-rooted fighting spirit born in the early days of World War I. In light of this fact, histories of American air power should spend more time studying the roots of this fighting spirit rather than focusing primarily on administrative links.

The fighting spirit that characterizes American air power today came from the former Legionnaires who flew in the Lafayette Escadrille. The veterans of the Foreign Legion had the most influence within the Lafayette Escadrille because of their previous combat experience and the unique effect that those experiences had on them. The Legionnaires carried a great deal of internal baggage with them to the Lafayette Escadrille. Many of them were physically impaired in some way, several of them had emotional scars, and almost all of them were dumbstruck by the senseless slaughter of the trenches. Compared to their previous experiences, flying in combat gave them freedom of mythical proportions. They were free from the humiliating episodes of hiding in underground tunnels and wondering how close the next shell would fall. They were free to roam, free to hunt, and free to attack when *they* chose to attack and on *their* terms. The significance of this freedom is absolutely essential to an understanding of air power. The former Legionnaires injected their new-found freedom into their style of fighting, and the result was a fighting spirit that differed significantly from ground combat or combat on the high seas.

Air combat in World War I relied heavily on the cunning and expertise of the individual. A soldier or sailor in battle during World War I could depend on assistance from hundreds of men in his battalion or on his ship. War on the ground or on the seas involved masses of men fighting masses of men, with death often striking from an unseen machine gun or artillery cannon. A pilot, on the other hand, fought most of his battles alone in the early years of the war. Air combat occurred in close quarters with individual pilots jousting for position and victories—it is no accident that pilots were known as "knights of the air." Even after both sides discovered the concept of mutual support, a pilot could expect, at most, little more than a half dozen other aircraft supporting him. The men of the Lafayette Escadrille quickly realized that they must strive for perfection in their skills as combat aviators—anything less would result in certain death. They knew perfection was impossible to attain, but demanding perfection prepared the men for the fire of air combat.

The former soldiers of the Foreign Legion quickly made their mark on the Lafayette Escadrille. They fought with abandon and embraced the freedom that they lacked in their previous lives. The weeks turned into months, and the men slowly began to replace their sordid memories of the trenches with glorious moments of fighting in the heavens. They inspired the new pilots, many of them former Legionnaires themselves, and the Lafayette Escadrille quickly developed a deep sense of unity and camaraderie. The first American combat squadron was truly a unique organization. But before delving into the story of the Lafayette Escadrille and what its pilots achieved, it is necessary to discuss how the squadron was born.

Many people knowledgeable on the subject of the Lafayette Escadrille give Norman Prince, one of the original pilots in the Escadrille, credit for founding the squadron. In reality, the formation of the Lafayette Escadrille was a carefully coordinated campaign among several individuals. Norman Prince received the most publicity for his role due to his family's influence, but it was truly a massive team effort among the Americans living in Paris. At the same time, the supporters interested in starting an all-American squadron needed Prince's help. Norman Prince was born at Prides Crossing, Massachusetts, and came from a prominent and wealthy family. His grandfather was a former mayor of Boston, and his father, Frederick H. Prince, was an investment banker who made a fortune in a variety of business ventures. Norman followed the route of many wealthy sons by studying at Groton and then attending Harvard. He graduated in 1911 from Harvard Law School and started practicing law in Chicago a few years later. Norman's father owned an estate in Pau, France, where the family enjoyed frequent hunting trips. He eventually made many friends and learned to speak French fluently on these various hunting excursions.[1]

When the war started in 1914, Prince chose to fight for France, just like many of the young American men who flocked to the Foreign Legion. He was an avid horseman and polo player at a time when horsemen and polo players were increasingly turning their attention toward the new flying machine. His emerging interest in flying took on new meaning after the opening salvo of the war. Norman Prince realized that if he became a pilot before offering his services to France, the French might receive him as a member of the Flying Corps.[2] In November of 1914, he enrolled in the Burgess flying school at Marblehead, Massachusetts, with Frazier Curtis, another Harvard graduate from the class of 1898. The two men learned to fly hydro-planes, and Norman Prince originally conceived the idea of organizing a squadron of volunteer American airmen while learning to fly at Marblehead.

Prince's goal of forming an American squadron in France was an extremely difficult endeavor. He sailed for France in January 1915 and immediately began to drum up support for the idea. For five weeks he worked incessantly to convince the French that they needed an American squadron. Many of his American colleagues thought the idea was foolish because of the neutrality of the United States. But enough individuals believed in the cause that Prince continued his efforts. Frazier Curtis joined Prince in February, and the two of them met with a pair of brothers named Jacques and Paul de Lesseps. They all drafted a letter to War Minister Alexandre Millerand for support, but the reply was disheartening. Millerand proclaimed that the aviation branch would not accept any American volunteers because it was already highly popular among the French soldiers.

Norman Prince was not the type to give up, however, and he decided to pursue additional options. A companion of his named Robert Bliss introduced Prince to a senior official in the Ministry of Foreign Affairs named Jarousse de Sillac. Unlike Millerand, de Sillac immediately saw the value of the plan. He wrote a friend of his named Colonel Paul Bouttieaux who worked at the War Ministry and said: "It appears to me that there might be great advantages in creating an American squadron. The United States would be proud of the fact that certain of her young men, acting as did Lafayette, have come to fight for France and civilization. The resulting sentiment of enthusiasm could have but one effect: to turn the Americans in the direction of the Allies…."[3] Thus, French support for the idea of an American squadron was purely a political endeavor. France needed the support of the United States, and French officials were willing to do anything necessary to gain American cooperation. De Sillac received a favorable reply from Colonel Bouttieaux, and the idea began to gain momentum.

The French referred to the idea as the *Escadrille Américaine*, but they needed a core group of American pilots before they could form an American squadron. While Prince and Curtis waited for their enlistment papers, they corresponded with an American volunteer named Elliot Cowdin. Cowdin was a 1907 Harvard graduate who was serving in the Ambulance Service ferrying the wounded from the front lines to hospitals in the rear. He was also ready to transfer to aviation and traveled to Paris to wait for his enlistment papers with Prince and Curtis. The three men signed the enlistment papers on March 9, 1915, and left immediately for Pau. Prince was ecstatic that his idea was working. James Norman Hall, a future member of the Lafayette Escadrille, described Prince's effect on the formation of his unit: "His enthusiasm and energy were irresistible; before his departure for Pau he had fairly launched the movement which resulted in the formation of the *Escadrille Américaine*."[4]

Once Prince, Curtis, and Cowdin all left for training, the idea of an American squadron needed additional support. The three men were too busy to organize the political capital necessary to carry the idea to fruition. They needed someone else but had not yet found an acceptable spokesman. Prince managed to secure the transfer of James Bach and Bert

Hall to Pau, so all the Americans currently serving in aviation could be in the same place. He tried to get Thaw to come to Pau as well, but Thaw would have none of it. He was already an experienced aviator before the war, so Thaw preferred going directly to the Front instead of waiting for the other Americans to finish training. Thaw did ensure Prince and the others that he would join the American squadron if it ever became a reality.

Progress toward the goal of an all-American flying unit languished while the men trained to fly the new machines. Prince and Cowdin finished their training and received their coveted brevet in two months. Curtis was not as fortunate. He suffered three successive crashes, and the French finally decided to discharge him. Curtis was heartbroken, but he decided to continue to assist the cause for which he originally came to France. He began searching for American volunteers who could fill the ranks of an American squadron, and after a short time he made the acquaintance of a man named Dr. Edmund Gros.

Dr. Gros was the man Prince needed to fulfill his dream. In fact, Dr. Gros had already been thinking, quite independently, of forming a squadron of American volunteer airmen.[5] He was one of the heads of the American Ambulance Service, and he saw how the young men in the Ambulance wanted to serve in a more active capacity. The American Ambulance started after the outbreak of World War I when young Americans living in Paris volunteered as ambulance drivers at the American Hospital in Paris. Members of the Ambulance (a total of 2,500) eventually participated in every major French battle and transported more than 500,000 wounded.[6] Many of the Ambulance men were university students, including several from Harvard. The vast quantity of Harvard graduates in and around Paris had a great deal to do with the university's commitment to service, but there were also Harvard connections at work. The president of the American Hospital that ran the Ambulance was Mr. Robert Bacon, a former ambassador to France and member of the Harvard Corporation, the smaller of Harvard's two governing boards. Bacon also became part of the Franco-American Committee that was forming the *Escadrille Américaine*. Dr. Gros worked with Robert Bacon to get the highest quality young men into the Ambulance Service.

Gros had already met dozens of Americans in the Foreign Legion, and it occurred to him that "both in the Legion and in the Ambulance there was splendid material which might be used to good advantage in the French Aviation Service."[7] Frazier Curtis was out seeking volunteers among the Ambulance in July 1915, heard of Dr. Gros, and decided to write him. The two of them met in Paris in early July, and Curtis introduced Dr. Gros to de Sillac. The men formed the Franco-American Committee that could lobby French authorities and arouse the interest of prominent Americans. They wasted no time, and de Sillac managed to schedule a luncheon attended by General Hirschauer, chief of the French Military Aeronautics, Senator Menier, Colonel Bouttieaux, and members of the Franco-American Committee. Dr. Gros and de Sillac argued persuasively, and General Hirschauer gave his blessing for the formation of an American squadron.

The details of forming the squadron took far more time to compile than the initial approval for the scheme. After the luncheon, the Franco-American Committee reached out to American volunteers in earnest. Kiffin had just arrived in Paris for his convalescent leave and quickly heard of the scheme. The growing momentum behind the idea of an American squadron firmly planted the desire in his heart to join aviation instead of continuing with the Foreign Legion. Paul Rockwell also followed the idea closely. He was well-connected with the American community in Paris, but he also had many connections in

French political circles through his fiancée's father, Georges Leygues. Paul threw his support behind the idea and advocated for the squadron in both French and American channels.

Progress continued to move slowly for the rest of the year. On August 21, 1915, after Kiffin rejoined the Foreign Legion to wait for his aviation orders, the Ministry of War and the Ministry of Foreign Affairs decided that all matters concerning the *Escadrille Américaine* should be referred to the Franco-American Committee. Dr. Gros also started pursuing the support of wealthy donors in the United States. He contacted William K. Vanderbilt to enlist his financial support because Vanderbilt's wealth, interest in aviation, and opposition to American neutrality were well known.[8] Herbert Mason also claims that Dr. Gros paid a visit to William Vanderbilt about the idea of the *Escadrille Américaine*. He discussed the idea with Mr. Vanderbilt and his wife, and after he had finished his proposal Mrs. Vanderbilt walked over to her desk, sat down, and wrote a check for $5,000. She then handed it to Gros and said to her husband, "Now, K. What will you do?" Vanderbilt then wrote a check for $15,000 and continued to support the Escadrille for the entire time the squadron served under the French flag.[9] The details of the exchange between Gros and Vanderbilt are probably embellished, but Dr. Gros did succeed in convincing William Vanderbilt to help fund the American squadron. By October 28, the Franco-American Committee heard from Rene Besnard, Sub-Secretary of State for Military Aeronautics, that the commander in chief, General Joffre himself, was greatly interested in the project. Unfortunately, all parties involved had a great deal more to accomplish before forming the squadron.

In the meantime, Kiffin Rockwell anxiously awaited a transfer to a front-line flying unit, while Victor Chapman continued working towards his brevet. By this time there

Kiffin Rockwell just after a flight (courtesy Virginia Military Institute Archives).

were a total of seventeen Americans in flight training or already flying in French squadrons. Adverse weather conditions slowed down the efforts of both men. In late October a storm blew down hangars and sent the flimsy machines cartwheeling along the ground. About fifteen machines were destroyed, which only caused further delays in training for Kiffin and Victor. In characteristic fashion, Kiffin became impatient and began seeking a transfer to the Serbian front, where he could begin flying in combat at once. His captain eventually squashed the idea but had no success in dampening Kiffin's impulsive desire for action. The inactivity exasperated Kiffin's concern for his friend Skipper. He heard that Skipper was again going into battle and feared that "the Boche will get him yet."[10]

Amid the weeks of poor weather, Kiffin received an eight-day pass to spend in Paris with Paul and Mrs. Alice Weeks, but the frustrations with weather continued when he returned. In

Flying temperatures, even in the summer, were frigid due to the cooler air at altitude and open, unheated cockpits (Rockwell family collection, courtesy Sybil Robb).

addition, the old captain had been fired and all the men described the new captain as a strict authoritarian. Without even meeting the new captain, Kiffin made up his mind to try to leave as soon as possible. However, when he went to the new captain, he discovered a Frenchman who was immensely proud of Americans serving in his country. The captain offered Kiffin his pick of any machine, so Kiffin naturally chose the most advanced aircraft flying at the time—the Nieuport. The Nieuport 11 biplane was known as the *Bébé* (baby) and was light, fast and extremely maneuverable. Its only major problem was the wing struts: in steep dives they would twist and occasionally the stress would cause the plane to break apart.[11] Before he could start on the Nieuport, Kiffin had to spend time on the Morane roller, the Bleriot roller, several low-powered versions of the planes, and then the Morane Parasol. The weather prevented any flying until a short five-day period toward the end of November, when Kiffin managed to sail through all the training.

With his training complete, Kiffin waited for his transfer to the General Reserve force.

Victor continued working on his brevet, but the poor weather had slowed the process significantly. His father and stepmother worried greatly about him, so he wrote them a letter. He understood their concern as it was "very parental" and he appreciated it, but he told them, "This is the first thing I have ever done that has been worthwhile, or may ever do, and you might just as well get the benefit of it without the heart-wringing worry."[12] He and Kiffin lived with a French marine in a town nearby with a "great luxury of soft beds and sheets ... combined with [an] enormous quantity of fresh air...."[13] They rose every morning at five thirty, cooked chocolate with breakfast, spent their day at the airfield, and then returned to eat a hearty dinner around the fire. It was a luxurious life compared to the trenches! Kiffin had his own Morane Parasol, which he flew whenever the weather cooperated, but he still had not started training on the Nieuport. Camp d'Avord actually had three or four Nieuports, but there were no instructors at the camp. Despite his frustration with more delays, Kiffin wisely decided to wait for instructors to arrive before he attempted to fly the unfamiliar Nieuport.

At the end of 1915, the Franco-American Committee finally had all the pieces in place to make an American squadron a reality. In October, Rene Besnard, the Military Aeronautics official, had requested the Committee's plan of action before the French authorities could proceed. The president of the Franco-American Committee responded on December 1, 1915: "A committee composed of Americans has been formed, with the object of making known to their compatriots the conditions under which they may enlist in the French Aviation, and to select the more desirable candidates from among those who offer themselves. The Americans who will lend their efforts to recruiting, and among whom are Mr. Bacon, Mr. Vanderbilt, Mr. Allen, Colonel Mott, and Dr. Gros, prefer, for the time being, to avoid publicity. In order to facilitate their work, they should be able to assure their compatriots that they will be well treated in the French Aviation, and not subjected to useless moving about or change of units."[14]

The American financiers of the plan worried that the French might reject some of the American recruits from flying and send them to infantry units on the front lines. The committee president outlined the example of Dudley Hill in his letter. Hill enlisted in September, passed a thorough medical examination in Paris, and went to Pau for training. Doctors at Pau then told him that he suffered from defective vision in one eye and tried to employ him as a mechanic instead. To prevent future incidents similar to Hill's, the Franco-American Committee asked for the following assurances to those who desired to enlist:

1. That every care will be taken to settle definitely at Paris [the recruit's] medical fitness for flying.

2. That if, once enlisted, they show inaptitude for flying, it be made possible to release them.

3. That they be treated, in so far as possible, with courtesy inspired by their generosity in offering their lives in the service of France.[15]

On Christmas Day, the Franco-American Committee received an official response from French authorities. The French provided guarantees to every American soldier leaving the Foreign Legion: "It is guaranteed to you that this act of engagement may be rescinded, either on your demand, or on demand of the military authorities, in case of proven inaptitude for service in the flying personnel of the Military Aviation."[16] This was welcome news for the influential Americans backing the Franco-American Committee. They needed assurances that the men would not be forced to return to the infantry if they did not pass all the qualifications necessary to become a pilot. With these guarantees in place, the Franco-American Committee entered the final stage of the lengthy process to create an American squadron in the French Aviation Service.

In the same month, December 1915, an incident occurred that nearly scuttled the entire process. Bill Thaw, Norman Prince, and Elliot Cowdin all traveled back to the United States after seeing that some weeks still remained before the new squadron could be formed. American soldiers in the Foreign Legion were very popular in the American press at the time, and the men who had started flying for the French were admired the most. When the aviators set foot on American soil again, they were instant sensations. Thaw and Prince, in particular, came from wealthy, distinguished families, so newspapers plastered their names all over the country. However, some Americans did not appreciate the exploits of American soldiers in the service of France. Neutrality was still an accepted foreign policy position in many circles, so the actions of men like Thaw, Prince, and Cowdin seemed like an affront to Washington's official stance. And then of course there were Americans who fully supported the German side. These men and women were incensed at Americans serving in the French military. The editor of the pro–German *Fatherland*, George Sylvester Viereck, immediately sent a letter to Secretary of State Robert Lansing stating, "I call your attention to the urgent necessity of taking action in the case of Thaw, Cowdin and Prince, of the French Army Flying Corps.... The United States cannot, without violating the letter and spirit of neutrality, permit these young men to rejoin the enemies of a country with which we are still at peace."[17]

From a legal standpoint, George Viereck was correct, and the three young men were in danger of being barred from returning to France. Thaw soon realized the delicate situation they were in when he went to a New York barbershop some days after their arrival. The German Ambassador to the United States, Count Johann von Bernstorff, was at the same barbershop when he arrived. The ambassador berated Thaw's actions and told him that he should voluntarily intern himself in order to avoid an international incident.[18] Thaw walked out on the ambassador, but Von Bernstorff formally called for their internment in a message to Secretary of State Lansing. Thaw, Prince, and Cowdin wisely recognized that it was time to leave, and they secretly boarded a ship in New York and sailed back to France. Upon hearing the news of the "Christmas Leave Incident," the Franco-American Committee worried that the U.S. State Department might kill the entire program. Fortunately for all involved, the State Department took no action, and the plan continued to move forward.

Meanwhile, the American pilots in training continued to wait for news concerning the formation of the American squadron. Victor Chapman finally received his brevet in the first week of January, and Kiffin Rockwell had moved to the General Reserve of the Aviation in Paris. In the Reserve, pilots flew as often as the weather allowed and waited for an assignment to an escadrille (squadron) at the Front. Bert Hall, the fib-generating former Legionnaire who left for aviation with Thaw, received orders as an instructor at Camp d'Avord in January 1916. He flew with Victor Chapman a few times, and the two seemed to enjoy each other's company. Kiffin finally started flying the Nieuport in the General Reserve and loved the new machine despite the bad weather and fiercely cold wind up at altitude.

As the weeks dragged by, all the men began to feel impatient, and they wondered whether the American squadron they were all waiting for was nothing more than a mirage.

The Franco-American Committee continued to push the French authorities as fast as the system would go. The committee sent another letter to Rene Besnard on January 24, 1916, requesting the General Headquarters to group the American pilots in the same squadron. The letter identified the following Americans who had distinguished themselves and could be grouped immediately: Lieutenant Thaw; Sergeants Cowdin, Prince, and Masson; Pilots Guerin, Hall, Balsley, Chapman, Rockwell, Rumsey, and Johnson.[19] The letter also mentioned that a Captain Thénault of the C.42, D.A.L., had requested to be the commanding officer of the squadron. The committee continued to receive assurances and favorable responses from French authorities, but the squadron remained an elusive, unformed dream.

The French did manage to group four of the Americans together. In February, Bill Thaw, Victor Chapman, and Kiffin Rockwell all climbed aboard a train and traveled to Plessis-Belleville about forty kilometers outside of Paris. They were the first men off the train when they arrived and hurried to the only hotel in town in order to reserve rooms. They booked four rooms since Norman Prince expected to join them the next morning. The weather was miserable all through February, and a virus plagued the impatient men sitting around waiting for action. Kiffin managed to travel to Paris every three days to see Paul, who was also feeling the effects of the flu. All in all, the men were beginning to feel jaded. They chose aviation in order to fight, but they were forced to sit in limbo due to the bad weather and the inability of the French to form the American squadron. At times, Kiffin wished his earlier idea of transferring to the Serbian front had worked. He wanted action and felt that he "had many scores to settle" on account of his friends who had been killed in the Foreign Legion.[20] Waiting and inaction were certainly not Kiffin's style, but the men's long wait would soon be over.

In early March, the Franco-American Committee complained that only Rockwell, Thaw, Chapman, and Prince were grouped together and that plans for the American squadron appeared to have stalled. The new Director of Aeronautics, Colonel Regnier, promptly wrote back on March 14: "I asked the Commander-in-Chief to advise me of his intentions. General Headquarters has just replied, informing that an American squadron will be organized with the pilots whose names follow: William Thaw, Elliot Cowdin, Kiffin Rockwell, Norman Prince, Charles C. Johnson, Clyde Balsley, Victor Chapman, Lawrence Rumsey, and James R. McConnell.... I have every reason to believe that the ... squadron will be constituted rapidly."[21] Rapidly constituting the squadron ended up taking a month, but the pilots waiting for the squadron's creation had no timetable. They sat around moaning about the delays and wishing for an assignment to the Front, whether it was with an American squadron or not.

Kiffin, as usual, was the most impatient and wrote to his friend the Vicomte explaining, "I have been more or less demoralized by never doing anything.... I ask each week to be attached to a regular French escadrille, but they continue to keep us all back, waiting until the Escadrille Américaine is formed."[22] James McConnell also described the painful process of waiting. He wrote, "Every day somebody 'had it absolutely straight' that we were to become a unit at the front, and every other day the report turned out to be untrue."[23] Most of the other pilots on Colonel Regnier's roster joined Kiffin and the other three Americans

9. The Creation of the Lafayette Escadrille

The Lafayette Escadrille in the summer of 1916. Many of the original members of the famous squadron are pictured here. From left to right: Bert Hall, Bill Thaw, Captain Georges Thénault, Lieutenant Alfred de Laage de Meux, Kiffin Rockwell, Escadrille mechanic, James McConnell, and Raoul Lufbery. At Kiffin's feet is Captain Thénault's dog Fram, the squadron's original mascot (Virginia Military Institute Archives).

at Plessis-Belleville by the end of March. And on April 20, 1916, the men finally received the news they had all been waiting for. The *Escadrille Américaine* was a reality, and the French had plans to send it to the Front immediately.

It was a momentous day for the young pilots. They were all capable of flying France's most effective aircraft, the Nieuport, and now they finally had a squadron to call their own. It would be composed entirely of American pilots except for a French commander and his deputy. The Americans were ecstatic and itching to get to the Front as soon as possible. But the campaign that awaited them was none other than the Battle of Verdun. The contest for Verdun would test the very fabric of France as a nation. The opening salvo of the battle had already begun in February and continued unabated into April. In the history of warfare, few battles can compare to the utter destruction wrought on the ground surrounding Verdun. It was a struggle for the survival of France, and the *Escadrille Américaine* was headed directly into the heart of one of the most devastating battles ever fought in Europe.

10

Verdun

For the French, the tale of Verdun is both glorious and tragic. Their line held. They repulsed one of the most enormous offensives ever assembled. France defeated Germany's advance on those hallowed fields, but the costs of victory were gigantic. Despite the victorious defense that occurred there, the name of Verdun brings chills to those who know it well. Even today a drive up the somber hills etched with the grooves of abandoned trenches is haunting. The French poured out their blood to protect their homeland and reveled in their success when the Germans finally gave up the attack months later. But the scale of bloodshed was cruelly part of Germany's strategy. For at the time, the French did not know that capturing Verdun was not the ultimate objective. Bleeding France to certain collapse was the real aim of the battle. It was quite a malicious plan, and the idea came very close to succeeding.

In the dawn of 1916, the German people were beginning to lose patience with their leaders. The armed forces had successfully expanded Germany's borders, but they saw no evidence that the end of the conflict was near. The previous year had been a good one in terms of holding the land they had captured, but there was enormous pressure on the German General Staff to take the offensive in order to end the war on favorable terms. The question for Chief of Staff Erich von Falkenhayn was not *if* Germany should attack but *where* Germany should attack. He and the Kaiser firmly believed the Western Front was the key to victory, but Paul von Hindenburg and General Erich von Ludendorff built a case for the Eastern Front after winning several victories there. Falkenhayn worried about the situation in the west because Britain was surging. The colonial juggernaut still commanded the seas and successfully maintained its blockade on Germany. Furthermore, Britain had mobilized its public and its massive industrial base, and its army was relatively fresh, so the chances of striking a fatal blow on Britain were slim.[1] Falkenhayn gained the support of the Kaiser for the idea of unrestricted submarine warfare which would address the issue of British naval dominance and their dependence on supplies from their colonies.[2] By 1916, Great Britain had become Germany's chief adversary.

Falkenhayn knew that Britain's most vulnerable weapon was the army of France. He believed "the strain on France [had] almost reached the breaking-point," and if he could direct a shattering blow on the French, he would strike "England's best sword" from her hand.[3] Since France was already exhausted, a merciless blow on its army might force the government to come to terms. Thus the key, according to Falkenhayn, was devising a campaign so destructive, so demoralizing, and so bloody that France would be forced to retire from utter exhaustion. He wanted the forces of France to "bleed to death."[4] His choice for this devious plan was the historic fortress of Verdun.

Verdun was an easy choice for Falkenhayn. The fortress lay in a salient, so the Germans surrounded the area in a half-circle and could attack from three sides. At the time, the French defenses around Verdun were unsatisfactory; the French had not yet completed their plans to bolster the front lines in the sector. Furthermore, the French lines were only twenty kilometers from German railway communications, which convinced Falkenhayn that the Germans could easily resupply its troops once the battle commenced.[5] The city also was located in a fertile area of France along the Meuse River, so it had some economic value as well. But the historic value of Verdun was perhaps the most important factor in Falkenhayn's choice. The Gauls had founded the city centuries before, and Verdun had been an important site for the Holy Roman Empire in the Middle Ages. In essence, Verdun "was a historic site associated with all the great military glories of France."[6] If Falkenhayn wanted the French to fight to the last man, Verdun was the ideal spot for such carnage.

After a series of devastating, unsuccessful offensives in 1915, the French were indeed exhausted as Falkenhayn correctly assumed. General Joffre had to draw up plans to reconstitute his force after the offensives in Artois and Champagne, and Verdun was not a major priority since no major operations had occurred there during the previous year. Joffre himself later wrote that Verdun did not "seem to me destined to become the theatre of the gigantic struggle which took place on its hills during the greater parts of 1916."[7] But foreshadowing of the great battle started as early as December 1915. In that month the Minister of War, General Joseph Gallieni, wrote General Joffre and informed him that the line of trenches in Meurthe, Toul, and Verdun did not appear to be completed, which presented a very grave danger. Joffre wrote back an incensed letter refuting the claims and downplaying the dangers involved while explaining why he chose to prioritize the reconstruction of trenches in other sectors.[8] However, by January 10, 1916, the French began to receive indications of a possible enemy attack in the region of Verdun. On February 14, they even received an intercepted order from the German Crown Prince that was to be read to the troops on the opening of the attack.[9] Joffre had twenty-six reserve divisions, but he chose to echelon them along the entire front because there were also rumors of coming attacks in other sectors. He could not afford to focus everything on Verdun if by chance the whole thing was a German ruse. But mostly, General Joffre was entirely confused. He wrote, "I was all the more induced to think that Verdun could not be the principal objective of the Germans, since the strategic results they could expect to attain there were entirely beyond my comprehension."[10] German intentions puzzled Joffre because he had no way of knowing that the strategic objective of Verdun was to bleed France to death.

In typical World War I fashion, the Battle of Verdun opened with titanic fury. Crown Prince Wilhelm deployed a million men to the field, supported by 1,120 artillery guns and 2.5 million shells. The French started with only 200,000 soldiers to oppose the German onslaught. At 7:15 a.m. on February 21, the Germans commenced a nine hour artillery bombardment and then sent 140,000 German infantrymen supported by almost one hundred flamethrowers in a pitched assault of the French front lines. The French put up a heroic defense, but the success of the German advance significantly alarmed the French General Staff by the evening of February 23. General Joffre wrote, "After long reflection, I came to the conclusion that the best way to bring this dangerous advance of the enemy to a standstill would be by sending fresh troops to the left bank of the Meuse with the double purpose of preventing the enemy from crossing the river and of receiving our troops in case they were driven over the right bank."¹¹ Joffre sent his deputy, General de Castelnau, to survey Verdun on February 25, and de Castelnau found the French leadership utterly demoralized. He viewed the fight for Verdun as a test of his country's capacity to defend their national territory and keep alive the hope of ultimate victory.¹² General de Castelnau was playing directly into the Germans' hands.

At this time, General de Castelnau made a momentous decision to appoint a man who would have immense historical impact on France for decades to come. De Castelnau found General Herr fatigued to the point of depression on February 25 and decided to place General Philippe Pétain in charge of the whole fortified region of Verdun. Joffre later wrote, "It was in this way that the solution of this delicate problem was arrived at—a solution which ultimately saved Verdun."¹³ Pétain was a perfect choice from the German point of view because he had a stubborn belief in the power of the defensive and ordered his troops to hang onto every yard of territory, and counterattack to regain any that was lost.¹⁴ The combination of Falkenhayn's deadly strategy and Pétain's unyielding beliefs jointly transformed Verdun into a cataclysmic struggle. Pétain wrote, "The Germans attacked with a force and violence never before equaled. The French accepted the challenge, for Verdun to them is even more than a great fortress, an outpost intended to bar the path of the invader on the east; it is the moral bulwark of France."¹⁵ He requested every available artillery piece for the Verdun sector and ruthlessly unleashed devastating fire on the advancing German troops. He relieved the French troops frequently in order to minimize their exposure to the deadly battlefield, and he widened the roads leading to the Verdun sector, enabling the French to supply an average of 50,000 tons of ammunition and 90,000 men a week.¹⁶ Pétain's efforts succeeded and stopped the German advance in February. Falkenhayn tried two more offensives in March and early April but could not break through Pétain's iron defenses.

Falkenhayn's strategy to bleed the French white did not have its intended effect. The French indeed suffered staggering losses, but the horrendous death toll did not succeed in convincing the French to raise the white flag. If anything, the casualties only steeled their resolve. At the same time, the Germans had nearly bled their own army to destruction. German losses in the opening months of Verdun were nearly identical to those of France, and Falkenhayn's job was increasingly in jeopardy in the spring of 1916. By the beginning of April, General Joffre grew impatient with Pétain because he believed Pétain needed to follow up his magnificent defense of Verdun with an equally brilliant attack to regain the lost ground. Joffre wrote, "I repeatedly urged upon General Pétain the need of striking back, pointing out to him that if we never recovered, little by little, the ground we had lost, we would be faced with a very dangerous situation."¹⁷ Pétain responded to Joffre's urging with a strong sense of caution and multiple demands. He cared a great deal for the lives of his men, and he was not about to sacrifice thousands of additional lives on a foolhardy attack. Pétain asked for additional artillery before he would do anything else, and Joffre eventually threw up his hands in exasperation. Joffre admired his subordinate, but he believed Pétain had too narrow a view on Verdun:

> General Pétain was the heart and soul of the action. Moreover, it should not be forgotten that it was his accurate and unceasing study of the enemy's fighting methods that brought about in our own army the greatest tactical improvement seen in it at any time during the war; this is especially true of the fruitful liaison he effected between the aviation and the artillery.... On the other hand, the very qualities of this most eminent leader were affected by a condition of mind which caused him to place an exaggerated importance upon the events happening at Verdun. If I had yielded to his demands, the whole French Army would have

been absorbed into this battle.... All this will explain how it came about that early in April I looked about for means of withdrawing General Pétain from the battlefield of Verdun, hoping that by giving him a more distant perspective, a wider front upon which to direct his action, he would take in the general situation with a clearer view.[18]

General Joffre quickly found a post with more significant responsibility for General Pétain. The tenacious defender of Verdun passed off operational command of the Second Army to General Robert Nivelle and took the promotion to Commander of Army Group Centre, consisting of fifty-two divisions. He and General Joffre continued to clash on strategic views, but Pétain never forgot the men he led at Verdun. The city and the soldiers who served with him found a special place in his heart. Years later he still reminisced, "Our men toiled and suffered more than can possibly be imagined. They did their duty simply, with no ostentation, and in so doing, they reached sublime heights."[19]

When the *Escadrille Américaine* finally came into being at the end of April, the Battle of Verdun was far from over. Pétain was preparing to transfer command to General Robert Nivelle, who was clearly cut from a different cloth from Pétain. Nivelle was an artilleryman and an ardent believer in the doctrine of the counterattack. He immediately began drawing up plans for a massive assault to regain the ground the Germans had captured since February. The Americans were just beginning to form their squadron when they were thrust headlong into one of the bloodiest battles in history.

When orders came in the spring of 1916 authorizing the formation of the *Escadrille Américaine* (later known as the Lafayette Escadrille), the Americans were overjoyed.[20] The directions called for the squadron to assemble at Luxeuil-les-Baines, in the Vosges sector near the Swiss border. James McConnell described the excitement: "The rush was breathless! Never were flying clothes and fur coats drawn from the quartermaster, belongings packed, and red tape in the various administrative bureaus unfurled, with such headlong haste."[21] McConnell was a native of Chicago and New York City whose father was a lawyer and then judge of the Cook County Circuit Court. He studied at the University of Virginia from 1907 to 1910, including a year at the university's law school, but he withdrew before graduating. McConnell arrived in France in 1915 to work with the American Ambulance and decided to join aviation in order to do more for the French cause.[22] He was thrilled when the Americans finally received orders to form an American squadron, and after only a few hours, McConnell, Norman Prince, Kiffin Rockwell, and Victor Chapman were on a train bound for Luxeuil, overjoyed with the opportunities that awaited them.

Their haste paid off, for they were the first pilots to arrive on April 20, 1916. A few days later, Bill Thaw, Bert Hall, and Elliot Cowdin joined the four others at their new home. The final roster for the Lafayette Escadrille did not match the list provided earlier by the French government. For reasons unknown, Charles C. Johnson, Clyde Balsley, and Lawrence Rumsey were not included on the final roster. The three Americans would join the squadron later, but for now the seven original members of the squadron relished their new surroundings.

Most of the nations involved in World War I referred to their pilots as knights of the air or some other aerial aristocracy, and they treated their aviators as such. For men of the Foreign Legion, like Kiffin, Thaw, Chapman, and Hall, the life of a pilot at the Front seemed like a fairy tale compared to their previous existence. Luxeuil-les-Baines was a small resort town surrounded by fertile hills, beautiful meadows, and nearby mountains. The small town had a long history stretching back to the time of the Roman conquests of Gaul. The Romans discovered the hot springs there, and over the years Luxeuil became a spa destination for the French. The destruction of the war remained well outside Luxeuil, so the peaceful little town with its picturesque surroundings was a small slice of paradise to the Americans. Its meandering streets were filled with cafés, bakeries, and well-built buildings with stone façades and turrets. Luxeuil symbolized the gift they had been given and the start of something special. James McConnell summed up their anticipations nicely: "For us all it contained unlimited possibilities for initiative and service to France, and for [the Legionnaires] it must have meant, too, the restoration of personality lost during those months in the trenches with the Foreign Legion."[23]

The French designated the Lafayette Escadrille as Escadrille N.124 and placed the squadron in the command of a French captain named Georges Thénault. Thénault was a pilot in Escadrille C.42 when William Thaw started flying after his stint in the Foreign Legion. The two men became good friends, and in May of 1915, Thénault received command of Escadrille C.42. Thaw convinced Thénault to volunteer for command of the Lafayette Escadrille and supported him wholeheartedly behind the scenes until the French chose Thénault as commander of the new American squadron.

Before the Americans arrived, Captain Thénault had already assembled the necessary personnel and equipment to make the squadron a reality. He chose his "faithful friend" Lieutenant Alfred de Laage de Meux as his deputy after observing his extraordinary character while commanding the C.42 at Verdun.[24] De Laage was born into an old Orleanist family and started the war as a cavalry officer in the 14th Regiment of Dragoons. He was wounded in the leg on August 31, 1914, after his horse was shot out from under him, and he entered aviation when his convalescence ended. De Laage started as an observer and gunner but later learned to fly while at the Front and was one of the few French pilots who never attended aviation training.[25] His brilliant actions over Verdun caught the attention of Thénault, and he accepted the deputy position with pleasure. The Americans admired him a great deal: "He represented all that is best in French character and had a power of personal magnetism which made him a natural leader. He gave to his pilots a new conception of the meaning of patriotism, and it is not the least exaggeration to say that the love which the Americans had for him bordered upon adoration. He led them out to their first battles, flew with them individually and in groups of two or three, instructing them in the tactics of combat, which, in those early days, had to be learned at the Front."[26]

Upon receiving command, Thénault went immediately to Lyons to acquire ten tractors, four trucks, and two automobiles for the squadron's use. He also enrolled eighty men who would act as mechanics, drivers, cooks, secretaries, and quartermasters. Thénault had the men escort the equipment on a special train from Lyons to Luxeuil. By the time the Americans arrived at Luxeuil, the wheels were already in motion. The Americans marveled at all the equipment that Thénault had assembled. Everything was brand-new, and the number of support personnel amazed the new pilots. They were accustomed to the harsh treatment of the Foreign Legion and the cash-strapped aviation schools. The mechanics, quartermasters, and other personnel were thrilled to work with the American squadron, so a tight bond quickly formed between the American pilots and their indispensable partners.

Despite the incredible dangers associated with flying in its original era, life on the ground was luxurious for pilots at the Front. In training the pilots had to deal with strict rules and regulations similar to the guidelines of an infantry unit. After arriving at the Front, however, all the pilots received "the treatment accorded an officer, no matter what his grade."[27] Pilots did not have to deal with roll calls or details, and they could do as they pleased when they were not flying. They had their own rooms with regular beds and orderlies to assist them. All of them received their own Nieuport aircraft, and Thénault assigned two mechanics to each pilot. It was quite a privileged lifestyle, especially considering what many of the men had been through earlier.

The pilots' specific accommodations at Luxeuil only magnified an already luxurious lifestyle. They lived in a stone villa just over one hundred yards from a two-hundred-year-old bathhouse built over the hot springs. Wide lawns and courtyards divided the various buildings spread throughout the compound. The bathhouse had large arched windows with a view of the lawns, flowers, and the city beyond the villa. It was a magnificent place to live. All of them dined at the Hotel Pomme d'Or where they ate trout, baked hare, roasted grouse, and chicken en casserole with bottles of Bourgogne wine and oven-fresh pastries.[28] Meals only cost a dollar, and the men could fish or hunt if they had extra time. At least a few of the men grew suspicious at the fine treatment. They knew the life expectancy of a pilot was depressingly low at the time, so McConnell remarked, "I thought of the luxury we were enjoying: our comfortable beds, baths, and motor cars, and then I recalled the ancient custom of giving a man selected for the sacrifice a royal time of it before the appointed day."[29] It certainly made the men wonder!

The Lafayette Escadrille's first assignment was to protect a madman and his subordinates. When the Americans arrived in Luxeuil, the French had not yet transported their Nieuports to the airfield. The aerodrome was south of the city about two kilometers from their villa. While they waited for their new aircraft, Captain Thénault drove them out to meet Captain Happe, the madman himself. Captain Happe was famous all along the Western Front as the Red Pirate. According to Thénault, his mad recklessness was only equaled by his luck.[30] The crazy aviator had bombed the Zeppelin factory and German trains so often that the Germans put a price of 25,000 marks on his head. Amazingly, he always flew alone in an old 80-horsepower Maurice Farman that could only fly a dreadfully slow forty miles an hour. Happe was a sitting duck for the speedy German fighters every time he flew on his bombing sorties, but he always managed to come back in one piece. His Maurice Farman would be shot full of holes, but Captain Happe always emerged unscathed. Happe's poor mechanic flew with him on every mission with a Winchester carbine or a cavalry musket, and the unfortunate soul did his best to pester attacking German aircraft with his primitive weapons. The French loved Happe's bravado, and when even his mechanic managed to survive every mission, they decided to cash in on Happe's reckless tactical approach.

Unfortunately, Captain Happe's luck did not transfer to those in his group. He commanded a bomber group of four escadrilles flying the same decrepit machines as his own. All of his men were brave individuals who volunteered to fly in Happe's group, but the French quickly found that Happe's approach was tantamount to suicide for most of the men. After sustaining significant losses, Happe's second in command convinced his crazy commander to fly at night until they received better machines and pursuit aircraft to escort them.

Thénault and the Americans had been assigned as escorts to Happe's bomber group in order to reduce some of the growing losses. When Thénault took the Americans into

Captain Happe's office, the bomber commander showed them eight sealed boxes containing war crosses for the families of eight men who had just died under his command. Thénault sarcastically stated, "As an introductory remark that wasn't very encouraging."[31] Happe welcomed the American pilots and told them to get ready as quickly as they could. The Americans left Happe's office with plenty of fodder for discussion over their evening meal. Kiffin was fascinated by the whole exchange and told his mother, "We are under the orders of the most famous man in French aviation … and we are to be guards for his outfit. He is a man absolutely without fear and one of the most interesting characters I ever met."[32]

Thénault did his best to keep the men busy while they waited for the Nieuports to arrive. He took them on long drives through the countryside in order to familiarize them with the area. There were only three aerodromes between Luxeuil and the front lines where the men could land if they had issues. During their drives, the men noted some of the open fields or cleared areas that they could use as a landing spot if they could not make it to an aerodrome. They all shuddered at the obstacles invariably around an emergency landing site—great trees, hills, ravines, and innumerable electric power lines that posed significant dangers to unaware airmen. Kiffin marveled at the stunning scenery along their drive through sections of Alsace with views of the Alps in the distance. Thénault also showed them the border of Switzerland so the men would not inadvertently fly into the neutral country. The Swiss put up a great fuss whenever French planes flew over their territory.

Kiffin was never good at waiting, but the presence of German aircraft in the skies above their aerodrome was enough to drive him absolutely crazy. He wanted to be airborne

Members of the Lafayette Escadrille posing in front of their formidable French Nieuport 11 aircraft. The Nieuport 11, nicknamed the Bébé, was a light, fast, and extremely maneuverable pursuit aircraft. Pilots pictured from left to right: Lieutenant Alfred de Laage de Meux, Charles Johnson, Lawrence Rumsey, James McConnell, William Thaw, Raoul Lufbery, Kiffin Rockwell, Didier Masson, Norman Prince, and Bert Hall (Virginia Military Institute Archives).

fighting for France, but instead he was stuck on the ground watching German planes lumber through their sector. Kiffin wrote, "We still have no machines, and the Germans continue to show up—three more yesterday. Great big slow things; one good man with a *Bébé* [Nieuport] could have gotten all three of them before they could have gotten back to their lines."[33] Thénault did not like the presence of German aircraft over his head either, but he needed the break that the supply delays offered him. He had fought over the Battle of Verdun from the beginning, "where nerves had been taut to the breaking point and one had to fight with every ounce of one's strength not to win, but simply to hold on; where ... we had to put up a defense ... against ten times our number of assailants."[34] Starting a new squadron was the perfect remedy for a commander whose already strained nerves would soon be put to the test once more.

Thénault sent telegram after telegram to hasten the arrival of the Nieuports, and on May 1, six of the speedy little aircraft finally arrived. The mechanics went to work at once since the planes had no armament or markings. Kiffin received one of the first six aircraft, and a few days later he decided to take it for a quick spin above the aerodrome. He was unaware that an incredible storm was headed directly for their sector. He could see a dark line along the horizon to the southwest, but the air at Luxeuil was calm and the sun was shining brightly. In an instant, the storm struck, lifted the unsecured aircraft off the ground, and smashed them to pieces. Canvas hangars fell over like a house of cards and observation balloons tore from their moorings. Most of the other pilots were out watching Kiffin fly, and Thénault described the scene that occurred:

> Suddenly this line [of dark clouds] seemed to rush upon him in a few moments at a terrific speed. It was a cloud of dust raised by the cyclone. The sun was hidden immediately, but from the ground we could witness Rockwell's struggle with the tempest. His Nieuport was thrown up and down like a dead leaf, but the pilot kept his head. He started descending head straight to the wind, with his motor full on and joystick right forward. The force of the wind was so great that he didn't go forward at all, but came down gradually. Our mechanics gauged the spot where this new fangled helicopter was going to land. They ran to meet it. Rockwell landed right in their midst and immediately a score of vigorous hands gripped his fragile machine by the wheels, the wings, the supports or the fuselage—anywhere, so as to prevent it being whirled away. Rockwell got out safe and sound and his machine was uninjured. It was a splendid piece of work.[35]

Kiffin was typically nonchalant after the harrowing experience. He told Paul, "I didn't think of any danger for myself, but was only afraid for my machine, as I knew I would have to wait a long time for another."[36]

His greatest fear from that day forward was not dying in the skies over France; the thought of being stuck on the ground for weeks at a time was far worse than his fear of death. Kiffin also needed to get away from the sudden rush of publicity that now surrounded the Lafayette Escadrille. He never liked when his fellow American soldiers did everything they could to get their names in the news. It had happened in the Foreign Legion and it was happening again in the new American escadrille. When Paul asked Kiffin for a photograph, Kiffin responded, "I had rather not bother with any of it as all this junk they pull off makes me sick."[37] Victor Chapman echoed his friend's disgust. The two friends had become incredibly close, and they both resented the popular drive for cheap notoriety. Although they continued to avoid the media, their attitudes gradually changed as they realized that the publicity encouraged other recruits and enhanced the cause of France over that of Germany. Kiffin also had no idea that he was about to be thrust into the national spotlight whether he liked it or not.

When the Lafayette Escadrille had all of its machines fully equipped with machine guns and other necessities, Captain Thénault took the pilots on their first combat patrol. They arose at dawn, studied the route Thénault had drawn on the map, and rose together into the crisp spring air. The French commander chose Kiffin Rockwell to lead the squadron's first patrol, and they flew in a wild-duck wedge with Thénault in the rear on one side to "keep an eye on [his] colts."[38] They cruised at ten thousand feet along the Swiss border near Belfort, where the weather turned hazy with the rising sun. James McConnell was afraid of getting lost, but he was having a hard time staying in formation with the others. As the haze increased, he climbed higher until the air became clear. To his horror, he realized that he was above a bank of clouds that looked like a white sea of majestic icebergs.[39] McConnell could no longer see his formation, and he was uncertain of his position. Being a wingman without a formation or flight lead can be a frightful situation, especially to a new aviator, but McConnell's fear subsided when he saw his comrades pop up through the cloud bank one by one. Thénault went to retrieve his young fledgling, and when they returned to the formation McConnell saw the Rhine River and "from a height of 13,000 feet over Dannemarie, a series of brown, woodworm-like tracings on the ground—the trenches!"[40]

As they passed over into enemy territory for the first time, the air around them exploded in little balls of flame. The German antiaircraft batteries opened up in full force at the sight of the American patrol. McConnell found that the roar of his motor drowned out the noise of the explosions so much that his "feelings about it were wholly impersonal."[41] Victor Chapman and Kiffin Rockwell must have felt a measure of vindication at the Germans' inability to target them with their dreaded artillery. In the trenches, the shells had been accurate and terrifying. In the air, the bursts could be deadly, but it was difficult for an antiaircraft battery to score a direct hit on a maneuverable plane like the Nieuport. Rockwell and Chapman took great pleasure in taunting the German artillerymen who used to have so much power over them. Much to Thénault's annoyance, the two former Legionnaires "deliberately amused themselves by diving at little smoke clouds [while] the strident explosions of the shells continued."[42] Kiffin figured the German aircraft would eventually come up to meet them after seeing the intense fire from the artillery batteries. His idea never materialized, so he decided to do the next best thing. With the rest of his patrol in tow, he dove straight "over the Habsheim aerodrome and there performed an aerial fandango to bring the Boches out."[43] But no German aircraft accepted the challenge, and Kiffin reluctantly decided to fly home, as they were running low on fuel.

The Americans made it back to Luxeuil safely and reported any of their machines' minor abnormalities to their mechanics. After the aerial exhibit over the front lines, Thénault wrote, "We followed Rockwell who as leader of the patrol we wouldn't have abandoned at any price."[44] One of the most hallowed truths of combat flying was beginning to form. The day of flying as individuals was rapidly coming to an end. The Germans designed patrols specifically for the purpose of jumping lone pilots, and the results were usually devastating no matter how skilled the pilot was. Flying in formation with mutual support was the only way to counter such tactics. Pilots still flew occasionally as individuals, but the practice was gradually dying out.

However, on May 18, 1916, one pilot in the Lafayette Escadrille took to the skies alone and unafraid. Kiffin Rockwell preferred flying with others, but on this particular day he was incensed at the enemy. German bombers often came on night raids to wreak havoc on French aerodromes. Kiffin was irate because the Germans had recently bombarded the airfield at Luxeuil and killed four of the Lafayette Escadrille's devoted mechanics. He already felt as if he had multiple scores to settle with the Germans on account of his friends in the Foreign Legion, and this raid only added to the list. When he took off on May 18, Kiffin was on the hunt and would not be deterred.

Kiffin flew across enemy lines in search of prey. The air was still bitterly cold at altitude, so he shivered as his eyes scanned the area below him. The dull roar of the engine masked any other sound, and he watched in silence as the menacing lines of trenches disappeared beneath the Nieuport's nose. Shortly after flying into enemy territory, the steady hum of his engine was interrupted by a surging and popping sound. He immediately recognized the distinct noise as his motor misfiring. Kiffin quickly turned back toward France, since a bad motor in a single-engine aircraft is a troubling issue.

As he started heading for Luxeuil, he suddenly saw a German aircraft loitering near the French lines below him. Kiffin's heart started beating rapidly. His chance had finally arrived! He forgot about his misfiring motor and dove headlong at his foe. As the Nieuport gained speed in the rapid descent, the engine caught and began operating normally again. A few seconds after Kiffin maneuvered downhill, the German pilot spotted him and plunged into a steep dive away from the attacking aircraft. The German machine was a two-seater with a gunner in the back manning two machine guns. Kiffin hurtled toward the enemy plane from the rear, and the gunner opened up a potentially deadly burst on the young novice pilot. A few rounds smashed into his machine, but Kiffin was locked onto his target. He closed fast on the plane, and when it felt as if a collision was imminent, Kiffin squeezed the trigger. Five rounds blasted out of the barrel, and Kiffin broke hard right to avoid crashing into the German. As he rocketed away from his prey, he saw the gunner fall dead and the pilot slumped over sideways. The smoking German machine fell to one side and then went into a vertical dive that ended in a fiery crash. The whole sequence happened in less than a minute, but the impact of the encounter made a permanent impression on the unit. The Lafayette Escadrille had its first victory and Kiffin Rockwell was the man of the hour.

The engagement on May 18 was a watershed moment for Kiffin. The Americans already knew him as a natural leader and fearless aviator, but his victory and his method of attack gave him a nearly mythical status in the squadron. Kiffin's last-second swerve to avoid a collision with his enemy became his trademark. His five rounds managed to kill the pilot, the gunner, and the engine. Before he landed, a French observation post had telephoned the news to the squadron, so the Americans welcomed him back like a returning king. James McConnell wrote, "All Luxeuil smiled upon him—particularly the girls."[45] Kiffin became known as the first American ever to down an enemy aircraft, and even though the claim was inaccurate it only added to his heroic status.[46] His brother Paul was absolutely ecstatic about his younger brother's success. The eighty-year-old bourbon he gave as a gift gave rise to one of the most hallowed traditions of the Lafayette Escadrille. The squadron's Bottle of Death was born and became a permanent fixture in the unit. Only those who scored a victory could have a taste of its contents, and once they took a sip they etched their names on the side of the bottle.

The bourbon sitting prominently on the shelf became a powerful motivation for all the pilots who served in the squadron. Pursuit pilots from every country desired aerial victories because they quickly became a status symbol. Five victories bestowed upon a pilot the title of "Ace," and in World War I the most successful aces had a status unequaled among any other combatant in the air or on the ground. Although the desire to rack up victories was often a selfish personal goal, the practice produced amazing results. Achieving superiority in the air over the battlefield required victories, and the pilots pursued those victories with a single-minded focus. Immediately after Kiffin's victory, the Lafayette Escadrille received orders to Verdun. Their time of incubation was complete—the French declared the unit ready for the fires of Verdun, and the pilots looked forward to their new assignment with great anticipation. Neither the French nor the Germans had fully grasped the concept of air superiority, but the outcome of the Battle of Verdun was one of the sparks that ignited the idea in the minds of the great air pioneers.

11

The Lafayette Escadrille Comes of Age

The aerial battle over Verdun was a defining moment in the history of air power. The war in the air matched the intensity and ferocity of the war raging on the ground. It was the first major confrontation of fighter forces, and more aircraft were marshaled against each other than any other previous battle in the short history of aviation.[1] The German High Command desired complete control in the skies over Verdun and assembled a massive force to achieve its aim. The Germans stationed most of their aircraft opposite Verdun, including two-seat planes designed to maintain a barrage patrol and 180 additional pursuit aircraft that could intercept French aircraft penetrating the aerial barrier.[2] The German strategy was devastating in its effectiveness during the opening weeks of the battle. Thénault's frayed nerves were part of the job. Before he took command of the Lafayette Escadrille, he had to fly this gauntlet daily. Fleeing from large German patrols became a common occurrence that many French aviators did not survive.

General Pétain changed the course of the battle in the air in the same way that he altered France's fate on the ground. He appointed Major Tricornot de Rose with the responsibility of defeating the Germans in the air. Pétain told him, "Rose, sweep the skies clear for me because I am blinded. If they chase us out of the sky, it's quite simple—Verdun will be lost."[3] Pétain also gave more detailed instructions: "Offensive patrols will be carried out on a regular basis at times fixed by the commander of the *groupe*.... The mission of the escadrilles is to seek out the enemy, to fight him, and to destroy him."[4] Major de Rose assembled most of France's greatest aviators in Verdun and went to work. By the time the Americans arrived in the Verdun sector, the French were well on their way to achieving air superiority. When the Germans finally gave up their frequent attacks in late June of 1916, the French had complete control of the air.[5] While the men of the Lafayette Escadrille missed the opening act of the aerial battle over Verdun, they played a major role in the decisive operations that resulted in air superiority in the sector. The Americans never forgot this lesson, and they managed to capture the spirit required to achieve aerial dominance. Over several months, the pilots of the Lafayette Escadrille refined this fighting spirit, and they injected it into the green and inexperienced aviators of the United States Air Service when they arrived in 1917 and 1918.

In May, the French issued orders moving the Lafayette Escadrille to Béhonne Airfield outside of Bar-le-Duc in the Verdun sector. The day after Kiffin's great victory, the pilots and support personnel began to pack up the whole squadron. They assembled all of the tractors on the edge of the field and loaded them with supplies. As the men trotted off to finalize their plan, a bomb exploded right in the middle of their parked vehicles. Seconds later there was a massive explosion as the gas in the vehicles ignited and consumed four of the tractors. The pilots looked up and cursed their luck as they saw a German aircraft pulling up from his bombing attack and wheeling around to strafe the rest of their assembled convoy. Some brave mechanics ran to the surviving tractors and saved them from the blaze while the German's bullets struck the ground around them on his next pass. Amazingly, no one was wounded, but the pilots left Luxeuil with an even greater desire to control the air.

The pilots took off in their Nieuports bound for Bar-le-Duc while the rest of the squadron's personnel escorted the convoy to their new home. Thénault had them stop for fuel at an aerodrome about halfway to their destination, and the pilots ate lunch with the local escadrille. As they ate, the droning of two motors reverberated through the building, and the Americans heard a cry that two Boche aircraft were over the field. Remembering the incident the night before, Thaw and Chapman raced to their Nieuports and flew up to meet them in battle. The Germans turned and fled, so the two men rejoined the rest of the Americans and flew to Béhonne Airfield.

Bar-le-Duc was another garden spot for the Lafayette Escadrille aviators. The town was built on and just below a high hill with a good view of the surrounding countryside. A river flowed just past the center of town. Willow trees and flowers covered its banks and gave the area a peaceful feel similar to that of Luxeuil. The Verdun battlefield and trench lines were far from the sleepy hollow that the Americans now occupied. The group commander, Major Fabiani, kindly situated the American squadron in a villa just inside the gates of Bar-le-Duc. The villa was very comfortable for the men, and all the French pilots from other squadrons would join the Americans at the villa for lunch.

The French threw the Americans straight into the inferno from the minute they arrived in the Verdun sector. The pilots began flying immediately after their arrival, and the first to score a victory was none other than Bert Hall. Kiffin was flying low over Fort Douaumont outside Verdun when Hall attacked a German high above Kiffin's position. Hall's machine was hit in the fight, but he managed to shoot down the German and watch it fall just inside the German lines. Only a day or two later, Thaw brought down a German at dawn on a patrol with Kiffin but told the exuberant squadron, "No credit to me. I just murdered him. He never saw me."[6] The pace of life was furious, and Kiffin explained, "This is a regular hell around here in the way of excitement and the world going crazy. Impossible to express with words one's impressions. I am badly played out for lack of sleep."[7]

Shortly after arriving in Verdun, problems began to surface among some of the personalities in the Lafayette Escadrille. Most of the men got along with everyone with the exception of Bert Hall and Elliot Cowdin. Hall was not popular due to his frequent embellishments and abrasive personality, while Cowdin liked to have his own way and became a bit of a troublemaker when things did not work out as he intended.[8] The rest of the Americans in the squadron wanted to preserve a sense of harmony within the group, so they managed the selection process of future members. Captain Thénault went on recruiting trips to flight schools and interviewed prospective candidates, and then the original members in concert with reliable follow-on members would select the new members of the Lafayette Escadrille. The process made the American squadron a very tight-knit organization. Since the Lafayette Escadrille could not absorb all the Americans flooding into the

French Aviation, the remaining Americans went to other French squadrons to form the Lafayette Flying Corps.

Kiffin must have been uncomfortable with the bad blood growing between Hall, Cowdin, and the rest of the Americans. He wrote a few letters to his brother that indirectly addressed the issue. In two different letters Kiffin asked Paul to give Bert Hall some publicity for his courageous actions. Most of the Americans received a great deal of press back home, but Bert Hall never seemed to garner much attention. After Hall shot down his first aircraft, Kiffin instructed his brother to write a story so Bert Hall could receive his due share of praise. While this probably helped the atmosphere in the squadron, Cowdin and Hall continued to vex the other members of the escadrille. Neither of the two men remained with the Lafayette Escadrille long.

When the pilots of the Lafayette Escadrille were finally all assembled at Bar-le-Duc, the French military commanders scheduled a massive counterattack in the region of Douaumont. The Americans received the task of patrolling one thousand feet above the area where the artillery battle was concentrated. The Lafayette Escadrille had the low patrol, while a second squadron flew a middle patrol at six thousand feet, and a third patrol covered

Kiffin testing the accuracy of his Lewis machine gun. The Lewis gun was mounted on the upper blade of the biplane and frequently jammed. To clear the jam, pilots had to stand up, brace against the wind blast, and attempt to fix the gun while flying with the other hand (Virginia Military Institute Archives).

the high ground at twelve thousand feet. Their stacked patrols were part of a tactic to ensure that no German aircraft could effectively control enemy artillery fire or push past the French lines. The low patrol was quite dangerous. Artillery shells frequently blazed through the formation, and occasionally an aircraft burst into pieces as a shell passed through the plane on its way to its intended target. In light of these obvious dangers, Thénault wrote with a dry sense of the obvious: "In war, life, or rather death, is only a question of meeting on your own route with the trajectories of any kind of projectile. To escape, the only thing to do is not to be at the meeting point at the same moment."[9] Unfortunately the men had little control over being in the wrong place at the wrong time.

Thénault was thrilled with the mission because it called for the entire Lafayette Escadrille to fly in force over the area. He laid out the plan in a simple manner and made it crystal clear that no pilot would attack unless he received a signal from him. Thénault knew something that the Americans may not have realized: "I knew the Boche, knew that he had all his great aces, [Oswald] Boelke and the rest of them, in the neighborhood, and I wanted to train my escadrille before trying to stack up against them."[10] Captain Thénault was an outstanding commander who knew his people and understood exactly how to take care of them. He had flown against the famous German aces and had no doubt that his men would be shredded by the experienced enemy pilots. Bravery was one thing—he knew all his men would not hesitate for a second before attacking a German ace. But foolishness was another thing—Thénault had a mission to accomplish in Verdun, and he knew they would fail if he threw his courageous pilots to the wolves too early. His plan prevented many untimely deaths and gradually prepared the men to take on pilots such as the famed Oswald Boelke.

Boelke was a young German ace who managed to revamp German fighter tactics with a focus on formation flying. He acknowledged the necessity of individual flying skills and encouraged training those skills, but he knew that the Germans would be more successful if they fought together. Boelke came from a strong German family and grew up as a sportsman who had little interest in studying. During school he secretly wrote the emperor about his desire to receive a nomination into the cadet corps, and the commander of the cadet corps later informed his parents that the emperor had granted his request.[11] After earning his wings, Boelke became a phenomenal pilot, and the Germans gave him a great deal of latitude to develop tactics. He and Max Immelmann competed early on for the title of Germany's premier ace, and on the same day Kiffin Rockwell shot down his first plane, Boelke took the lead over Immelmann for good with sixteen victories. When the Americans arrived in Verdun, Boelke was incredibly famous, and the Americans respected his success as much as they hoped to meet him in battle.

Boelke also trained and mentored Germany's most famous ace of World War I. Manfred von Richthofen was earning his spurs as a brand-new pilot in the skies over Verdun. Before the battle, he was an observer and a gunner in a two-seat aircraft and developed a great deal of frustration with his inability to shoot down the enemy. He decided to raise his concerns with Boelke: "So I asked him: 'Tell me, how do you manage it?' He seemed very amused and laughed, although I had asked him quite seriously. Then he replied: 'Well, it is quite simple. I fly close to my man, aim well and then of course he falls down.' I shook my head and told him that I did the same thing but my opponents unfortunately did not come down. The difference between him and I was that he flew a Fokker and I a large battle plane."[12]

Shortly after this interaction, Richthofen resolved to fly a Fokker and threw all his aim and ambition into learning how to fly. He graduated from observer to pilot in March of 1916, and even though it did not get counted officially, he brought down his first aircraft (a French Nieuport) over Verdun on April 26, 1916. Boelke would later choose Richthofen as his pupil in the Somme sector, and the Red Baron would quickly eclipse the fame of his tutor after Boelke's death in October 1916. The German pilots were certainly a force to be reckoned with over the fields of Verdun, and the Americans were eager to test their mettle against some of the greatest pilots in the world.

Thénault was cautiously optimistic about their first trip over enemy lines as a complete squadron. He had instructed them concerning the dynamics of the low patrol and incessantly reminded them of his order not to leave formation without a signal from him. It was a mission he would remember for the rest of his life. Thénault, de Laage, and the Americans all took off, and the men flew through a swarm of antiaircraft shells, "so numerous in this sector that even later we never saw them thicker anywhere else."[13] When they turned north and established themselves on a vector for Verdun, they soon witnessed a sight that rattled their souls. Down below them they saw "a strip of ground several miles wide without a tree, without grass, brown and yellow in color, where the soil was pitted with shell-holes innumerable that touched each other, without roads, without houses, nothing—nothing, as if the very bowels of the earth had been torn open. It was the battlefield of Verdun."[14] Thénault's description captured the utter destruction that had befallen the old city. Entire villages had disappeared into muddy pockmarks, and the lack of vegetation in a fertile region made the entire area feel eerie and malformed.

As the pilots gazed down on the battlefield, the excitement of the day began in earnest. Thénault spotted about twelve German two-seaters flying low over their lines but gave no indication that he saw them: "They were too low, too numerous, and too far behind their own lines for us to attack on this first expedition, especially with pilots who had yet to get thoroughly acquainted with a redoubtable enemy."[15] As these wise thoughts traveled through Thénault's mind, he suddenly noticed with horror that someone (even years later he never knew who it was) had broken formation and dove like a meteor towards the Germans. The others naturally followed immediately, and Thénault had no choice but to dive after his rebellious pupils.[16] All of them pushed forward on the stick and opened the throttle to travel at maximum speed. Thénault described the melee: "Everyone picked out his opponent, but the Boches were so startled to see this pack of devils falling upon them that they turned tail and ran for all they were worth."[17] The ensuing dogfight was a mass of twisting and looping aircraft so low to the ground that German soldiers in the town of Etain started firing at the French planes.

The Lafayette Escadrille's first squadron-size engagement was a partial success and a major learning point. The Germans eventually spun around to meet the Americans and the machine guns from both sides flashed as streams of lead rocketed back and forth. Kiffin attacked one in his typically thunderous style, but as he was following the aircraft to the ground, another German raked his machine with bullets. This particular German was using explosive bullets, which were considered illegal in warfare at the time, and the bullet exploded through the windshield directly into Kiffin's face. Four or five pieces penetrated his skin around his mouth, and he staggered back to the lines covered in blood and slightly in shock. He managed to land in French territory and later spent two days in Paris recovering from wounds that were fortunately not life-threatening. The Lafayette Escadrille seriously damaged at least three German aircraft, but the enemy planes were able to land, since the engagement happened inside their front lines.

The aftermath of the intense aerial battle was quite uncertain for several hours. Thénault arrived in an angry mood due to the disobedience of his American pilots, but discipline was a sensitive issue in the squadron. He was a Frenchman commanding an all-American squadron and had to tread carefully due to the high visibility of his famous unit. Thénault eventually embraced the difficult situation as a diplomatic necessity, but the inability to discipline angered some of his future French deputies.

Only this particular day, Thénault never had a chance to remain angry at his young aviators because upon landing, "A big fellow, his face all covered with blood, was waiting for me. It was Kiffin Rockwell, who burst into a flood of abuse against Germany and her disloyal methods."[18] Thénault sent Kiffin off to the hospital in Paris and quickly hurried around the camp accounting for his young pilots. Everyone had arrived except for Bill Thaw. The men were shocked since Thaw was the most experienced among them. During the fierce dogfight, the unseasoned Americans had completely lost track of one another, so no one knew of Thaw's fate. After several hours, they finally received a phone call. The men's fears melted away when they learned that Thaw was in a hospital near the front lines. Most of the squadron went to visit him and found out that a German bullet had struck him in the elbow and shattered the bone. Thaw had steered his machine with his good arm, but the loss of blood and the shock made his condition deteriorate rapidly. He landed in a patch of barbed wire without knowing which side of the lines he was on, but he was relieved when he saw men in blue uniforms running towards him. The hospital had put his arm in plaster, and Thaw was out of the action for the time being.

The trial by fire in Verdun had only just begun. The life of an aviator in World War I was incredibly dangerous. The casualty rate among pilots was dreadfully high, but the danger only seemed to further energize the Americans. Their new lives, despite the perils involved, were infinitely better than their former existence in the trenches. They engaged the enemy on a daily basis, and rarely encountered the feeling of helplessness that had penetrated every facet of the trenches. Victor Chapman wrote his father soon after the squadron's first major engagement and said, "This flying is much too romantic to be real modern war with all its horrors. There is something so unreal and fairy like about it, which ought to be told and described by Poets, as Jason's Voyage was, or that Greek chap who wandered about the Gulf of Corinth and had giants try to put him in beds that were too small for him, etc."[19] The idealists among them could not believe that they could live a life more rich than the one in the Lafayette Escadrille. They had a cause they believed in and the means to achieve it. What more could they desire?

About a week after the battle that wounded Thaw and Rockwell, another extraordinary man showed up at the door to the Lafayette Escadrille's villa. His name was Raoul Lufbery—a pilot of humble origins destined for greatness. Thénault described him thus: "Simple, modest, silent and hardworking, always getting his plane ready himself—it was Lufbery."[20] At thirty-one years old, he was older than most of the Americans in the Lafayette Escadrille but was actually born in France to French parents. His mother died when he was one, and his father remarried and emigrated to the United States when Lufbery was five years old. His father left him and his two brothers in France in the care of his grandmother, but by the turn of the century Lufbery earned enough money working at a chocolate factory to travel to America. After spending a few years in the United States, Lufbery decided to see the world. At nineteen years old he traveled to Algiers, Tunis, Egypt, and then Constantinople. He left Turkey and went to the Balkans and Germany; at every place, Lufbery would accept any sort of employment that he could find. In Germany, he signed a three-month contract for a steamship company that employed him on a ship traveling between Hamburg and German South Africa.

Lufbery arrived home in New York three years later to spend some time with his father, but his father had just left on his own travels. He stayed at home for two years but left again when his father did not return. He traveled to Cuba, worked in a bakery in New Orleans, and served as a waiter in a San Francisco hotel. Lufbery then decided to join the U.S. Army and went to the Philippines for two years. He completed his enlistment and continued his travels to Japan and China, where he worked in the Chinese Customs Service.

His travels finally culminated in India as a ticket agent in Bombay. Lufbery fortuitously met a French pilot named Marc Pourpe in Calcutta in 1912. The Frenchman had come to make a series of exhibition flights throughout the region, and Lufbery was fascinated by the man and his machine. Pourpe's flying partner died in a flying accident while in India, and his mechanic left shortly afterwards due to illness. Pourpe asked Lufbery to be his new mechanic, and the two then showed their machines to inquisitive people around the world. They traveled throughout the Far East and then Egypt and the Sudan. Lufbery provided valuable insights into weather patterns and other potential flying dangers because Pourpe had never visited most of the places.[21] In the summer of 1914, they finally returned to France as the war broke out, and Pourpe immediately enlisted in aviation while Lufbery joined the Foreign Legion. Lufbery transferred quickly to aviation as Pourpe's mechanic, but was devastated when his friend was killed three months later on December 2, 1914.

Raoul Lufbery resolved to avenge his great friend, and he joined the aviation school at Chartres. He received his brevet, but much to his dismay the French sent him to a bombardment squadron. He tried the Nieuport but struggled so much that the French declared him as "inapt for combat training and more fitted to be a *pilot de bombardement*."[22] This proclamation did not sit well with Lufbery, and he continued pushing until he finally finished Nieuport training. The clumsy, inexperienced pilot bore no resemblance at all to the victorious aviator he would become. By the end of May, a humbled Lufbery joined the Lafayette Escadrille, but his desire to avenge Pourpe was as strong as ever.

Several other pilots joined the Lafayette Escadrille at the same time as Lufbery. Charles Chouteau Johnson, a native of St. Louis and fellow University of Virginia graduate with James McConnell, joined the squadron on May 29, 1916, with Lufbery and another man named Clyde Balsley. Johnson and Balsley, a San Antonio resident, both came from the American Ambulance and served with the Air Guard of Paris before starting with the Lafayette Escadrille. Laurence Rumsey and Dudley Hill served in the American Ambulance as well and joined the squadron in early June. Rumsey was a 1908 Harvard graduate from Buffalo, New York, but ill health kept him grounded for much of his time at the Front. The French would later declare him unfit for aviation in November 1916. Dudley Hill, on the other hand, was a survivor. He was originally from Peekskill, New York, and mostly blind in one eye. For pilots, eyesight is everything, so Hill had to tread carefully around physicians. When he left the American Ambulance, he received a pass for his eyesight from Dr. Gros because the demand for pilots was so high. The French eventually found out and decided to remove him from Aviation, but by the time they issued the order he had nearly completed his brevet.[23] The French relented when they realized that he was able to perform successfully as a pilot with defective vision.

The final man in the first group of recruits was a pilot named Didier Masson. Masson was actually born in France and served in the French Army for three years, from 1904 to 1906. He learned to fly in 1909 and traveled to the United States to hone his skills. In an amazing turn of events, General Obregon of Mexico commissioned Masson as his Chief of the Air Service in 1913.[24] General Obregon opposed the military coup of Victoriano Huerta and fought the Mexican Federalist troops throughout 1913. Masson pioneered several innovations, including aerial bombs made out of tin cans filled with explosives that he tried to drop on Huerta's gunboats.[25] When the war broke out in 1914, Masson left his Mexican adventure behind and enlisted in the French Army again. He fought with the army until October 1914 when he transferred to Aviation and started flying with the French. Masson joined his adopted countrymen in the Lafayette Escadrille on June 19, 1916.

All of the pilots in the Lafayette Escadrille wanted revenge after an event on the first of June. A group of German bombers managed to evade the French air defenses and mercilessly bombed the town of Bar-le-Duc and neighboring areas. The attack killed forty people (many of them women and children), and the pilots of the Lafayette Escadrille were ashamed to walk down the streets under the glare of the survivors. Kiffin was incensed because his machine was still being repaired after all the damage caused by the explosive bullets. He told Thaw that the two of them could have downed multiple Germans that day and prevented the loss of innocent lives.[26]

In the meantime, Kiffin's friend Victor Chapman was beginning to make a name for himself in the squadron. Several days after the bombing of Bar-le-Duc, Chapman was on a patrol with Thénault, de Laage, and Balsely on the west bank of the Meuse when he spotted some Germans on the other side of the river. He hurtled towards them with de Laage and Balsley following at a distance. The Germans quickly enveloped Chapman in a swarm, but de Laage and Balsely managed to break up the fight. Instead of returning to the Béhonne aerodrome, Victor landed at a nearby field, gassed up his plane, and took off alone in search of more Germans. He found what he was looking for, except this German was an ace and had four other aircraft supporting him.[27] Chapman bravely but foolishly attacked the formation alone. The German ace was none other than Oswald Boelke himself, who told the story of the fight in one of his letters.[28]

Chapman fought like a tiger in the aerial death-match and somehow managed to escape the wrath of the famous German. His aircraft was riddled with bullets, several of which had cut the wire struts between the wings, and he set his crippled plane down at a field just inside the French lines. Victor only received a minor gash when one of Boelke's bullets grazed his head. Despite his wound, Chapman tried to get airborne again immediately, and the French commander of the airfield had to forcibly keep him on the ground. He was extremely lucky to be alive, and he proudly wore his bulky head bandage like a badge of honor. All the Americans loved Victor, but his courage often bordered on the insane. Kiffin began to grow worried about his friend. Their months of living and learning together in pilot training made them extremely close, and they were very much alike in many ways. But Victor's insatiable appetite for danger and extreme odds was more than

Kiffin in Paris on leave from the Escadrille in June of 1916 with his brother and his brother's fiancée. Seated left to right: Paul Ayres Rockwell, Marcelle Guérin de Précourt, Kiffin, Anne Marie Françoise Jeanne Leygues (Paul's fiancée), and unknown (from the archives of Loula Rockwell Brown, courtesy W. Vance Brown II).

Kiffin could handle because he feared that Victor would take on a fight he couldn't finish. Kiffin even told Paul that he nearly lost his own life trying to support Victor. He wrote, "Chapman has been a little too courageous and got me into one of the mess-ups because I couldn't stand back and see him get it alone. He was attacking all the time, without paying much attention."[29] James McConnell also described his daring friend Victor: "Considering the number of fights he had been in and the courage with which he attacked it was a miracle he had not been hit before. He always fought against odds and far within the enemy's country. He flew more than any of us, never missing an opportunity to go up, and never coming down until his gasoline was giving out. His machine was a sieve of patched-up bullet holes. His nerve was almost superhuman and his devotion to the cause for which he fought sublime."[30]

The fighting over Verdun grew even more intense in the days and weeks that followed. A few days after Chapman's duel with Boelke, four of the pilots had another serious encounter with the Germans. Kiffin, Balsely, Prince and Thénault were on a patrol when a large number of Germans surrounded them and commenced a coordinated attack. Balsely had only been with the squadron a week, so the veteran pilots did not think much of him at that point due to his inexperience. Kiffin had the same feelings about the new pilot until he saw that "he had plenty of good will to work and was not afraid."[31] Just after Kiffin and the other three flew over the German lines, they ran across forty enemy aircraft flying at different heights in one small sector. The Germans surrounded them and had the men totally hemmed in for about ten minutes while they made long-range passes at them. The veterans saw their chance when only one aircraft was between them and the friendly lines, so they shot towards the lone German in a desperate escape attempt. The Germans countered this by pouncing on them all at once. Kiffin and Thénault made it out of the deadly ring, but they thought Prince or Balsley was dead because they had seen at least one French aircraft go into a death spiral.

The Americans soon found that the spiraling aircraft was piloted by Clyde Balsley. Prince landed soon after Kiffin and Thénault, so they rushed to the telephone to inquire about their young comrade. As information came in, they pieced together Balsely's fate. Balsley attempted to fire on a German aircraft in the middle of the aerial brawl, but his gun jammed and forced him to exit the fight to clear his weapon. While he tried to clear the jam, another German aircraft attacked him, and one of the bullets exploded in the thigh, causing "appalling injuries, literally splitting the pelvis bone."[32] With incredible strength, Balsley recovered from his death spiral and set the machine down right by the front lines. In accordance with the tactics of the time, the German artillery opened up on the haplessly grounded and injured aviator, but some brave French infantrymen dashed out to the plane and rescued Balsley. The exploding fragments from his aerial duel had wounded him grievously, and he required an immediate operation. The French managed to get him to the hospital in time, but Balsely's life was still very much in danger.[33]

June 23 was an even more fateful day than the day Balsley was wounded. The Americans received a telephone message from Balsley requesting some oranges because the doctors would only allow him to suck on an orange due to his intestinal injuries. The always-caring Victor Chapman purchased some oranges and loaded them into the bottom of his Nieuport. On his way to the hospital, Chapman could not resist attacking five Germans with Thénault, Prince and Lufbery in tow. Chapman's good fortune finally eluded him. He screamed into the melee in typical fashion but was quickly surrounded by the enemy aircraft. Victor dove and turned through a number of maneuvers and then tried to disengage. His efforts were useless—the Germans had pinned him in and were swarming around him. One of the Germans finally picked up an accurate bead on Victor and fired a lethal burst into his aircraft. Victor Chapman was hit and slumped over as his Nieuport dove straight down toward the earth. An observer on the ground called and said he saw Chapman's plane disintegrate in the air during its dive. The utterly fearless and eternally thoughtful Victor Chapman was the first to fall in the Lafayette Escadrille.

Kiffin Rockwell was devastated by the death of his best friend and constant companion. He loved Victor's courage, but every night in their room Kiffin begged him to be more prudent: "He would fight every Boche he saw, no matter where or what odds, and I am sure that he had wounded if not killed several.... His head wound was not healed, yet he insisted on flying anyway, and wouldn't take a rest."[34] After Victor's death, Kiffin tried to write Chapman's parents several times, but it took a few days before he had the courage to take up his pen. His words are still the best and most fitting tribute to his friend:

> To start with Victor had such a strong character. I think we all have our ideals when we begin, but, unfortunately, there are so very few of us that retain them; and sometimes we lose them at a very early age, and after that, life seems to be spoiled. But Victor was one of the very few who had the strongest of ideals, and

then had the character to withstand anything that tried to come into his life and kill him. He was just a large, healthy man, full of life and goodness towards life, and could only see the fine, true points in life and in other people. And he was not of the kind that absorbs from other people, but of the kind that gives out. We all had felt his influence and seeing in him a man made us feel a little more like trying to be men ourselves.... He died the most glorious death, and at the most glorious time of life to die, especially for him with his ideals. I have never once regretted it for him, as I know he was willing and satisfied to give his life that way if it was necessary, and that he had no fear of death, and there is nothing to fear in death.... Yet he is not dead; he lives forever in every place he has been, and in everyone who knew him.... He is alive every day in this Escadrille and has a tremendous influence on all our actions. Even the [mechanics] do their work better and more conscientiously. And a number of times I have seen Victor's [mechanic] standing (when there is no work to be done) and gazing off in the direction of where he last saw Victor leaving for the lines.[35]

Victor Chapman left a large hole in the tight-knit group of Americans in the Lafayette Escadrille. He was the heart of the squadron, and his courage inspired all of the men in multiple ways. But Chapman certainly died doing what he loved. After years of searching, he had found his calling and performed his task with unparalleled energy. Kiffin and the others missed their friend dearly, but they all sensed that Chapman's death was not in vain. He died for a cause, and he died in support of his fellow Americans. The others, Kiffin included, moved on with the knowledge that their time might come as well. The survival rate of pilots was still depressingly low, but they continued to fight regardless of the odds.

The fire of Verdun still raged on, so the men had little opportunity to rest and reflect on the passing of their comrade. The spirit of the Lafayette Escadrille did not break with Chapman's passing, but grew stronger and more refined. The American pilots were gradually transforming into the noble group that would later shepherd hundreds of additional pilots from the United States. Victor Chapman was the first to place his eternal mark on American air power. In the words of his classmate, John Temple Jeffries: "If a long and distinguished ancestry, the presence of all a man's virtues and the absence of all vices count for much, then Harvard has lost one of the greatest gentlemen that ever studied at that university."[36]

12

Passing the Torch

The Lafayette Escadrille continued shoring up the skies over Verdun, but major operations in Verdun were mostly complete by the beginning of July 1916. The Germans had not managed to bleed the French white and force them from the war, and as a consequence General Falkenhayn soon lost his job. At the same time, the French Army was a wreck. Defending Verdun cost the French dearly—they lost 362,000 men in the gigantic clash of opposing armies. The German strategy of attrition was a complete failure because France did not seek terms and the German Army suffered 336,000 casualties—a number nearly equal to French casualties! Earlier, as the Germans prepared their final attempt to inflict a decisive blow on the French, General Joffre thundered one final appeal to his exhausted army at Verdun: "Soldiers of Verdun! It is our valor which has made this possible, for your heroic resistance was the indispensable condition to our success. Upon it still depends our future victory.... I make one more appeal to your courage, your ardor, your spirit of sacrifice, your love of country. Hold fast and strive with all your might to shatter the last desperate efforts of an enemy now at bay."[1] The weary French soldiers answered their commander's plea, but the horrendous loss of life in just a few months nearly brought the country to its knees.

By the middle of June, General Joffre needed an outlet to relieve the pressure in the Verdun sector, and he needed it quick. The British had successfully raised a massive army along the lines in northern France, so General Joffre appealed to the British commander, General Sir Douglas Haig, to prepare a major offensive in a separate sector. General Haig complied, and an Anglo-French offensive on the Somme commenced on the first of July. The plan was essentially the same archaic scheme that had already resulted in hundreds of thousands of deaths throughout Europe. The battle was a disaster. In one month, the British and French lost 200,000 men while the Germans lost another 160,000. The catastrophe on the Somme was the greatest loss of life in British military history.[2]

Meanwhile, the fighting in the air over Verdun was still intense. The focus of aerial operations would ultimately shift to the Somme sector, along with the Lafayette Escadrille, but for the time being the American pilots had a job to finish over the scarred terrain of Verdun. Promotions and decorations were in order after all the fighting the Americans had done thus far. Prince and Hall were promoted to the rank of adjutant, and Kiffin, McConnell and the rest of the corporals received the rank of sergeant. Kiffin and Hall also received the *Médaille Militaire* and the *Croix de Guerre* for their earlier victories, while Bill Thaw was awarded the Legion of Honor for his victory. Thaw came up from the hospital with his arm in a sling to receive his decoration with Kiffin and Hall. The men all took the recognition in stride and continued their mission.

The Americans quickly settled into a routine in Verdun. Every single day, as long as the weather permitted, the Lafayette Escadrille launched several sorties starting at sunrise. An orderly would come and wake up the pilots while it was still dark, and the men would gulp down some coffee before heading to the airfield. McConnell claimed that "as a rule the most successful sorties are those in the early morning," so the ambitious pilots were ready to go out at first light.[3] Typically about four to six pilots launched every morning, and the men made sure to wear their fur-lined boots and jackets to combat the cold at altitude. The morning ritual consisted of a great deal of jibing and excited conversation since none of them could talk once they were airborne. When the aircraft were ready, the pilots yelled "Contact!" and started the motors. The men took off one at a time and then circled above the field at about 4,500 feet waiting for the rest of the flight to join. Once they all rejoined, the Americans set off in hunt of German aircraft.

The Nieuport was a thrilling aircraft to fly, and the men loved their machines like children of their own. All of them had distinguishing markings, usually the first letter of their last name written in large, bold print on the side of the fuselage. Bert Hall wrote "BERT" from left to right on the left side of his aircraft, and the same name spelled backwards on the right side, "so an aviator passing him on that side at great speed [would] be able to read the name without difficulty...."[4] It was an interesting idea that likely did not make much sense to pilots unfamiliar with the Lafayette Escadrille. All the pilots of the Nieuport referred to it as "the machine of Aces and the Ace of machines," and it clearly outclassed the Fokker in combat over Verdun.[5] Flying the Nieuport was a great honor in France; consequently, an American aviator in the Lafayette Escadrille was "stamped at once as a great pilot and the crowd of other pilots envied [him] bitterly."[6]

Aerial tactics progressed rapidly throughout World War I. Maneuvers like the spin, the barrel roll, the renversement, and the loop became basics of aerial combat, and pilots constantly sought to innovate in order to gain an advantage. In air combat, the pilots searched for maneuvers that allowed them to point at another aircraft first or position themselves behind their adversary. Successful maneuvers such as these spelled doom for opposing aviators and were the first step to achieving the victories that led to control of the skies. But even if a pilot maneuvered to an advantageous position, he still had to know how to shoot.

Poor aim, jammed guns, or effective defense maneuvers by the adversary made victories elusive for an inexperienced aviator. The wings of the Nieuport had an upper plane and a lower plane connected by wooden struts and metal cables—thus the term biplane. The Nieuport carried a Lewis gun fixed on the upper plane of the machine in order to prevent shooting through the propeller. Germany had already devised a brilliant solution to this problem by creating a synchronized machine gun capable of successfully firing through the spinning propeller. Because the Nieuport's Lewis gun was mounted on the upper plane of the wing, the gun frequently jammed. Thénault claimed, "[O]ur Lewis gun used to jam in 75 per 100 of our attacks owing to the effect of vibration, and many a Boche owed his life to that."[7] Many a Boche probably also owed several victories to the unreliable Lewis gun because clearing a jam was treacherous in the middle of an aerial duel. In order to fix the Lewis gun, a Nieuport pilot had to push his body out of his seat, strain to reach the port of the weapon while dealing with wind blast, and somehow clear the jam and reload a round. During the entire process, the pilot had to maneuver the aircraft with one hand

and evade incoming German fighters eager for a kill. Many a Nieuport pilot did not survive this complicated process. Nevertheless, the men regarded the Nieuport as far superior to the better-armed Fokker on account of its power of maneuvering and the confidence which it gave to pilots.[8]

July passed with multiple engagements but few victories for the Americans. Kiffin described his frustration to his brother in several letters. In one instance, he attacked a machine with forty-four rounds and then turned off to let Lieutenant de Laage engage the German. De Laage shot over eighty rounds followed by another twenty by Bert Hall, but the German kept flying as if nothing happened. Kiffin and the others then attacked three more German aircraft, and Kiffin's bullets sent one of them plunging through the clouds. He later heard that an observation post reported seeing his falling enemy right himself under the clouds and fly to safety. On one day, Kiffin flew for eight hours but could only assist in forcing a German to land inside of German lines. He complained to Paul, "I have had about twenty fights lately, sometimes going as close as ten meters to the Germans, and I almost ran into one two or three days ago. But I haven't had the luck to have one of them smash to pieces in our trenches...."[9] McConnell noticed Kiffin's ongoing offensive as well: "Rockwell, who attacked so often that he has lost all count, and who shoves his machine gun fairly in the faces of the Germans, used to swear their planes were armored."[10]

During one of these unlucky encounters, the men of the Lafayette Escadrille crossed swords with Boelke once again. Ironically, the day of the duel was none other than Independence Day: July 4, 1916. Boelke wrote in his diary that the aerial activity over Verdun had been slight until the Fourth of July. He was sitting idly at the aerodrome when he saw one of his fellow German pilots get jumped by a Nieuport. The German landed quickly and breathlessly declared, "The devil is loose at the Front. There are six Americans out there. I distinctly saw the flag on the machine! They are very bold and come far on our side of the lines."[11] Boelke was undeterred and decided to see for himself how bold the Americans were. He discovered them flying in a group and attacked the first aircraft, which he believed to be flown by a beginner. Boelke's gun jammed during his attack, and the other five Americans pounced on him. He managed to "[slide] down on [his] left wing" two times to escape the American onslaught and had to dive down to two hundred meters above the ground in order to finally get away.[12] Describing this engagement, Boelke wrote, "[I] flew back to camp, little pleased, although untouched, while the Americans continued on their flight along the Front."[13] After Boelke's translated diary appeared in France, the Americans found that the pilot who barely escaped Boelke's initial attack was Elliot Cowdin. Kiffin was almost certainly one of the other five Americans since Thénault and a few other pilots had gone to a Fourth of July celebration in Paris.

By the end of July, the squadron's victories finally began to increase. On one morning, de Laage and Kiffin found a solitary German near the French lines, and Kiffin jumped him immediately. After Kiffin's attack, the German nosed over, and de Laage managed to finish him off. Kiffin was happy for de Laage because it was the courageous lieutenant's first victory, but he was irritated about some of the practices of some of the pilots in the Lafayette Escadrille. It was common in World War I to "cherry-pick" near the French lines, since any victory over the lines was easily confirmed by observers on the ground. Others like Kiffin roamed far abroad in search of German fighters and engaged many more aircraft because of it. Kiffin, in his role as the informal leader of the Lafayette Escadrille, complained loudly to Captain Thénault about those who hung near the French lines. In his view, and that of many others, the point was not racking up victories inside French lines but seeking and destroying the Germans wherever they roamed. Kiffin, always somewhat impetuous, told his brother that he would leave the American squadron if the issues continued.[14]

Kiffin's threat never materialized because, despite his frustrations, he loved the Lafayette Escadrille, and he quickly developed a deep friendship with the newcomer—Raoul Lufbery. Since he arrived in the escadrille, Lufbery learned his new craft very slowly and had been unable to bring down a German for a variety of reasons. Like the others, Lufbery became aggravated and resolutely continued to work for his elusive first victory. He and Kiffin flew together often and had the same idea of how to take the fight to the Germans. On July 31, Lufbery finally succeeded. He brought down a German aircraft just before lunch, which launched a string of additional successes. A few days later Lufbery downed two more Germans near Fort Vaux and then his fourth on August 8. It was an amazing feat, and Lufbery's achievements made the Lafayette Escadrille's fame skyrocket. Once Lufbery started gaining victories, the other pilots followed suit, and any bad blood remaining among the squadron members rapidly dissipated.

The flying in August continued in earnest, and the men logged a great deal of time in the sky above Verdun. Kiffin had flown eighty-one hours in July and recorded thirty or forty fights with German aircraft. Since most of his engagements took place well within enemy lines, the French only officially reported twenty-one of the fights. Some of the aircraft tumbled from the sky but none of them were confirmed. The desire for victories often led to inaccurate or untruthful claims. Kiffin and de Laage shot down a German one day in August, but the plane recovered just prior to impact and flew back into Germany. An observer did not see the aircraft recover, so he reported a victory. After hearing of the observer's confirmation, Kiffin did not feel right claiming the victory since he had seen the German recover, but two well-known French pilots stepped in and claimed it the next day. Victory claims could be a vicious game.

The desire to attain the title of Ace was an ever-present aspiration in the Lafayette Escadrille, but the Americans' ambitions soared with the arrival of one famed aviator. At the end of July, a young, brash, highly confident Frenchman joined the Lafayette Escadrille on a temporary basis. His name was none other than Charles Nungesser, the renowned French Ace who had multiple victories before he began flying with the Lafayette Escadrille. Nungesser was already a legend, and the Americans viewed him with a great deal of respect. His body was a mess due to multiple accidents and close calls, but the Frenchman was resilient. He flew with a "ghoulish insignia" including a death's-head and crossbones, but the startling image only added to his fame.[15] Nungesser's presence pushed the Americans in the same way that a star athlete can inspire his teammates to perform at a higher level. The Americans enjoyed his company for the short time he flew with the Lafayette Escadrille. Nungesser returned to his old squadron, N.65, in August, but his short stint left an indelible impression on the young squadron. Nungesser shot down one German with the Lafayette Escadrille and would go on to score forty-three victories, which earned him the title of France's third-highest ace behind René Fonck and Georges Guynemer.

The month of August started fairly eventfully, and the lively action continued through September. Lufbery's earlier victories ignited the already surging Lafayette Escadrille. Some of the pilots who had yet to score a victory were willing to try nearly anything to join the exclusive club. Norman Prince became obsessed with the idea of bringing down a German "sausage," since the German aircraft had so far eluded him.[16] A sausage was an observation balloon that looked very similar to a German sausage and was prevalent all along the Front at the time. Prince acquired aerial rockets that he could attach on each side of his machine in order to take down the enemy balloons. The rockets were designed to burn for 600 feet, and a well-aimed shot would set the gases inside the balloon alight. Norman Prince mapped out his plan and executed it with great passion. For a time, he had the same luck with balloons as he had with airplanes. The balloons would either land quickly or German aircraft would guard them fiercely. Prince "stuck to it, however, and finally his appetite for 'sausage' was satisfied. He found one just where it ought to be, swooped down upon it, and let off his fireworks with all the gusto of an American boy on the Fourth of July."[17] The balloon disintegrated in flames, and Prince won his victory.

James Rogers McConnell (right) with Kiffin Rockwell. McConnell studied at the University of Virginia before leaving to join the American Ambulance in 1915. He served with distinction in the Ambulance before becoming one of the Lafayette Escadrille's original members. After Kiffin's first aerial victory, McConnell wrote, "All Luxeuil smiled upon him—particularly the girls" (from the archives of Loula Rockwell Brown, courtesy W. Vance Brown II).

Not long afterward, Prince finally downed an aircraft as well. On August 23, he shot down an Aviatik and was able to claim his first victory. At the same time, Kiffin's dear friend from the Foreign Legion, Paul "Skipper" Pavelka, finally joined him in the Lafayette Escadrille. Skipper and Kiffin were supposed to leave the Legion at the same time, but events beyond the control of either of them kept Skipper with the Legion for a few additional months. He managed to survive the extra time in the trenches and finally received the coveted transfer to Aviation.

Skipper Pavelka was the thirteenth pilot to join the Lafayette Escadrille, and the "unlucky" number immediately convinced him that he surely must be cursed. Thénault gave him the "hoodooed machine" that Thaw had been seriously injured in and that Prince had wrecked shortly before.[18] Skipper's concerns were quickly confirmed. On his second flight, the machine caught fire, and Skipper had to masterfully maneuver his aircraft toward the ground without getting burned in the process. He slammed the Nieuport onto the ground, jumped out of it, and as he walked from the wreckage, the fuel tank exploded. The

Germans used the smoke from the burning Nieuport to direct their artillery, and the jinxed little aircraft finally ceased to exist.[19] Skipper Pavelka was now fully initiated into the American squadron!

The month of September was the most significant month to date for the Lafayette Escadrille. It would also turn out to be one of its darkest months in the whole war. Most of the original hands remained; Chapman had fallen in glory and Cowdin had to retire from active service due to ill health.[20] The French eventually released him, but he later came back to France in 1918 as a major in the U.S. Air Service. Kiffin Rockwell inaugurated the momentous month of September by finally destroying and gaining confirmation of another German aircraft. Immediately after his victory, the Lafayette Escadrille received orders to leave Verdun. Thus, Kiffin's victories served as bookends to the American squadron's amazing time over Verdun. He was the first of the squadron to gain a victory, and he was the last pilot to score a victory in the Verdun sector. The Americans left the war's most destructive battlefield to date with a proud sense of accomplishment.

In his book about the Lafayette Escadrille, Captain Thénault provided an excellent account of their actions in the sky above the great battle. He began his summary with the words, "So ended for us the Battle of Verdun, which went down in the Escadrille's record as the hardest struggle we had to face.... Every one had to fight with all his soul to hold his own against a tenacious foe."[21] During the battle, the Americans had 146 aerial engagements, thirteen confirmed victories, one pilot killed and three wounded. Thénault continued: "The Escadrille's baptism of fire at Verdun was an undying memory for all the pilots who took part in it, and later the survivors were wont to recall this terrible period when they had hardly time to sleep or eat, when they used to sleep fully dressed in their flying suits beneath their planes so as to be ready to start at the first glimpse of dawn. Those were the heroic days of the Escadrille, its glorious prime. Prince, Lufbery, Rockwell, and Chapman, were you not worthy rivals of the greatest Heroes of any age or country?"[22] Thénault's tribute to his beloved squadron was moving, and it certainly exhibited the admiration he had for the Americans' daily sacrifice over his country. They won multiple confirmed victories, had untold numbers of other victories that could not be confirmed, and the squadron "had become known throughout the world...."[23]

Victories, bravery, and renown are important measures of success, but even such significant accolades are empty assessments if the enemy prevails. Yet in the Lafayette Escadrille's case, the enemy did not prevail. The Americans and their hundreds of fellow French pilots routed the Germans in the skies over Verdun. The most telling measure of the Lafayette Escadrille is Thénault's following evaluation: "By this time the enemy was much less numerous and above all showed much less dash. The main body of his air forces had moved over to the Somme, where the Allied offensive was in full swing."[24] This was the ultimate assessment. At the end of the battle, the French owned the skies. Verdun taught the Americans in the Lafayette Escadrille how to achieve air superiority and how decisive superiority of the skies could be.

The fires of Verdun also fortified the bond among the Americans in the Lafayette Escadrille. Months of living together, flying multiple sorties a day, and defending their brothers in combat produced a rock-hard bond between the men. They spent hours after dinner playing games, listening to music, and talking—always talking. As the night wore on, a few would always remain and the talk became "more personal and more sincere."[25]

They lived together, and they died together. Their differences began to melt away, their passions began to merge together, and their collective soul began to form. The squadron was born in April of 1916, but its soul rose from the ashes of Verdun. From that point forward, the Lafayette Escadrille was truly a band of brothers. Their little organization was now an unrelenting force, and its existence would soon shake the foundations of their native country thousands of miles away.

The monumental month of September was not over yet, though. Starting on the fourteenth, the men received a much-needed week's rest in the capital city of Paris. Jim McConnell spent most of his days holed up in Paul Rockwell's apartment trying to recover from a back injury he received when his plane crash-landed in a field. The rest of them were naturally elated at the chance to blow off some steam, and they wasted no time getting themselves into mischief. The Americans were already famous, so their unannounced arrival in Paris caused quite a sensation among the American reporters. They were all tired of reporters by that point, so one of the men decided to have a little fun with one of the reporters. He made up the following story about Bill Thaw: "Bill was flying alone over German territory, about twenty miles behind the lines, when an Archie shell almost got him. Bill got mad as hell at the Boche for almost killing him, or what was worse, making him a prisoner. Old Bill got so mad in fact that he landed his Nieuport right beside the German battery and took his Lewis gun from the top wing. Then he charged those Germans, spraying hot lead all around him. When Bill had emptied the drum, all the Germans lay dead. That satisfied Bill, so he put the machine gun back on the wing and took off and flew home."[26] The reporter amazingly believed the above story, but the madness of their leave in Paris was only just beginning. Thénault busied himself bailing Lufbery out of jail because he had broken six teeth of a railroad employee who had insulted him.[27] The Americans also toured the factories to have a peek at future machines still in development.

Perhaps the most outrageous activity of the trip to Paris was the acquisition of a baby lion cub. A Parisian man was in the possession of a lion cub that had been born on a boat crossing from Africa. The Americans saw the advertisement in the paper and thought a little lion would be a perfect mascot for the Lafayette Escadrille—particularly when it was full grown. Dudley Hill, Bert Hall, Kiffin Rockwell, Bill Thaw, and Norman Prince all chipped in money to buy the lion, and they named it Whiskey. The men loved their little "cute, bright-eyed baby lion who tried to roar in a most threatening manner but who was blissfully content the moment one gave him one's finger to suck."[28] When they finally received orders to head back to Luxeuil, the men tried to bring little Whiskey into the passenger department of the train. The conductor was appalled at the sight of a lion, despite its diminutive size, and ordered it off the train immediately. Thaw had to stay behind and escort the lion cub back to Luxeuil in a crate the next day. The week of fun in Paris was over and it was time to get back to business once again. Paul Rockwell escorted the group to the train station and fretted over his younger brother as he often did. Kiffin shook Paul's hand, smiled broadly, and said, "Cheer up, I'll be back again soon on permission."

The men enjoyed their return to Luxeuil, the location where the Lafayette Escadrille had started. A large British aviation contingent had also moved to the airfield earlier, but the early tension between the British and the Americans quickly turned into a veritable Anglo-American alliance.[29] In Paris, another pilot named Robert Rockwell (a distant cousin of Paul and Kiffin) had joined the squadron. Rockwell was a native of Cincinnati, Ohio, who had originally traveled to France to work as a surgeon in the American hospital. After some time working in the hospitals, he realized that he would rather enlist in aviation instead of remaining in the rear.[30] The Americans welcomed the new "Doc" Rockwell with open arms.

Whiskey the lion cub became an immediate hit at the Pomme d'Or Hotel, where the pilots stayed while in Luxeuil. The hotel owner's daughters adored Whiskey and spent several days figuring out exactly what the lion liked to eat. A mix of bread and milk did the trick, and the cub happily gulped up the concoction at every meal. The Americans quickly realized they needed to restrain Whiskey's instinct to extend his claws on occasion, but after some strict reprimands the lion cub "soon became the best behaved of lions."[31] Whiskey became the inseparable companion of Thénault's dog Fram, a former police canine, who had been the sole pet of the Lafayette Escadrille until the lion cub arrived. The two animals played so well together that even when the lion was full grown, and could have eaten Fram fairly easily, the two still played nicely as long as Fram left Whiskey alone during mealtimes.[32]

In the meantime, the Americans waited anxiously for their new machines. The French scrapped the Nieuports they used over Verdun because the planes were completely worn out after months of combat. The new model of Nieuport was larger, with an extra twenty square feet of surface area on the wings. The extra surface area improved the stability of the new aircraft and enabled the Nieuports to climb faster to higher altitudes. Most important to the pilots, however, was the fact that the new models dropped the forty-seven-shot Lewis guns for a five-hundred-round, double-barreled Vickers machine gun.[33] The Vickers held a great deal more ammunition, but it was also mounted in front of the cockpit and fired through the propeller with a synchronized gear similar to the one used by the Germans. This update made the Vickers gun far more accurate and ended the perilous task of reloading the Lewis gun mounted on the upper plane. The men were excited to break in the new machines.

While they waited, the pilots fished for trout in nearby streams and threw parties for the British pilots. On one occasion, the Americans challenged the British to a game of football in a British shed at the airfield. They did not get around to starting the game until midnight and had to extinguish all the lights so the German bombers would not find an easy target. The state of the shed after the game was an utter disaster. The Americans reciprocated by organizing dances in their hotel where the foreigners and the locals tried out all the modern steps. After a week of waiting in Luxeuil, the first six machines arrived at the airfield on September 19.

Captain Thénault did not have to think long about who would receive the first available aircraft. When the mechanics finished preparing the first two aircraft for combat, Thénault gave the Nieuports to Kiffin Rockwell and Raoul Lufbery. The commander of the Lafayette Escadrille wrote, "But think of restraining fanatics like Lufbery and Rockwell, when they have at their disposal superb new machines, fitted with the latest devices."[34] Thénault of course had no intention of attempting to restrain his finest fanatics, so he let the two leaders begin flying on September 22. The two friends were thrilled and declared themselves ready after their cursory test flights that day.

The following day, September 23, was a fateful day for the Lafayette Escadrille. Kiffin and Lufbery took off together and scoured the Alsace region for Germans. It did not take long for them to find three Fokkers who screamed upward to meet them. They both picked

Picture of the actual medals presented to Kiffin Rockwell by the French government. The most significant medals are France's highest decoration, the Legion of Honor (top left); France's third highest decoration, the *Médaille Militaire* (top row second from left and bottom row second from right); the *Croix de Guerre* (top row third from left); and the Insignia for Military Wounded, equivalent to the Purple Heart (bottom row third from left) (from the Rockwell family collection, courtesy of Sybil Robb).

an adversary and commenced a coordinated attack. Lufbery's brand-new machine gun jammed on his first pass, and he cursed as he tried to clear it.³⁵ He dove away from the engagement, but several German rounds found their target and damaged the framework of one of his wings. Kiffin escorted his friend back to Fontaine Field, but decided to continue the patrol alone rather than land with Lufbery. Flying alone in the Alsace sector was a dangerous thing to do because the Germans had stationed large numbers of pursuit squadrons in the area to oppose the British and French bombing squadrons.³⁶ Kiffin, however, was not easily frightened or deterred by danger. As Thénault described it, "It was dangerous, but that was Rockwell all over, and no one who knew his character could expect him to act otherwise. He was a born fighter and the blood of his soldier ancestors ran ever hot in his veins."³⁷

Kiffin climbed high above the French lines and continued to search his sector. He finally spotted a German Albatross a few thousand feet below him and was clearly satisfied to see an enemy aircraft inside friendly lines. McConnell wrote, "Rockwell had fought more combats than the rest of us put together, and had shot down many German machines that had fallen in their lines, but this was the first time he had an opportunity of bringing down a Boche in our territory."³⁸ Kiffin plunged headlong at the enemy as a captain stationed near an Alsatian village witnessed the engagement. The fearless American rocketed downwards so close to the German that it appeared the two aircraft would collide. The rear-gunner in the Albatross fired first at long range, but Kiffin continued his attack. In standard fashion, Kiffin opened fire at a very close range and broke away. This time was different, however. At first, the German aircraft looked as if it was falling, but then Kiffin's machine turned rapidly nose down and broke apart. The French captain watched helplessly as Kiffin and the remains of his aircraft crashed into a small field of flowers a few hundred yards behind the trenches. It was a terrible moment. In what seemed like a blink of an eye, the Lafayette Escadrille's world turned upside down. The fearless American, their natural leader who had just turned twenty-four years old, was now dead.

The whole fight took less than a minute. Kiffin Rockwell had been shot down on the same kind of pass that he had performed dozens of times before. It was an inconceivable loss, especially considering the fact that none of the other Lafayette Escadrille members were there to witness it. Kiffin continued his mission without his friend Lufbery and was all alone when he finally fell. The men in the squadron were in shock and disbelief when they heard the news. Kiffin was their rock—the one who always came back. He always knew when to attack and when to disengage, and by that point he was by far the most experienced combat aviator in the squadron. His death was thus thoroughly unexpected.

Lufbery heard immediately about the fate of his brave companion. With tears in his eyes, Lufbery swore revenge and took to the skies with an entire band of cartridges and fury in his heart. He sped up and down the French lines, searching and hoping to find a German, any German, to attack. As if in solemn tribute to the fallen American, the normally crowded skies were eerily silent. Lufbery flew in circles over the German field at Habsheim, but the enemy did not show. Low on gas and pained to the limits of endurance, Lufbery reluctantly returned home.

The location of Kiffin's fall was only two miles from the spot where he had earned his first victory in May. The German artillery batteries commenced their bombardment of the wreckage, but some French artillerymen ran out and saved Kiffin's body from the approaching shells. The Frenchmen discovered "a hideous wound in his breast where an explosive bullet had torn through."[39] A surgeon who examined Kiffin's body would later say that the brave aviator probably would have survived if he had been hit with a normal bullet. But the Germans had used the explosive kind—a brand of bullet outlawed at the time—and Kiffin never had a chance.

Kiffin's death was heartbreaking to the squadron he loved and led. Thénault ordered a tractor to recover Kiffin's body, and with a heavy heart he sent Paul Rockwell a telegram informing him of his brother's death. The commander then ordered all the Americans to convene in the room of the hotel and tearfully broke the news to them. The men were shocked and devastated. Kiffin was their leader and the one they all looked up to. McConnell described the sorrowful feelings pulsing through the squadron that night:

> No greater blow could have befallen the escadrille. Kiffin was its soul. He was loved and looked up to by not only every man in our flying corps but by every one who knew him. Kiffin was imbued with the spirit of the cause for which he fought and gave his heart and soul to the performance of his duty. He said: "I pay my part for Lafayette and Rochambeau," and he gave the fullest measure. The old flame of chivalry burned brightly in this boy's fine and sensitive being. With his death France lost one of her most valuable pilots. When he was over the lines the Germans did not pass—and he was over them most of the time. He brought down four enemy planes that were credited to him officially, and Lieutenant de Laage, who was his fighting partner, says he is convinced that Rockwell accounted for many others which fell too far within the German lines to be observed.[40]

The night before Kiffin was killed, he told Skipper Pavelka and a few others that if he was ever brought down he would like to be buried where he fell. When the news of his death reached Skipper and the rest of the Americans, they desperately wanted to fulfill Kiffin's wish. Unfortunately the plan was infeasible, since the site of his crash was so close to the lines. The Lafayette Escadrille decided to do the next best thing. Paul Rockwell arrived the night of Kiffin's death, so most of the squadron escorted him the following morning to the spot where his brother had fallen. Paul was "utterly overcome at the thought of never seeing again his dearly loved brother," and all the pilots honored the memory of their hero by saluting and standing in silent prayer.[41]

Kiffin's funeral took place on September 25, 1916, with his body and coffin draped in a French flag at a church in Luxeuil. He was posthumously promoted to the rank of second lieutenant and given the Legion of Honor. His funeral was worthy of a general.[42] Paul Rockwell silently escorted his brother's bier from the church to the cemetery as every Frenchman in the aviation at Luxeuil marched behind. The sky above buzzed in unison with dozens of Allied aircraft flying over to render homage to the famous American aviator. The British pilots from Luxeuil marched behind the French pilots, and a detachment of an additional five hundred British soldiers followed the pilots. An entire battalion consisting of hundreds of French troops brought up the rear. It was an amazing and awe-inspiring sight: "As the slow moving procession of blue and khaki-clad men passed from the church to the graveyard, airplanes circled at a feeble height above and showered down myriads of flowers."[43]

At the gravesite, more than a thousand tearful pairs of eyes gazed at Captain Thénault as he stood before them. The cemetery was covered with flowers from the townspeople who adored all the Americans but particularly Kiffin Rockwell. Thénault began speaking with a lump in his throat, but he gave a fitting tribute to the foremost leader among the American pilots:

> Here by this tomb so recently closed, we meet today to pay our final duty to our comrade.... Learning of the cowardly aggression of which our country was the object, and loving France as a second motherland, he, with his brother, here present, hastened to France to enlist in the Foreign Legion ... he joined the aviation corps, where he obtained his *brevet* in an exceptionally short space of time. On the formation of the American escadrille, he came with it to Luxeuil.... Ordered to Verdun, he took part in every expedition against the enemy. He was happy in the midst of danger; the greater the strength or the number of the enemy, the more anxious was he to attack. Never did Rockwell consider that he had done enough.
>
> His courage was sublime and when the flights prescribed by the Commandant were accomplished he would set out again on his "Baby," barely allowing his mechanic time to refill his tanks.
>
> Indefatigable, he would fly over Vaux and Douaumont, above the crash of the enemy's guns. Where Rockwell was the German could not pass, but was forced rapidly to take shelter on the ground....
>
> Glory be to him who fell valiantly in the pursuit of his dream of love and justice. He met the glorious death he so much desired.... Glory be to his noble family and to his brother, whom a serious wound has forced to leave the field of battle. We share in their great sorrow.
>
> And to thee, our best friend, in the name of France I bid thee a last farewell. In the name of thy comrades, who have so often proved that they know how to keep their promises, I salute thee reverently. And with the memory of those who have already fallen, and whom we here invoke, we swear faithfully to guard thy memory and to avenge it.[44]

There was not a dry eye in the cemetery after Thénault finished his tribute to Kiffin Rockwell. Lieutenant de Laage wept like a child, and, "Indeed every man wept, for Rockwell had been the life and soul of the squadron."[45] Newspapers all over France and America ran stories praising the life of Kiffin and his hearty band of American pilots. One French reporter wrote, "The name of this young hero will live on in fond memories and grateful to France."[46]

Even the German newspapers covered Kiffin's death. Berlin sent a dispatch to the *Journal de Genève* declaring that Rockwell's fall deserved the greatest attention since it demonstrated Germany's outrage at America's breach of neutrality.[47]

Kiffin's mother Loula was heartbroken when she heard the news, but she was prepared. She knew why her boys were in France, and she had supported his actions ever since she received the letter Kiffin wrote from the hospital. The French ambassador to the United States wrote her a brief letter in which he simply said, "All France mourns with you. Your son will live forever in the hearts of the French people."[48] Loula was mourning, but she knew why her son had fought for France. She later wrote: "When the word came ... that Kiffin was killed in an encounter with three enemy airplanes, I could thank God that he died facing the enemy of civilization as he had expressed a wish to die. And while I am proud of the record he made as a soldier and the standard he set for those who shall fight after him, I am proudest of the character that I have seen develop, through their letters, in both of my boys. I would not change it if I could, and if I had a dozen sons I should want them, too, to fight for France."[49]

Even the words of Loula Rockwell's late husband comforted her. One of James Chester Rockwell's poems seemed to foreshadow the death of his son. Kiffin had done his duty and he had done it well:

> He came and went. Why question further,
> If he performed his mission well?
> For he who judgeth all things rightly,
> Alone can tell.
> This much we know: that he was faithful
> And e'er on duty was intent.
> Ask me no more. This is his story:
> He came and went.[50]

The outpouring of praise and admiration for Kiffin Rockwell was unequaled among the deaths of any other American aviator during the First World War. All of the survivors in the squadron believed Kiffin was the heart and soul of the Lafayette Escadrille. No other man matched his bravery, his commitment, and his devotion to the cause. He characterized everything the Americans were fighting for, and he died in pursuit of the dream that brought him to France. Kiffin was irreplaceable. He was an extraordinary man among exceptional men. The Americans could not replace him, but they did far more than avenge him. For what Kiffin stood for, what he believed in, and what he died for became eternalized in the spirit and soul of the squadron. Kiffin's sacrifice and the impact it had on the squadron transformed over many years into one of the greatest gifts ever given to the United States Air Force. He gave his life for France, but he gave his soul to America. Walk into any U.S. Air Force squadron and see for yourself. As Captain Thénault so eloquently stated, "The best and bravest of us all is no more."[51]

13

The Climax of the Lafayette Escadrille

Kiffin's fall, shocking as it may seem, was only the beginning of the story. His fellow comrades may have wished that their friend and leader would fight on with them, but it was not to be. He may have died in a field full of flowers near the Front, but his soul lived on in the Lafayette Escadrille. Even if they had wanted to, the Americans had little time to mourn him. Kiffin was gone, but the others would tenaciously continue the fight. They knew Kiffin would have it no other way.

At the same time, the remaining pilots did not forget him. Kiffin was an ever-present fixture in the squadron because he had touched the lives of so many of them. The Bottle of Death was shared dozens of times over the coming months, and the men always remembered the original bearer of the bottle. Kiffin's death "urged the rest of the men to greater action, and the few who had machines were constantly after the Boches."[1] They sought to emulate his actions and his ideals, especially his close friends. Those who knew Kiffin well ensured that his memory would never die by molding the squadron's character after their dear friend. And the men would not have to wait long for someone to avenge their friend. Norman Prince brought down a German soon after Kiffin's death, and the Americans never looked back.

Kiffin's spirit lived on though all the men, but primarily through Lufbery. He flew the most with Kiffin and learned the most from Kiffin. And when the brave aviator finally fell, Lufbery picked up the torch and advanced it proudly. The men in the squadron redoubled their efforts to destroy the Germans' flying force, but Lufbery shined above all the rest. He put on the mantle of leadership that fell with Kiffin, and he carried it for the remainder of the Lafayette Escadrille's existence. From that day forward, Kiffin was gone but far from forgotten. His fighting spirit lived on through Lufbery, and the other Americans did everything they could to live up to Kiffin's legacy and Lufbery's example.

The day after Kiffin's funeral, Lufbery sailed up into the big blue expanse in search of retribution. He ventured far over enemy lines and taunted the Germans by circling aggressively over their airfields. One day the Germans accepted his offer of battle, but Lufbery had gone home due to low fuel by the time they launched. Prince had followed Lufbery and flew into a hornet's nest. The German machines surrounded him and battered his plane with exploding bullets. Prince barely made it back to Luxeuil in his damaged aircraft. Lufbery refueled and took off again to meet his foe. He found a German whom he had fought before, and the two swirled around each other in a furious engagement. Lufbery and his German adversary were both incredible aviators, and neither of them could gain an advantage. When Lufbery saw a cloud of flak rising from the French lines, he knew another German was penetrating French airspace, and he was responsible for the threat. Lufbery waved to his equal, who waved back, and he left in pursuit of the other German.[2]

The Lafayette Escadrille nearly lost its greatest pilot only days after losing its greatest leader. After leaving his previous fight, Lufbery attacked the German machine that had penetrated the French lines. As he closed in for the kill, an unseen adversary pounced on him at the same time. The German's aim was sound—three bullets ripped through his motor, two sailed through his fur-lined clothes, and another split his flying boot in half. One final bullet tore through the elevator controls, and Lufbery's plane began to drop like a rock. With seemingly superhuman skill, Lufbery gained control of the aircraft and ditched the machine just inside French lines—"had he not been an exceptional aviator he never would have brought safely to earth so badly damaged a machine."[3] Lufbery survived, but his plane did not. His machine was so riddled with holes that the mechanics had to scrap the aircraft.

On October 12, the Lafayette Escadrille executed one of its most successful missions of the war. The squadron knew it was tasked to provide air cover for the massive British and French bomber force assembled at Luxeuil, but the orders continued to get delayed. On the twelfth of October, the orders came. The target was the Mauser factory at Oberndorf, and the English launched scores of Sopwith machines loaded with four bombs each. The French contributed Breguets and Farmans, each loaded with numerous explosives as well. Lieutenant de Laage, Lufbery, Norman Prince, and Didier Masson escorted the bomber force to its target. The Sopwiths reached their targets quickly and landed safely with close protection from the Lafayette Escadrille. Unfortunately, the Farmans were much slower and could only manage to fly at a low altitude due to the weight of their bombs. Antiaircraft shells accounted for one Farman, and the German pilots took out another five when the Lafayette Escadrille pilots were forced to refuel. Nevertheless, the bombers caught the Germans mostly unaware and obliterated the rifle factory. Every one of the Americans scored a victory on the mission. De Laage and Masson blasted two German machines away as they attacked a French bomber, and Prince downed one after the Americans refueled quickly at a nearby airfield. When the men of the Lafayette Escadrille were airborne, the Germans were helpless: "So well did they work that several convoys were thus protected, each one by a single fighting plane."[4]

Raoul Lufbery hurtled into stardom that day. He jumped three Germans and expertly drove two away with a quick turn to attack the third. His engagement with his unlucky victim only lasted seconds. Lufbery sent the German tumbling down in flames and received credit for his fifth victory. Raoul Lufbery was an Ace! He was the first Ace in American history and instantly became a national hero.[5] Newspapers throughout France emblazoned his name in headlines, and American newspapers soon followed. The mission was an unqualified success. Not only had the bombers successfully destroyed their target, their American escort had accounted for four of the six victories won that day. The Lafayette Escadrille had truly arrived as a powerful force on the Western Front.

Unfortunately, tragedy struck the Lafayette Escadrille once again that night. Prince and Lufbery stayed aloft until after nightfall in order to escort the last of the bombers under their protection. Lufbery landed at a small field near the lines, and Prince followed about ten minutes later. In the darkness Prince never saw the power lines on final approach. His wheels struck the taut lines, and the machine snapped forward. The nose of his Nieuport slammed into the ground, and Prince crashed through the wreckage when his seatbelt ripped from its moorings. Prince did not lose consciousness, but his wounds were serious. He had broken both of his legs, and the men suspected that he suffered internal injuries, so Lufbery escorted him in an ambulance to a nearby hospital. The entire squadron was shocked when Prince went into a coma the next day. The Americans had not fully realized how critical his injuries were—the accident had caused severe internal bleeding, and a blood clot in his brain induced the coma. On the 15th of October, he passed away in his hospital bed. As they had done for Kiffin Rockwell, the French promoted him to second lieutenant and decorated him with the Legion of Honor. The man most responsible for the formation of the Lafayette Escadrille was now dead.

Rather than fostering a spirit of hopelessness, Prince's death encouraged the pilots of the Lafayette Escadrille to fight harder and for other men to take his place. All of the Americans knew that Prince did not mind dying as long as he did his part before he fell.[6] Prince had certainly done his part, and far more, before giving his life for France. After his funeral, one of Norman Prince's uncles told Captain Thénault, "No, his death will not be in vain for hundreds of others in America will come to take his place. Even after his death he will be serving France."[7] His words were prophetic. Within days, the Lafayette Escadrille received three new members, one of whom was none other than Frederick H. Prince, Norman's older brother. Americans continued to come to France in waves, filling the Lafayette Escadrille and fanning out into scores of additional French escadrilles. Well over a hundred Americans became pilots for France and served the country faithfully until America entered the war.[8] Two days after Norman Prince died, the Lafayette Escadrille received welcome orders to transfer to the Somme. The British threw the Americans a fabulous banquet and toasted the Yank pilots as their "Guardian Angels."[9] The Americans left knowing they had done their duty, but they all looked forward to serving in the Somme sector.

The Battle of the Somme was another grand example of the importance of air superiority. The massive offensive had already cost the British and French hundreds of thousands of casualties by the time the Americans arrived. It was a classic World War I battle with slight territorial gains and enormous human losses. In the air, however, the Battle of the Somme was the scene of a considerable fight for control of the skies. Major General Hugh Trenchard, commander of the Royal Flying Corps, understood the value of air superiority and massed so many aircraft in the sector that the Germans were outnumbered nearly three to one.[10] The Royal Flying Corps managed to gain a degree of air superiority from the very beginning, but the Corps lost twenty percent of its aircraft in the first few days of the battle.[11] The Germans needed to turn the tide somehow, so they turned to Oswald Boelke. The famous German ace returned from the Eastern Front to form his own *Jagdstaffel* which was designed to counter the British air threat in the Somme sector. Boelke set up the squadron at the end of August and chose Manfred von Richthofen as one of the first members of the unit.

Boelke's *Jagdstaffel* quickly became a force to be reckoned with over the Somme, but he did not survive the battle. In less than two months, Boelke managed to shoot down a number of British aircraft over the Somme. His squadron garnered respect from all sides, and the Americans certainly knew they would once again have their hands full countering Boelke. In an interesting twist of fate, however, the Americans only had to deal with the

James McConnell (left) with Paul Rockwell shortly before McConnell's death (from the archives of Loula Rockwell Brown, courtesy W. Vance Brown II).

great German ace for little more than a week. On October 28, 1916, Boelke, supported by Richthofen and four other German Fokkers, jumped two British aircraft. As he attacked his chosen victim, one of his best friends collided with him in the ensuing melee, and Boelke fell to his death. Manfred von Richthofen witnessed Boelke's death firsthand and sadly described the loss of his greatest mentor: "The only man who was perhaps more intimate with him than the others was the very man who had the misfortune to be in the accident which caused his death."[12] The British were relieved that their most successful foe was gone, but Richthofen quickly replaced Boelke as the most fearsome German fighter on the Western Front.

When the Americans arrived at the Somme, the Germans had stiffened their resistance in the air, and the Allies no longer had air superiority.[13] The British, the French, and the Americans in the Lafayette Escadrille faced an angry and slightly desperate German foe who was not about to back down. The veterans of the Lafayette Escadrille received three new members to assist them in their new mission above the Somme. Norman Prince's brother Fred joined the squadron on October 26 with Willis Haviland and Robert Soubiran. Haviland, a Chicago native, left the American Ambulance to join the famous American squadron. He served continuously over the Front until transferring to the United States Naval Air Service in 1918. Bob Soubiran had served in the Foreign Legion from the beginning of the war until he was wounded in 1915 during the Champagne offensive. He transferred to aviation after his lengthy recovery and served with distinction in the Lafayette Escadrille.

The Lafayette Escadrille traveled to the Somme with Captain Thénault as their commander and Raoul Lufbery as their standard-bearer. The squadron joined the 13th Combat Group commanded by Major Féquant, and some of the men soon received the newest French fighter—the mighty Spad. Thénault, one of the first to receive the new machine, described the Spad as a "new machine of meteoric speed, 125 miles an hour, terror of novices, who spoke of it with bated breath ... which from the outset, handled by Guynemer and his comrades, literally pulverized the enemy."[14]

The superiority of the Spad, the massing of effective escadrilles and famous Aces, and the development of new tactics eventually gave the French and British a clear advantage over the Germans. According to Thénault, the Germans were completely outclassed from the beginning. Germany's fighter forces received a drubbing over Verdun and the Somme, but bad weather in the wintertime later gave them the breathing space they desperately needed.[15] Thénault summed up the tactics that made the French and British so successful over the Somme:

1. Never attack without looking behind you.
2. Attack a single-seater from behind and above, then break the combat by a "chandelle," and *always maintain a superiority of altitude.*
3. Attack a two-seater by getting under its tail in the "dead" angle formed by the stabilizator [sic], and stay there to prevent him [from] taking you unawares.
4. Fly always waving around and break combat when expedient by a clever "renversement."[16]

Compared to their previous locations, the Lafayette Escadrille's accommodations at the Somme were far from luxurious. Their quarters were portable barracks "newly erected in a sea of mud."[17] They slept in shoddy sheds that provided no protection from the cold and allowed rain to drip through the cracks. The pilots had to sleep in their flying gear for quite some time because the squadron had no blankets. They also did not have a kitchen, so the men had to live off the generosity of the other French squadrons stationed at the field. As the men's spirits fell under the "thick mist, for which the Somme is famous," Bill Thaw and Didier Masson traveled to Paris to alleviate the situation. They acquired a stove, cooking utensils, and other supplies and quickly transformed their area into something more comfortable. Renovating the quarters became a welcome mission due to the weather on the Somme. The low fog and rain prevented much flying that winter, so the Americans used the restoration work to keep them busy when they could not fly. Thénault wrote that there were only about a dozen days suitable to fly from the 15th of November to the 15th of January. Mud seemed to be the only real memory of that time: "What mud! What mud! 'twas enough to make you think that all the quagmires of Poland, so dreaded once by Napoleon the First, had made their rendezvous on the banks of the Somme."[18]

After improving their quarters, the Americans busied themselves with various tasks during the long winter. Some of them would write memoirs, while others would play poker or rowdy dice games. They all enjoyed rifling through American newspapers and reading stories about the Lafayette Escadrille. On several occasions, the men read about American aviators who falsely claimed gallant deeds and received spectacular receptions in the United States despite never setting foot in France. Thénault wrote, "This used to make my pilots absolutely furious and if they could have laid their hands on one of these imposters he would have fared pretty badly."[19] Other pilots kept busy by decorating the rooms with original drawings of air battles. Dudley Hill also brought back records from America that the men would play on the gramophone as they sat around and listened.

During these down times, the men talked as fighter pilots often do. The veterans shared their stories and lessons with the new pilots, and they all discussed how to effectively prosecute an aerial attack. The time on the ground paid dividends in the long run because for the first time the pilots of the Lafayette Escadrille actually had a chance to reflect on their experiences. They analyzed their previous engagements and devised new ways to counter the tactics of their enemies. It was an incredibly useful endeavor and the Americans were well prepared when they began flying again in earnest. Many of the discussions usually ended around the gramophone, and Lufbery's taste in music was memorable: "Lufbery preferred strange melodies, often melancholy in character, which are, it appears, very popular in America. It was Hawaiian music, tunes played by a sort of banjo called a Ukulele. These tunes were generally very beautiful and in listening to them Lufbery used to dream of distant lands where he had lived and their spreading palm trees. But the note of melancholy was quickly forgotten and Lufbery himself was the first to shake it off by telling some of his innumerable experiences of travels far and wide."[20]

During the long winter, three additional Americans joined the squadron. Ronald Hoskier came from the Ambulance Service with a devotion to the cause that must have reminded Paul Rockwell of his brother Kiffin. Paul wrote, "From the day of his departure for the Front, every time I have met one of the pilots or have received news from the Escadrille, Hoskier has been mentioned as one of the most active members of the unit … the Squadron has not made a single sortie in which he has not taken part."[21]

Edmond Genêt was the great-great-grandson of Citizen Genêt, the Ambassador to America from the Revolutionary Government in France in 1783. At the age of eighteen, he had already bound himself to service in the United States Navy, but he approached the French Consul in New York and obtained permission to enlist in the Foreign Legion. James Norman Hall wrote, "Technically, perhaps, his act may be called desertion, but it was desertion with a noble purpose, from a safe and easy berth at home to a post of danger in the trenches of the Western Front."[22] Genêt joined the Legion in February of 1915 and fought with distinction in numerous offensives during his fifteen months of service. Genêt had originally sailed for France on the same ship as Norman Prince in 1915, so he knew all about the plans for the Lafayette Escadrille. He was finally able to join the squadron in January of 1917.

Edwin Parsons was from Massachusetts and attended the University of Pennsylvania before moving to California in order to learn how to fly. He served in the American Ambulance briefly and then transferred into Aviation. When he started flying with the Lafayette Escadrille, the French referred to him as *un chic type*. Hall described Parson's title as "about as far as Frenchmen can go in the matter of compliment. One must have been born to the distinction, and then, in war-time, to have earned it all over again at the Front."[23] Parsons would eventually become one of the more famous aviators in the Lafayette Escadrille.

The French government finally decided to officially change the American squadron's name in the winter of 1916. From its inception, the French called the squadron the *Escadrille Américaine*, but Thénault received a cryptic message in November of 1916 stating the following: "For diplomatic reasons Escadrille 124 will henceforth be called the Volunteer Escadrille. It is expedient to abandon the title 'American Escadrille.'"[24] The Americans later found out that Herr Bernstorff, the German ambassador in Washington, had lodged a formal complaint with the United States government concerning the fact that the French had a squadron called the *Escadrille Américaine*. Washington notified the French Ministry of War, and the French General Headquarters directed a name change. When Dr. Gros heard that the new name would be Volunteer Escadrille, he believed the name was too colorless and suggested the title of Lafayette Escadrille in honor of the famous Frenchman who helped America during the Revolutionary War.[25] The name stuck, and the *Escadrille Américaine* is now known primarily as the Lafayette Escadrille.

Near the end of the year, the men once again had an opportunity to remember their fallen leader Kiffin Rockwell. On the fourth of December, Paul Rockwell married Jeanne Leygues in Paris at the Sainte-Clotilde Basilica. The Lafayette Escadrille sent James McConnell to represent them, and Paul chose the Vicomte de Peloux as his best man. The pain of Kiffin's passing naturally still gripped Paul, but the wedding was simple and elegant. Jeanne Leygues's father Georges invited a few of his fellow high-level French politicians to the ceremony, but Loula Rockwell was unable to attend. She was still grieving over the loss of her son, and the ongoing war made travel to Europe difficult. Furthermore, Kiffin's sister Agnes was also married in December of 1916. Five days after Paul's wedding, Agnes married the Reverend Leonidas Braxton Hayes on December 9. The Reverend Hayes was the pastor of a Methodist church in Wilkesboro. The wedding that day was private and held in Loula Rockwell's home. Loula managed to give away her daughter, and her grief subsided slightly in the joy of knowing her two surviving children were now married. Ten months later, in

October of 1917, the Reverend Hayes and Agnes had a baby boy. Fittingly, they chose to name their oldest son Kiffin Rockwell Hayes.

Kiffin's immediate family would carry on his legacy in their own lives. His mother Loula would go on serving others and caring for them throughout the rest of her life. She dedicated herself to honoring the cause that had driven her sons to France, and she encouraged her own countrymen to take up the cause as well. Kiffin's sister Agnes was a devoted wife and mother who demonstrated an unquenchable spirit. Unfortunately, she died early, as so many in the Rockwell family had done. She passed away giving birth to a baby boy in 1926. Nevertheless, she lived her days with the same indomitable passion as her brother. At her funeral, the Reverend Charles C. Weaver stated, "The blood of the brother who died for his land was in her veins also and right bravely she showed it. No whining, no shirking, no evasion, she faced life with a smile and met it with a valor worthy of the best traditions of all womanhood."[26]

Paul Rockwell lived a long, productive life in the service of the United States and his adopted country of France. He returned to the U.S. after the war ended in 1918 to spend time with his mother, but France soon beckoned him back. Between the wars, he joined the French Air Service as a reserve officer to fight what he believed was a Communist threat in Morocco. He served as a bombardier on Breguet bombers until he became disillusioned with the war and the methods used during the fighting. When Germany invaded France in 1939, he rushed once again to the aid of France and tried to create a second Lafayette Escadrille for the French. After France fell, he joined the U.S. Army Air Corps and served with distinction. He continued his passion for writing after the wars and finally settled down back in Asheville, North Carolina. For the rest of his life, he kept alive the spirit and memory of the Lafayette Escadrille in the U.S. and France, and he died at the age of 96.

As the spring of 1917 approached, the men of the Lafayette Escadrille could sense the tension in the air. After nearly three years of constant fighting and unbelievable casualties, the Allies and the Central Powers were stretched to the breaking point. Falkenhayn's departure initiated a significant alteration in German strategy. The new commander, Field Marshal Paul von Hindenburg, decided to adopt a defensive posture in the west while striking a decisive blow against Russia in the east.[27] In many ways the strategy was brilliant. Russia was weak and on the verge of collapse, so the Germans knew they had a chance if they concentrated their forces on the Eastern Front. In order to shore up their western flank, however, the Germans needed a defensive line that would be nearly impossible to breach. They built a massive line of defense consisting of deep, well-engineered trenches, reverse slopes, and up to five successive lines of fortifications.[28] The new German defense, known as the Hindenburg Line, was one of the most formidable defensive structures ever built. They completed the line in January and fully occupied it by the 18th of March 1917.

At the end of January, the Lafayette Escadrille received orders to move to Ravenel in preparation for the Nivelle Offensive. The French did not know of Hindenburg's plan, and General Nivelle had devised a massive attack designed to finally inflict a decisive blow on the Germans. Little did he know that Germany had anticipated this move and had built an impenetrable defense structure. The Lafayette Escadrille certainly knew nothing about the Germans' grand design. Their orders at Ravenel were to show themselves as little as possible so as not to attract the attention of the enemy.[29] This naturally did not sit well with Lufbery,

Members of the Lafayette Escadrille in late 1916. Fram the dog remains, as well as the lion cub Whiskey. Pilots standing left to right: Lawrence Rumsey, Paul Pavelka, Emil Marshall, Didier Masson, Dudley Hill, and Robert Rockwell. Seated left to right: Bert Hall, Lieutenant Alfred de Laage de Meux, Captain Georges Thénault, William Thaw, a chaplain, and Charles Johnson (from the Rockwell family collection, courtesy of Sybil Robb).

who had shot down an additional two aircraft during the winter, and the rest of the Americans. But the men obeyed their orders and waited for the battle to commence.

Raoul Lufbery received the coveted Cross of the Legion of Honor on the 23rd of February, and another quartet of pilots joined the escadrille. Stephen Bigelow, Edward Hinkle, Harold Willis, and Walter Lovell reinforced the squadron in advance of the upcoming offensive. Bigelow was from Boston, Massachusetts, and had served in another French squadron for a short time before transferring to the Lafayette Escadrille. At forty years old, Hinkle was an old man compared to the others and did not last long at the Front. He grew ill after two months and the French released him from the service. Lovell and Willis were both Harvard graduates who served in the American Ambulance before enlisting in the French Air Service. Lovell was the deputy commander of an American Ambulance section and his natural leadership abilities enabled him to quickly attain the position of patrol leader in the squadron.[30] Willis served in the squadron faithfully but would later be the first man in the Lafayette Escadrille to become a prisoner of war.

When the Germans abandoned their front lines in early March, the soldiers on the ground were ecstatic at their good fortune. They surged forward and at first the advance seemed like the breakthrough everyone had anticipated. Thénault wrote, "It seemed to everyone that we would never stop before the Rhine, or at least the Meuse."[31] But the pilots of the Lafayette Escadrille knew better. They had scouted out the Hindenburg Line and reported its formidable defenses to their superiors.[32] The joy of the French soldiers quickly evaporated when they too saw the looming ramparts of the Hindenburg Line. But General Nivelle would not quit; he secretly continued his plans for a major offensive along the Western Front.

In the meantime, the Lafayette Escadrille continued its operations against the enemy. Before the fighting started, Thaw took a quick trip to Paris with Whiskey, who was nearly full grown, to try to restore the poor lion's eye. Rumsey had struck Whiskey with a stick and knocked out the lion's eye. Thaw tried to convince a veterinarian to construct a glass eyeball for Whiskey, but none of the veterinarians in Paris were willing to perform such an operation. Thaw did happen to hear of a lioness with a new batch of cubs, so instead of bringing Whiskey back with a new eye, he brought back Whiskey and *another* lion cub aptly named Soda. The squadron was quite the exotic zoo from that day forward.

When Thaw returned, he and De Laage used some clever tactics to spot enemy positions near St. Quentin.[33] Later that day, James McConnell took Genêt out on a sortie, and three German aircraft jumped them near St. Quentin. Genêt fired at one of the aircraft but received a return burst of incendiary bullets that cut one of his struts and wounded him in the cheek. He lost sight of McConnell and found his way back to the airfield. The pilots found out later that McConnell had been killed in the dogfight.

Thénault took the news hard. He had a photo in his office that everyone already called the "tragic photograph." It was a memory of times past because it included Victor Chapman, Kiffin Rockwell, Norman Prince, James McConnell and himself. The photo was a constant reminder of Kiffin and his close comrades who had helped Thénault build the squadron into a formidable fighting force. Now another pilot from the photo had fallen. Thénault was the only one left of the group of five. In his memoir he wrote:

> Poor Jimmy! We were all so fond of him. Looking at the first photograph taken at Luxeuil of the first five members of the Escadrille, three of whom, Chapman, Rockwell, and Prince, had already disappeared, McConnell, who with me was the only survivor, once said to me: "It is my turn next, and it would have been better that I had been killed rather than Chapman. He would have done better work than I for he was a cleverer pilot."
>
> What a modest fellow he was and what a noble spirit of calm philosophy was taken from us at his death. And when I look at the tragic photograph, as we used to call it, in which I alone am left alive, my heart is very heavy at the thought of my brave comrades.[34]

In April the Lafayette Escadrille moved closer to the new front lines with the 13th Group. Their new airfield was located near the village of Ham, and the Lafayette Escadrille quickly took advantage of their new position. Lieutenant de Laage shot down two enemy aircraft on April 8 and later received the Legion of Honor for his performance. Chouteau Johnson joined the club with his first victory on the 16th of April, and Thaw partnered with Haviland to down another on the same day. The squadron's victories were quickly overshadowed by a few tragic events. On April 16, a German shell obliterated Genêt's aircraft and killed its occupant. Thénault praised the young man as "one of our best pilots, the type of man who always had to be restrained rather than encouraged; always ready to sacrifice himself."[35] A week later, on April 23, Hoskier also fell after three German aircraft attacked him. Lufbery avenged Genêt and Hoskier on April 24 with another victory, but it was a sad month for the American squadron.

Four more Americans arrived in April to replace the fallen aviators of the Lafayette Escadrille. Kenneth Marr joined the escadrille from the American Ambulance, and the gregarious man seemed to know half of the personnel in the entire French Air Service.[36] William Dugan was an assistant manager of a banana plantation owned by the United Fruit Company in Central America when the war broke out. He gave up his position in the company and joined the French Foreign Legion, where he served in all of the great battles of 1915 and 1916. James Norman Hall wrote, "It was at this period that he gained his intimate knowledge of the courage of men and of their powers of endurance, which was so great an inspiration to him, serving him well in later emergencies."[37] Thomas Hewitt was a New York native who had served earlier in the American Ambulance, but he transferred for training as a bombardment pilot after a few months with the American squadron. Andrew Campbell was a fantastic joker from Chicago who quickly earned the distinction of being the only pilot to completely lose the lower wing of a Nieuport and land safely.[38] Campbell and the others were required to learn quickly because events were heating up on the Western Front.

The month of May was a trial by fire for the new pilots as well as the veterans. Manfred von Richthofen and the other heirs of Boelke had fully implemented their master's vision of armed scout patrols along the Front. The Germans, "who in 1916 had been distinctly beaten as far as aviation was concerned, had carried out during the winter an enormous program of production under the direction of General Groener."[39] Germany combined their massive aircraft buildup with competent new pilots, and the Allies had a tough time adjusting to the changes. Thénault described the tactics of the new German flying circuses: "Seven or eight Albatros would fly in a circle of great circumference, round and round like horses in the ring at a fair. Woe to the rash pilot who attacked one of them. The German, who was thus attacked, dived towards the interior of the circle and broke the combat by sudden maneuver while his assistant was attacked in turn, in an unfavorable position, by another enemy, the next in order of the circle."[40] The German flying circuses dramatically eliminated American victories in the month of May. The Lafayette Escadrille flew over 350 sorties, including thirty-four combats, but not even Lufbery could claim a victory.[41] While the Germans stymied the Americans in the air, something far more sinister was occurring on the ground. Nivelle's offensive of over one million men was yet another catastrophe of epic proportions. The Hindenburg Line became a slaughter zone, and the French Army finally cracked after suffering over 187,000 casualties.[42] The French Army mutinied under the stress of years of killing, and Nivelle lost his job to the much-loved General Pétain. The army of France was shattered by the time Pétain took command—he had to employ every device of discipline, diplomacy, and empathy to regain control of his forces.[43]

In May of 1917 the pilots of the Lafayette Escadrille were fighting for their lives and flying over a decimated and demoralized force. The Russian czar had abdicated, and his country was on the brink of revolution. France and Britain knew they could not rely on Russia, which meant that Germany would soon bring its entire force to bear on the Western Front. France was in the midst of a national crisis after the failed spring offensives and subsequent mass mutiny of 1917. The historian John Keegan appropriately summed up the situation facing the leaders of France: "Defend the homeland the soldiers of France would; attack they would not. Their mood would not change for nearly a year."[44] The only glimmer of hope left was the United States. America finally gave up its neutrality on April 6, 1917, and declared war on the Central Powers. The Americans in the Lafayette Escadrille were initially overjoyed at the news, but a month later they were all concerned. France was mutinying and suffering from a national crisis, the situation in Russia was desperate, and Britain did not have enough strength left to carry the Allies. The United States was France and Britain's only hope, but would the Yanks arrive in time?

14

The Transition to the U.S. Air Service

The entry of the United States into the war was a welcome development for the Allies, but the outcome of the war was far from certain. Germany's strategy for countering Russia worked. The Germans fought a ferocious campaign against the Russians on the Eastern Front, and the empire to their east collapsed into political chaos. Their strategy against the French came close to succeeding as intended. While France was not willing to strike terms and sue for peace, its army in 1917 would do no more than defend the territory it held. The most difficult part of German grand strategy in World War I, countering the British, nearly succeeded as well. Admiral Henning von Holtzendorff had calculated that sinking Allied ships at a rate of 600,000 tons a month would bring the British to the brink of starvation within five months.[1] The impact of unrestricted submarine warfare on Britain was astounding. German submarines decimated the royal island's lifeline, and the situation was desperate.

Germany's cunning strategy to counter Britain had one critical unintended consequence. German submarines were too effective at sinking ships, and when the United States lost three merchant vessels in one day, even President Wilson could no longer maintain his pacifist stance. Wilson instead seized the war as a divinely bestowed opportunity to fulfill his idealist aspirations. He threw his support behind the politicians who clamored for war, and Congress declared war on April 6, 1917. Unfortunately, the United States was woefully unprepared for combat of the scale seen in the Great War. The U.S. Army had a paltry force of 108,000 men the month Congress declared war, and few of them were adequately trained for the fight that awaited them. Nevertheless, America's entry into the war was inevitable, and the Allied commanders knew that if they could survive long enough, the contribution of the United States would be decisive. General John J. Pershing, commander of the American Expeditionary Force, arrived in France in June and put his force on display in Paris for the Fourth of July. America had officially arrived, and its leaders promised to deliver a decisive blow by mobilizing nearly three million men in eighty divisions.[2]

The contingent of Americans already in France took pride in the fact that their country was finally joining them in the cause of their generation. They knew American soldiers were fresh and ready to fight. But at the same time, they also knew that the state of aviation in the United States was abysmal. When World War I started in 1914, the U.S. Army had a grand total of eight aircraft in its inventory.[3] By December of 1914, America had yet to realize the potential of the aircraft, judging by the statement of the U.S. Air Service's Chief

Signal Officer: "As a fighting machine the airplane hasn't justified its existence."[4] In 1916, when Kiffin Rockwell and the other Americans in the Lafayette Escadrille won their spurs over Verdun and the Somme, the U.S. Air Service struggled mightily during the Punitive Expedition in Mexico. General Pershing wanted his aircraft to perform reconnaissance missions and maintain contact with advance element troops, but the poor-performing aircraft could not climb over the windy mountain passes of Mexico. Pershing praised his airmen for their courage, but dismissed their aircraft as useless due to their inability to fulfill the mission.[5]

President Wilson withdrew American forces from Mexico in January of 1917, and the Army aviators left Mexico with some painful lessons about conducting a lengthy campaign.[6] Across the Atlantic in France, however, the Americans in the Lafayette Escadrille had been successfully flying in combat for over a year. The dichotomy was clear—the men of the U.S. Air Service were totally unprepared for the task ahead of them, but the Americans fighting for France were ready and willing to use their experience to rapidly bring their fellow countrymen up to speed. They waited patiently for their country to call them for their expertise, but the call never came. The men of the Lafayette Escadrille would eventually make a great mark on the United States Air Service, but how events initially transpired left them sorely disappointed.

In the meantime, the Lafayette Escadrille pilots could not let their thoughts linger on the impending arrival of their fellow Americans. They had a mission to accomplish, and the German pilots were well-prepared for the battle of the skies in 1917. Richthofen and his pupils gave the Royal Flying Corps such a mauling in April 1917 that Britain referred to the period as "Bloody April."[7] The veteran Allied aviators knew how to achieve air superiority; they had accomplished the feat over Verdun and the Somme. But they also knew that Germany wanted the same superiority and seemed capable of achieving it. In the summer of 1917, the Allies continued the fight with renewed vigor.

The Lafayette Escadrille resumed its astounding success along the Western Front. During their stay at Ham, when the Germans drastically outnumbered Allied fighters, the Americans still managed to maintain a winning record. They participated in sixty-six aerial battles and shot down a total of seven enemy aircraft while losing three pilots and one wounded.[8] Lufbery continued to distinguish himself in the air, and he received the English Military Medal from King George V of England as well as the grand gold medal of the French Aero-Club. The French promoted him to the rank of second lieutenant right as a new batch of American pilots joined the squadron. Seven new recruits joined in the months of May and June, and the Lafayette Escadrille was at its full capacity. Characteristically, the new pilots looked to Lufbery for guidance: "They set themselves to follow in Lufbery's footsteps, and what with their own qualifications and an example like his they fully maintained our standard."[9] The tradition of excellence that Kiffin had started was alive and well.

One of the new pilots was a young author named James Norman Hall. When the war started in 1914, he was on vacation in Britain. Hall wanted to be a writer, but he decided to enlist as a Canadian in the British Army after the war broke out. He served as an infantryman "with Lord Kitchener's first hundred thousand" and later received an honorable discharge after he was wounded.[10] Hall traveled back to the United States and wrote a book titled *Kitchener's Mob: The Adventures of an American in the British Army*. The draw of the Lafayette Escadrille soon became too strong to ignore, so Hall joined the famous unit like many other adventurous Americans. Thénault described him as "brave to a degree that bordered on rashness," but he loved Hall's spirit.[11] Hall would go on to be one of the famous members of the Lafayette Escadrille. He teamed up with Charles Nordhoff to write the *History of the Lafayette Flying Corps*, which is still the premier source for the Americans who flew for France. Years later he and Nordhoff also wrote the famous novel *Mutiny on the Bounty*. For its entire existence, the Lafayette Escadrille always managed to attract amazing personalities such as James Norman Hall.

Just before Hall and the other new recruits showed up, the squadron lost one of its most experienced aviators. Lieutenant de Laage, always the daredevil, decided to take his new Spad for a trial flight on May 23. He took off, kept the Spad low to the ground until he was at a terrific speed, and then pulled up into a steep climbing turn. Unfortunately, he was not familiar with the new plane, and the engine failed, causing a low-altitude stall. The men could only watch as his machine spun out of control and smashed into the ground. The second in command of the Lafayette Escadrille was killed instantly. Thénault and the Americans buried their friend at Ham and continued moving forward as they always did.

The summer of 1917 was an epic battle in the air. The squadron left Ham on June 3 and shifted to the Aisne sector, where armed escort was their primary mission. The American pilots protected five French reconnaissance squadrons and grew an enviable reputation for their triumphant efforts. Thénault claimed that "no fighting escadrille was more sought after than our own. That was very complimentary. The sheep were always delighted with their watch-dogs and that is a proof that the wolves were kept at a distance."[12] During their time in the Aisne sector, Hall attacked seven enemy aircraft single-handed and narrowly escaped death when a German bullet left a tidy hole in his chest. He left for the hospital only ten days after arriving with the escadrille and did not return until October. The Americans continued flying in the Aisne sector until they received orders on July 17 to shift to Flanders.

The Lafayette Escadrille's move to Flanders was into uncharted territory. The Americans were stationed right by the North Sea less than two miles from Dunkirk, and they had orders to gain control of the skies prior to another offensive. The upcoming battle was the ill-advised Third Battle of Ypres. Field Marshal Sir Douglas Haig wanted to break through the lines into Belgium and seize the ports that Germany used to launch their dreaded U-boats.[13] The shelling of the German lines commenced the day the Lafayette Escadrille arrived and continued for two weeks until July 31. The British launched 4,283,500 shells (100,000 of which included deadly gas) while the Germans retaliated with their own chemical attacks.[14] The British began the offensive at the end of the month and once again achieved nothing of consequence while suffering 240,000 casualties. John Keegan wrote, "The point of Passchendaele, as the Third Battle of Ypres has come to be known, defies explanation.... The Germans may have suffered worse ... but, while the British had given their all, Hindenburg and Ludendorff had another army in Russia with which to begin the war in the west all over again. Britain had no other army."[15]

The battle above Ypres was somewhat muted due to the weather. The fog was thick around Dunkirk and the North Sea, so good flying days were few and far between. When the weather did cooperate, the Lafayette Escadrille and their Allied brethren often fought Richthofen's circus. The dangers included more than weather and the Germans, though. At the time, the sky was full of novice pilots, so experienced pilots had to worry about being attacked by their own side! Thénault described one such incident: "Our greatest Ace [Georges Guynemer], whom I have just mentioned, was once attacked by an Allied novice, and only managed to get rid of him by landing after various maneuvers. His assailant, who by this time had realized his mistake, did the same and hurried up to apologize. Guynemer replied curtly: 'If I'd thought myself in danger there would have been only one thing for me to do—to bring you down.' The other looked rather sick, but I need hardly say that the whole thing ended happily over a cup of tea."[16]

By early August, the offensive on the ground in Flanders sputtered, and the French decided to shift the Lafayette Escadrille back to the Verdun sector. The squadron had performed tremendously for over a year, and the French knew that the American squadron deserved a citation in the Army Orders. The pilots of the Lafayette Escadrille had shot down twenty-eight confirmed enemy machines and forced many more to land behind enemy lines.[17] Their success came at the cost of nine killed and five wounded, but according to their Group Commander Féquant, "These losses have increased, rather than diminished their ardor.... The splendid spirit of the Escadrille Lafayette and its devotion to duty has been a matter of pride to all Americans and has helped to bring their country to our aid in the war."[18] Féquant's nomination resulted in an official citation from the commander in chief, General Pétain. He wrote:

> Escadrille composed of American volunteers who have come to fight for France in the purest spirit of sacrifice. Has carried on ceaselessly, under the command of Captain Thénault, an ardent struggle against our enemies.
> In very heavy fighting and at the cost of serious losses, which far from weakening it, exalted its morale, has brought down 28 enemy planes.
> Has roused the deep admiration of the chiefs, who have had it under their orders, and of French Escadrilles, which, fighting beside it, have wished to rival its courage.[19]

The Lafayette Escadrille met nearly the same crowd of Germans in the skies over Verdun. The concentration of artillery and subsequent bombardment in the sector had forewarned the enemy of future action, so most of the German fighter force actually preceded the Americans' arrival. A group of some of the most famous German pilots faced the Lafayette Escadrille once again.[20] The French called them the "Tangos" because they painted the body of their planes an orange shade called tango. The Lafayette Escadrille escorted multiple bomber formations on several raids targeting German airfields. On one such expedition, Harold Willis went down in flames fighting bravely. The Americans thought he had been killed, but after several weeks they heard he became a prisoner of war. Willis was the Lafayette Escadrille's first prisoner of war. During his aerial battle, the Germans riddled his machine with bullets, and Willis had no choice but to set his plane down behind enemy lines because his machine had thirty bullets in the fuselage, motor, and radiator. He wrote in a letter from Germany that the German aviators who forced him down landed next to him and took him to lunch before they transferred him to a prison camp.[21] Near the end of the war, Willis helped plan the only mass American escape from a German POW camp during the war. He and a fellow escapee named Edouard Izac were two of only five men who managed to avoid recapture. Izac, a U.S. naval pilot, won the Medal of Honor for his actions during the escape. Willis evaded with Izac through enemy lines and a freezing river crossing into Switzerland. Miraculously, the young Lafayette Escadrille aviator arrived in Paris in time to witness the celebrations on Armistice night.

Raoul Lufbery continued his dominance in the air. He normally flew three or four times a day and humbly made his reports upon landing. After his flights, Lufbery (a former mechanic himself) spent hours with the mechanics trying to perfect his machine and its armament. The lions adopted him as master: "It was a sight to see the brave Whiskey, when he spotted Lufbery, hurl himself upon him at full gallop as if to devour him, but it was to devour him with caresses.... Lufbery was the only one for whom Soda was good and gentle."[22] By any standard, Raoul Lufbery was a remarkable man. Captain Thénault had a deep respect for the famous American under his command and wrote, "His Spad was always the highest and every day he won new victories. He seemed to hardly care about having them confirmed. Calmly he reigned as sovereign lord in his chosen element and beat down his foes to accomplish his duty and not for the sake of glory."[23]

The flow of American recruits into the Lafayette Escadrille finally ended in the summer of 1917. A couple of pilots joined in the fall, but the United States gobbled up the majority of the volunteers as it built up its force. One of the last pilots to join was a man named Douglas MacMonagle. He was killed on the 24th of September in a furious fight between the Argonne and Verdun. His mother was a devoted woman who volunteered in Paris as an aid worker for wounded soldiers. She accompanied her son to his burial at Triaucourt, and for the first time a member of the Lafayette Escadrille was buried with American soldiers as the guard of honor and with an American band to play the funeral dirge. Thénault described the touching scene and left with one thought: "MacMonagle had fallen but America was coming."[24]

America was indeed coming, but the transition would be a long and painful process. The United States had no aircraft capable of successfully tangling with the advanced German fighters, and it had only a small pool of trained aviators. The task of building an armada of flying planes was formidable, so the Army turned to a little-known officer who would soon become famous and highly controversial. William "Billy" Mitchell was the son of a wealthy Wisconsin senator who had fought in the Spanish-American War and eventually gained a commission in the Signal Corps. He was flamboyant and outspoken but known as an outstanding junior officer who displayed a rare degree of initiative, courage, and leadership.[25] A few days after the United States declared war, Mitchell traveled to France to evaluate the French and British air operations. He soon crossed paths with the Lafayette Escadrille.

Lieutenant Colonel Mitchell quickly realized that the Americans in the Lafayette Escadrille were a gold mine for the inexperienced American force on its way to France. He met with Dr. Edmund Gros and learned of the Lafayette Escadrille's exploits. Gros also told him of the Americans flying in French escadrilles that everyone referred to as the Lafayette Flying Corps. The meeting energized him about the idea of making the veteran American pilots the foundation of his buildup. He wrote, "A good many Americans were there who had enlisted in the French Foreign Legion, probably two hundred of them. These were the men I was so anxious to get for our own aviation as they would have several months start on any we could get from the United States, besides their experience in actual air fighting."[26] Mitchell met the Americans of the Lafayette Escadrille shortly thereafter and came away impressed: "The squadron was under the command of the French Captain Georges Thénault. The pilots were lined up to meet us, with Lieutenant Bill Thaw at their head. I was especially glad to see them because a squadron formed principally of American volunteers could assist us greatly as trained leaders."[27]

Mitchell's ideas needed clearance from his superiors, however. General Pershing divided the Air Service of his American Expeditionary Force into two segments. Mitchell commanded the Zone of the Advance, which would eventually become the combat elements of the Air Service. Colonel Raynal Bolling commanded the Zone of the Interior and was responsible for the supplying, equipping, and training the future combat units. Pershing appointed Brigadier General William Kenly as the chief of the Air Service to "bridge the gap and provide the necessary coordination between the two segments."[28] Mitchell advanced the idea of building his future units around the veteran American aviators to General Kenly, who directed a medical board to evaluate the capabilities of the men. The subsequent board classed aviators into one of six categories:

1. Capable of commanding a squadron—rank, major.
2. Capable of commanding a flight of six aeroplanes—rank, captain.
3. Capable of command, but not to be commissioned as a flight commander until later, owing to present experience—rank, 1st lieutenant.
4. Capable of being pilots—rank, 1st lieutenant.
5. Capable of being an instructor, 1st Class—rank, captain.
6. Capable of being an instructor, 2nd Class—rank 1st lieutenant.[29]

Dr. Edmund Gros came out to visit the Lafayette Escadrille in early October with a four-man team in order to gather evidence for the medical board. The men were naturally suspicious since the doctors were from the U.S. Army, and many of the pilots had significant injuries from their service in the Foreign Legion and in aviation. The U.S. Army doctors promised to take their previous flying experience into account if their medical examinations were not up to standards.[30] The doctors were shocked at what they found—partial blindness, immobility of limbs, scarred bullet wounds, and frayed nerves. The board judged nearly every man as physically incapable of flying an aircraft, but General Kenly persuaded General Pershing to recommend unconditional waivers for the men.[31] In the end, despite its judgments on the health of the American aviators, the board still gave the Lafayette Escadrille a glowing recommendation: "[The men examined are] valuable as a nucleus of aviators, experienced at the Front, around whom can be grouped the less experienced pilots recently trained or undergoing training here. It is capital with which to build and should be preserved...."[32]

Overall, the men of the Lafayette Escadrille ranked well on the board. Thaw, Lufbery, Bridgman, Hall, Hill, Marr, Peterson, Doc Rockwell, and Soubiran all received recommendations for the rank of major. Dolan, Dugan, Jones, and Chouteau Johnson received recommendations for the rank of captain. The men were pleased with the results and looked forward to the day when their nation was ready to take up the fight on its own. Unfortunately, the full Army staff had just begun to arrive, and the plan quickly stalled. As is typical of large, inefficient bureaucracies, the arriving officers decided to do a full review of the previous recommendations. Billy Mitchell was irate. He believed he had a competent plan in place that was based on meticulous research in the field. The fact that a group of unproven staff officers had the authority to alter his detailed blueprint was a slap in the face to him. Mitchell responded in characteristically ruthless fashion: "A more incompetent lot of air warriors had never arrived in the zone of active military operations since the war began.... As rapidly as possible, the competent men, who had learned their duties in the face of the enemy were displaced and their positions taken by these carpetbaggers."[33]

Calling someone a carpetbagger is a fairly serious insult, but Mitchell's choice of words clearly demonstrated the disdain he had for the incoming officers. The target of his tirade was a Signal Corps officer named Benjamin Foulois. Foulois was a Connecticut native whose career mirrored Mitchell's in many ways. He enlisted during the Spanish-American War, served in the infantry during the campaigns in the Philippines, and received a commission shortly after the war. He remained in the infantry branch of the U.S. Army until transferring to the Signal Corps in 1905. While Mitchell served on the War Department General Staff, Foulois imbedded himself in some of the Signal Corps' most important projects. He operated the first dirigible balloon purchased by the U.S. government and was one of the first three officers in the Army to operate the initial military aircraft purchased by the government from the Wright brothers.[34] Foulois then commanded the First Aero Squadron during the Mexican Punitive Expedition, where he developed a close relationship with General Pershing. Foulois and Mitchell were definitely rivals. They had a dreadful relationship to begin with, and the fires of combat only raised the tension between them to epic proportions.

In the last few months of 1917, the pilots of the Lafayette Escadrille fell victim to the infighting between Foulois and Mitchell. They wanted to raise the American flag over the Lafayette Escadrille and formally fight for the United States, but the rivalry between the two senior American officers prevented a timely transition. Foulois had been selected to replace General Kenly as the chief of the Air Service in France, so Mitchell's greatest rival became his boss. Billy Mitchell had gone to France senior in rank to Foulois (who was then a major), but Foulois's appointment as chief of the Air Service allowed him to skip two ranks, jump over Mitchell (who was now a colonel), and establish himself as the highest-ranking U.S. aviator in France. The situation was absolutely intolerable to Mitchell. Serving under his rival was one thing, but dealing with the decisions of his boss was another. One of Foulois's first acts was to replace Colonel Bolling and cancel all the contracts Bolling had made with the French for aeronautical material.[35] Foulois's additional review of the Lafayette Escadrille pilots was the final straw for Mitchell. He made it known that his superior's actions were unnecessarily delaying the process of creating American aviation units in France. General Foulois wasted no time expressing his own opinion of Mitchell: "The seeds of insubordination had already been sown when I relieved [Mitchell], and his memoirs prove how distorted an opinion he had of himself as an expert on air matters. Here was a man who had not had one minute's flying time as a rated Army pilot since he had not yet been through any official instruction course."[36]

The men of the Lafayette Escadrille quickly became disillusioned with their own leaders when the effects of this feud rolled downhill. As the infighting occurred, the American pilots continued their brilliant performance. While supporting a limited operation in the Aisne sector in October, Lufbery brought down six enemy machines in one day, but the infantry was in full movement, which prevented official confirmation.[37] The other Americans participated in multiple engagements and added to the victory total of the squadron. Through October and November, the men waited anxiously for news of an official transfer. They could not understand why the delays continued to occur—it made no sense to them. They had aircraft, they had experience, and they had an existing organization. The Americans only needed an official order stating that their squadron was formally part of the U.S. Air Service, and they would be off to the races. Unfortunately, the situation was far more complex than they appreciated at the time. General Foulois's belief in his experience as a logistician and Mitchell's failure in the area were the primary reasons General Pershing hired him for the job.[38] Thus, he meticulously reviewed everything within his realm of responsibility, including the fate of the American pilots in the Lafayette Escadrille.

The Lafayette Escadrille's final movement occurred in December, when the French reassigned the squadron to La Noblette field in the Champagne sector. The weather prevented large numbers of sorties, but the men flew whenever they had a chance. Commander Féquant finally made the Americans get rid of Whiskey and Soda because the lions had grown so large that the French were worried they might attack someone. The Americans transferred them to the Paris Zoo and would often visit them during leave periods in the capital city. The departure of the lions heralded the end of one era and the beginning of another. On January 1, 1918, the transfer to the United States Air Service finally occurred. Unfortunately, Foulois's review was not yet complete, so the Americans were in limbo until they heard the results of the review.

The Lafayette Escadrille's record on the Western Front was impressive. Kiffin Rockwell and his contemporaries took the opportunity given to them and exceeded all expectations. Before he died, Kiffin helped mold the squadron into a powerful fighting force with the skill and the passion to succeed at all costs. He was the soul of the squadron, and when he died Lufbery took his place and continued the marvelous performance. During the Lafayette Escadrille's operational period, the Americans received thirty-nine confirmed victories over enemy aircraft, while six pilots were killed in aerial combat, one killed by antiaircraft fire, two killed in operational accidents, and five required hospitalization from wounds.[39] Lufbery accounted for sixteen of the escadrille's victories and was America's greatest Ace when the United States started flying over the Western Front. Captain Thénault stepped down as commander of his beloved squadron and gave a stirring tribute to his American friends. With his mind full of visions of Kiffin Rockwell, Raoul Lufbery, Norman Prince, and Victor Chapman, Thénault proudly declared:

> Let us bow low before them and salute them very respectfully. Glory to all these volunteers. Glory to all these noble heroes, these noble forerunners. The Nation which bore them is a great nation, and I am sure that Remembrance will keep fresh their names and teach their deeds to its children and children's children.
>
> To my former comrades in arms, to all those who have fallen, I can give the assurance that despite her sufferings France will never forget them in her eternal gratitude.[40]

The decommissioning of the Lafayette Escadrille marked a significant milestone for American air power. The men of the Lafayette Escadrille had proven themselves on the Western Front. They built a strong, passionate, and thriving organization that had a great deal to offer to the thousands of newly arrived Americans preparing to do battle in the skies of France. Kiffin Rockwell and many of the founding members were gone, but their souls continued to fuel the organization they left behind. The Lafayette Escadrille was furling its flag and shutting its doors, but its pilots would continue to fight in the skies over France. The unit may have been disbanded, but the heritage and legacy of the unit was only just beginning. The veteran pilots of the Lafayette Escadrille were ready to lead their countrymen to glory, but only time would tell how much influence the battle-tested warriors would have over their eager but untested fellow citizens.

15

The Dawn of American Air Power

The United States Air Service came to France in 1918 as a very inexperienced force. Not a single pilot had ever attacked an enemy aircraft. The only Americans with any experience in aerial combat were the men who fought for France or Britain. The vast majority of this pool of experienced aviators (about 267) fought for the French. Only thirty-eight of these pilots served in the Lafayette Escadrille—the remaining 229 all flew in different squadrons as part of the Lafayette Flying Corps. Is it really possible that a few dozen pilots made such an impact on America's fledgling flying force? The answer is yes. The men of the Lafayette Escadrille, while few in number, had flown *together* as a unit and had developed their own culture, tactics, and fighting spirit. The other Americans placed among the French and British did not have the luxury of operating in unison day after day. Even though the Air Service leadership (minus Billy Mitchell) never fully grasped the potential of the Lafayette Escadrille, the men still managed to plant their spirit firmly within the culture of the Air Service. The surviving veterans of the Lafayette Escadrille took the soul that Kiffin Rockwell so proudly represented while he was alive, and they delivered it to the new American pilots. It is impossible to appreciate American air power without acknowledging the impact of the Lafayette Escadrille.

Most historians credit Billy Mitchell as the father of American air power. There were certainly other airmen who thought similarly to Mitchell, but Mitchell receives and deserves the credit because he forced air power strategy into the limelight in the United States. Yes, he was brash, arrogant at times, and overly ambitious. But it often takes a man like Billy Mitchell to give an idea the hearing it deserves. Mitchell vocally advocated for the idea of air power and all it could achieve. He taught others *why* ideas such as air superiority and strategic bombing were important. Unfortunately, most historians neglect the importance of *how* air power is achieved. Air superiority, strategic bombing, and other central air power principles are critical, but if pilots do not know *how* to achieve these objectives, then the ideas are worthless. This was the Lafayette Escadrille's greatest contribution to American air power. Kiffin Rockwell and the others were the first Americans to test and prove air superiority—the central tenet of air power. By the time the United States finally showed up in Europe, the men of the Lafayette Escadrille knew how to achieve air superiority. The pilots of the Escadrille developed the tactics, the culture, and the fighting spirit required to attain control of the skies. They refined these ideas and bestowed them upon their countrymen. Their great gift is woven within the fabric of what is now the United States Air Force.

15. The Dawn of American Air Power

The process of transferring their experience to the new American aviators was agonizingly slow at first. The men were still in limbo until Foulois's board finished its review and provided recommendations. Lufbery and the others could hardly stand waiting for a decision. They originally had high hopes for the arrival of their nation's armed forces, but as the weeks went by most of them began to have misgivings. Some of them even wished they had chosen to stay in the French Aviation Service. But the men finally received the news they were waiting for in February. General Foulois signed the "Conventions Concerning the Creation of an Escadrille, called 'Escadrille Lafayette'" on February 14, 1918, which spelled out the terms of the transfer. William Thaw received the rank of major and would command the squadron of American pilots, but the squadron would fly French aircraft and use French mechanics until the American mechanics were adequately trained. Foulois designated the new unit as the 103rd Aero Squadron of the Air Service.

Unfortunately, the order came with some bad news. Foulois accepted the recommendations of the earlier board with one major exception. He reduced the proposed ranks of all the men by one. The American pilots were infuriated because they felt betrayed by their own country. Many of the new arrivals had little flying experience but held ranks higher than the ones given to the Lafayette Escadrille airmen. It was an unfortunate decision for the Americans because they were expecting the ranks that the Air Service previously promised them, but the pilots had no control over the outcome. To be fair to Foulois, the approved organizational plans called for captains to command U.S. squadrons, so the ranks he handed out were in line with the organizational structure.[1] Once the men started flying combat sorties again, they quickly got over the controversy and served their country proudly.

All of the veterans of the Lafayette Escadrille transferred to the 103rd Aero Squadron except for Edwin Parsons and Raoul Lufbery. Parsons decided to remain with the French Air Service and ended the war as an Ace with eight confirmed victories. The Air Service leadership had chosen Lufbery to command the 95th Aero Squadron, so he was forced to leave the friends and the unit that he loved. The veterans would certainly miss him as well. They revered him for his mastery of the air and his concern for fellow aviators. Parsons flew with Lufbery a great deal and described him in his book: "I was in daily contact with a figure of flesh and blood, but know [Lufbery]? Not a chance. In contrast to him, the Sphinx was a child's primer. He kept his real self shut up like a clam in a shell. He was a man seemingly devoid of fear, or, in fact, emotion of any kind. But what a man he was in the air! He had forgotten more about combat flying than most men ever knew."[2]

Ultimately, the men loved Lufbery for taking care of them while they built experience in the hostile skies above France. Parsons wrote, "Ofttimes sacrificing a sure kill of his own, with his uncanny faculty for watching everything that transpired in a dog fight, he'd swoop through the lead-filled sky to some isolated spot where a desperate youngster was waging a losing fight."[3] He was a special individual and would be sorely missed in the new 103rd Aero Squadron.

Fortunately, the veterans of the Lafayette Escadrille retained William Thaw as their leader. Thaw was a great pilot, but his chosen task was much different from the one of legends like Kiffin Rockwell and Raoul Lufbery. Captain Thénault was always the commander of the Lafayette Escadrille, but Bill Thaw was the Americans' informal commander and advocate. They desperately needed him. Discipline was a constant issue in the Lafayette Escadrille due to the stresses of combat and the differences in customs between the Americans and their French leaders. Thaw masterfully placed himself between the unruly Americans and their French commanders. Parsons wrote, "According to the French brass hats, all Americans were slightly, 'teched in the haid....' We were as far apart as poles, and it was Bill's superhuman task to act as a buffer and maintain some sort of cohesion and cooperation."[4] In the end, the men revered Bill Thaw as much as they did Lufbery, but for different reasons. Parsons described their relationship with Thaw: "We never questioned Bill's decisions. We knew he'd give us better than an even break. We didn't squawk or alibi with him. His word was law, not because he was our superior officer, but because he was Bill."[5] The new 103rd Aero Squadron was in great hands.

Thaw had little time to prepare his squadron for the German onslaught that began in the spring of 1918. He took command on February 18 at La Noblette when his enlisted troops arrived. The French mechanics helped the American enlisted men learn how to maintain Spad aircraft while the American pilots continued flying daily patrols. After one short month of executing their mission as a team, the 103rd Aero Squadron responded to the crisis unfolding along the Western Front. The Germans had launched Operation Michael.

In 1918 the German High Command knew they had to strike a decisive blow in the spring or the war would be lost. The United States had mobilized its massive industrial and manpower base. The Germans recognized they could not counter the enormous amount of men and material crossing the Atlantic Ocean. General Erich Ludendorff, the commander of the German armies, chose to attack an unfinished section of the lines in a sector near St. Quentin occupied by the British Fifth Army. On March 21, the Germans launched their offensive by bombarding the British lines with a mix of high-explosive, smoke, tear-gas, and poison gas shells. Small, well-equipped German units called "storm troopers" exploited the gap with light machine guns and grenades. The mobile units bypassed strongholds and penetrated enemy lines while the supporting troops completed the envelopment and destruction of the opposing forces.[6] The Germans broke through the British lines and forced a massive retreat that alarmed the French and the Americans.

Throughout the spring and early summer of 1918, the Americans of the 103rd Aero Squadron helped the French and British Armies repel the advancing Germans. The battles were fierce and oftentimes the situation on the ground was highly uncertain. The 103rd transferred twice during this period to support operations in different sectors along the Front from Champagne to Dunkirk. The Germans nearly destroyed the British Fiftieth Army during Operation Michael, but casualties were high on both sides. The Germans lost 239,000 men while the British suffered 177,739 casualties and the French lost 77,000 men. In its first four months of existence, the 103rd earned fifteen confirmed victories and two balloons at the cost of five pilots.[7] The fight to the finish had begun and it promised to be a bloody conclusion.

Thaw kept his men in fine fighting form throughout the spring and summer, but he had a difficult job. The Germans were desperate and many of the veteran American pilots were fatigued. Most of them knew of the short life expectancy of a pilot in World War I, but they could not stop. One aviator summed up the dilemma neatly: "I don't want to quit. My nerves are all gone and I can't stop."[8] Thaw was brilliant at calming the men in his command and drawing the best out of them: "On the ground and in the mess, during times of great nerve-strain, Thaw was a tonic for all his pilots. He was never flustered, never frightened, never excited."[9] Many a young airman took heart when they saw Thaw's big "T" on the side of a Spad. He encouraged the men and urged them on to greatness. But even Thaw could only do so much. The greatest aces of the war were often convinced they would not survive. They fought on because they loved their countries, their mission, and their cause. Major Brocard probably described the paradox the best when he wrote of one of France's greatest aces: "Guynemer was only a powerful idea in a very frail body, and I lived near him with the secret sorrow of knowing that some day the idea would slay its container.... Those who find it difficult to believe this self-destructive tendency among the great aces of World War I should consider this paradox: Those who were the very best at aerial combat had the poorest survival rates."[10]

Raoul Lufbery, America's greatest ace at the time, displayed no apparent self-destructive tendencies, but according to the statistics he was living on borrowed time. The unflappable Lufbery left the Lafayette Escadrille in January and prepared to take command of the 95th Aero Squadron. His first order of business was to inspect the airfield at Villeneuve where his squadron would be stationed. Lufbery had no way of knowing that he was about to become the center of another U.S. Air Service family feud. Foulois had tasked Major Bert M. Atkinson with the responsibility to prepare the first Air Service pursuit squadrons for combat. Atkinson was the son of a former governor of Georgia and a veteran infantry officer. He had flown in Foulois's squadron during the Punitive Expedition and was best friends with another future air power legend, Carl Spaatz. Even though he was not a West Point graduate, Atkinson was a blue-blood Army regular bred on formality and discipline. The ways of the Lafayette Escadrille were an anathema to him.

Nevertheless, Atkinson knew he needed men like Lufbery to help him. Describing his job, Atkinson wrote, "The purpose of this Center, as I interpret it, is to form pursuit squadrons from completely trained personnel, both commissioned and enlisted, and to coordinate and adjust them to their equipment.... At the same time, with the aid of the French here, to break the pilots in over the front."[11] Lufbery could help him achieve his goals, so Atkinson was willing to take a chance on a wandering vagabond turned major in the U.S. Air Service. Unfortunately, Atkinson's willingness to rely on Lufbery lasted only a few days. Lufbery did not like the airfield at Villeneuve, and after taking command of the 95th at Issoudun, he suggested that Atkinson move the group to La Noblette with Thaw and the 103rd Aero Squadron. Lufbery's innocent suggestion based on his experience was apparently too much for Atkinson. In a letter to his superior, Atkinson wrote, "I strongly recommend that [Lufbery] be not placed in command of a squadron at present.... He would be of great value here to take small patrols over the lines for the first time and as a general instructor in combat work."[12] With the stroke of a pen, Lufbery lost his command and quickly found himself living a fighter pilot's worse nightmare—behind a desk.

For a flying ace who had never done anything other than travel the world, life behind a desk was no life at all. Lufbery was adrift in his new American world and had no idea where, or when, it would end. James Norman Hall masterfully portrayed Lufbery's pitiful existence at Issoudun:

> Not knowing what to do with him, they sent him to the American A.I.C. at Issoudun, where they gave him a roll-top desk, a writing-pad and pencil, and absolutely nothing to do. There he sat day after day, whittling his pencil, or making little curlicues on his writing-pad. Any average judge of character could have known after a five-minutes talk with Lufbery that he would never make a paper-work squadron commander. He knew nothing, and wanted to know nothing, about the routine of making reports and of keeping lists and records and indents. His place was at the Front, leading his patrol in combat. One of the men who knew him

at Issoudun said that he was pathetically helpless in that den of the more or less typical kind of American officer. In his loneliness he used to confide in his orderly, and ask his advice as to the best means for getting out to the Front![13]

Lufbery eventually became the 1st Pursuit Organization and Training Center's chief of training and started flying again when the Americans received their aircraft. Atkinson passed over all the rest of the American veterans to choose Captain James E. Miller, a 1904 Yale graduate, as Lufbery's replacement. Captain Miller took command of the 95th Aero Squadron and asked Major Davenport Johnson and Major Millard Harmon to fly with him over the lines. He told them, "I am ... in command of the first American Pursuit Squadron on the front [but] I have never seen the lines from the air.... I need the experience for myself but I need it more to give me some prestige with these pilots."[14] Miller, Johnson, and Harmon took off on March 9, and Miller was last seen going down in a tailspin inside German lines with two Germans in pursuit. Without Lufbery, the 95th Aero Squadron had an inauspicious start to its operations on the Front.

Major Johnson took command of the 95th Aero Squadron after Miller's death, but the 94th Aero Squadron received all of the aircraft because the 95th pilots had not completed gunnery training. Johnson and the 95th Aero Squadron moved to Cazeaux for the gunnery course, and the 94th Aero Squadron quickly shot to stardom with the aid and encouragement of the Lafayette Escadrille veterans. The commander of the 94th was Major Jean Huffer, an experienced Lafayette Flying Corps veteran, who knew the ins and outs of aerial combat. His job of preparing the fledgling aviators became easier when Major Atkinson instituted a rule requiring one experienced pilot leading two new pilots who could not engage in combat unless attacked.[15] In order to facilitate his new policy, Atkinson allowed Lufbery to lead new pilots on patrol and transferred James Norman Hall, Kenneth Marr, and David Peterson (all Lafayette Escadrille veterans) to fill the three flight commander positions in the 94th Aero Squadron.

Atkinson may have erred greatly by recommending Lufbery's removal from command, but his decision to fill key positions in the 94th with Lafayette Escadrille veterans was historic. The 94th Aero Squadron would go on to have the best record of all American pursuit squadrons in the First World War. This remarkable fact came about in no small part from the influence of the Lafayette veterans. Lufbery led the 94th Aero Squadron's first combat patrol with two men destined for greatness. He chose First Lieutenant Douglas Campbell and First Lieutenant Eddie Rickenbacker to fly with him on the historic flight. Campbell was a Harvard University student who dropped out of school to enlist in the Air Service with his best friend Quentin Roosevelt, the son of former President Theodore Roosevelt. He was cut from the same mold as many of the other Lafayette Escadrille veterans from elite families. Rickenbacker, on the other hand, was a chip off the old Lufbery block. Like Lufbery, he was not well-educated, was from working-class origins, and loved working with machines. Reed Chambers, a fellow pilot and working-class man like Rickenbacker, wrote that he and Rickenbacker were ostracized and that anyone associating with Eddie was considered a lowlife.[16] Lufbery, of course, had no problem with lowlifes, so taking young Rickenbacker under his wing was an easy decision.

Campbell and Rickenbacker remembered their first combat patrol with Lufbery for the rest of their lives. In his autobiography, Eddie Rickenbacker vividly recalled his first flight with Raoul Lufbery. He described his horror at the thought that he might throw up after following his leader through some acrobatic maneuvers. Just as he felt his airsickness becoming uncontrollable, the explosion of Archie shells around him jolted his mind back to reality. He recalled the fear that gripped him as the shells exploded near his flimsy machine, but through it all Lufbery was right there beside him. "I shall never forget how scared I was and how enraged I felt at the old pilots back home, who pretended to like the Archies," he wrote. "Never before did I, and never again will I quite so much appreciate the comfort of having a friend near at hand. I suddenly noticed Major Lufbery was alongside me … and gradually I began to realize that each maneuver he made was a direct word of encouragement to me."[17] Campbell and Rickenbacker revered their tutor for safely taking them over enemy lines and back.

As they shut off their engines and met with Lufbery following the sortie, they thought his instruction was complete. Unexpectedly, Lufbery asked them with a chuckle what they had seen. Both of them knew how much they had to learn when he told them that they had missed two formations of friendly Spads flying within 500 yards of them and four German Albatros machines five miles ahead of them. Lufbery ended his lesson with a grin and said, "You ought to look about a bit when you get in enemy lines."[18] As the great American ace sauntered off, the two men shook their heads in amazement and resolved to be just like the man walking away from them.

Hall and Peterson finally joined the 94th several days later and helped Lufbery mentor the new aviators. Rickenbacker wrote, "We had all heard of these boys and idolized them before we had seen them. I cannot adequately describe the inspiration we all received from the coming of these two veteran air-fighters to our camp."[19] After learning from these famous aviators, the men of the 94th Aero Squadron began to forge their own name and reputation. Douglas Campbell took off with Alan Winslow on April 14 after German fighters were reported in the sector, and each man shot down a German aircraft. Campbell and Winslow became the first American-trained pilots to shoot down an enemy aircraft. Rickenbacker wrote, "Lieutenants Campbell and Winslow were overwhelmed with telephone calls and cablegrams. From all parts of the United States congratulations came to them.… It was particularly fortunate for the squadron that such an extraordinary success should have marked the first day of our operations…."[20]

Eddie Rickenbacker struggled during his first few weeks of combat operations. He flew with Lufbery often but had no luck bringing down a German. The life of America's most famous aviator in World War I almost ended before it fully bloomed. On a cloudy day over France, Rickenbacker spotted a German observation plane flying straight and level below him. As he eagerly pressed the attack, the young aviator recalled something critically important. "I remembered the often repeated instructions of Major Lufbery about attacking enemy observation machines," he wrote. "'Always remember it may be a trap!' I hurriedly looked over my shoulder,–and just in time! There, coming out of a cloud over my head, was a beautiful black Albatros fighting machine that had been hiding about, waiting for me to walk into his trap."[21] Lufbery's past instruction saved Rickenbacker's life that day, and the young pilot made his salvation worthwhile in the coming months.

On April 29, 1918, Rickenbacker finally earned his first of many aerial victories. He was flying with none other than James Norman Hall, the gifted author and Lafayette Escadrille veteran. Rickenbacker almost ended the sortie in shame when he left the formation without permission to attack what he believed was a German aircraft off in the distance. Just as he was about to open fire, he was horrified to see a French insignia on the wings of his victim. Rickenbacker held his fire and sheepishly returned to Hall, who was graciously waiting for him a few miles away. Shortly afterward, the two discovered an enemy aircraft flying in their sector, and they pressed the attack. Hall attacked first but pulled up abruptly, leaving Rickenbacker with an open lane toward the German. The young aviator took the gift, opened his throttle, fired his gun, and sent the German down in flames. The French had telephoned in confirmation of his victory before he even landed, and Rickenbacker wrote with great candor, "It was with a very humble gratitude then that I received the warm congratulations of Lufbery, whom I had always revered for his many victories.... I was glad to be at last included in the proud roll of victors of this squadron. These pals of mine were to see old 94 lead all American squadrons in the number of successes over the Huns."[22]

Unfortunately, the 94th Aero Squadron lost James Norman Hall about a week later. Hall led Rickenbacker and another pilot named Eddie Green out over the lines on May 7, and they quickly became entangled in a fierce aerial engagement. Rickenbacker lost track of the others as he attacked a German and saw it fall away. He rejoined with Green after his squadron-mate sent another German down full of bullets, but Hall was nowhere in sight. When they got on the ground, Green told Rickenbacker that he last saw Hall going down in a tail spin with his upper wing gone. The pilots of the 94th were devastated, but they later found out that Hall had lost his wing in the dive and managed to crash land his aircraft. He became a prisoner of war, but he was alive! Rickenbacker wrote, "Captain Hall's disappearance that day was known to the whole civilized world within twenty-four hours. Widely known to the public as a most gifted author, he was beloved by all American aviators in France.... Every pilot ... burned with a desire to avenge him."[23] Vengeance fell to Lufbery, as it so often did. When he heard that his old friend had fallen, Lufbery took off without uttering a word and sent a German aircraft down in flames near St. Mihiel—his seventeenth victory. The loss of Hall had a profound effect on the 94th Aero Squadron. Rickenbacker said, "I am convinced that the memory of him actually did much to account for the coming extraordinary success of his squadron. Every pilot in his organization that day swore to revenge the greatest individual loss that the American Air Service had yet suffered."[24]

Lufbery, America's Ace of Aces, officially passed the torch to Eddie Rickenbacker almost two weeks later on May 19, 1918. In the morning a German photographing machine flew directly over the airfield while the other pilots were away. Lieutenant Gude was the only pilot ready for flight, so he took off to attack the German Albatros. The squadron personnel watched as Gude opened fire at an impossible range and expended all his ammunition. Lufbery saw the entire engagement from his barracks and quickly rode a motorcycle to the squadron hangars. His plane was out of commission, so he ran to an operational machine belonging to Lieutenant Davis. The mechanics assured him that the aircraft was ready, and he blasted into the air in pursuit of the Albatros. Again, the personnel on the ground were able to witness the entire aerial duel. Lufbery fired several short bursts at the Albatros, but he had to pull away in order to fix a jammed gun. When he pressed the attack again on the hapless Albatros, the onlookers saw his engine and machine burst into flames.

As the flames engulfed Lufbery's aircraft, the men on the ground watched with horror as a figure jumped out of the burning plane. "Lufbery had preferred to leap to a certain death rather than endure the slow torture of burning to a crisp."[25] His body landed in a garden of a peasant woman who lived in a small town just north of Nancy. By the time the Americans arrived, the villagers had carried his body to their town hall and covered it with flowers. The Americans buried Raoul Lufbery in their "Airmen's Cemetery" near the airfield. General Gerard, the commander of the Sixth Army; General Liggett, the 26th Division commander; and Colonel Billy Mitchell attended Lufbery's funeral along with hundreds of others. Rickenbacker, now a flight commander, flew his flight directly over the open grave and they dropped flowers on his final resting spot. He remembered the somber flight back from the cemetery: "Returning then to our vacant aerodrome we sorrowfully faced the realization that America's greatest aviator and Ace of Aces had been laid away for his last rest."[26]

Eddie Rickenbacker proudly accepted the torch from Raoul Lufbery, who had earlier accepted it from Kiffin Rockwell. In two short years, the United States had established its first direct lineage of aerial heroes. Kiffin Rockwell had been the soul of the Lafayette Escadrille, and he passed his duties onto Raoul Lufbery upon his death. Lufbery carried the Escadrille for nearly a year and a half before bringing a new set of American aviators under his wing. When Lufbery died, it was only natural that Eddie Rickenbacker, his constant companion and greatest pupil, would keep the tradition alive. Rickenbacker ended the war as America's Ace of Aces with twenty-six confirmed victories. He eventually commanded the 94th Aero Squadron, and his leadership enabled his squadron to become the highest scoring American pursuit squadron with sixty-seven kills. Douglas Campbell was the first American-trained ace in World War I, and many of Lufbery and Hall's other pupils achieved greatness in the skies over France.

The connection between Kiffin Rockwell, Raoul Lufbery, and Eddie Rickenbacker is only one of many links between the Lafayette Escadrille and America's successful World War I aviators. A vast number of Escadrille veterans commanded squadrons during the last year of the war and influenced countless other young aviators. William Thaw commanded the 3rd Pursuit Group after relinquishing command of the 103rd. David Peterson commanded the 95th Pursuit Squadron, Ray Bridgman commanded the 22nd Pursuit Squadron, and Dudley Hill commanded the 128th Pursuit Squadron before leading the 5th Pursuit Group. Henry Jones and Charles Dolan became instructors in the United States. Robert "Doc" Rockwell and Robert Soubiran both commanded the 103rd Pursuit Squadron at different times after Thaw moved up to be a group commander. Each of these Lafayette Escadrille veterans had a profound impact on the men in their units, and their exploits could fill additional books.

The critical point is that by the end of World War I, Kiffin Rockwell and the men of the Lafayette Escadrille had achieved their destiny. They were the vanguard of American combat aviators. None came before them but thousands came after them. Colonel Billy Mitchell gave their pupils the plan for his St. Mihiel offensive, and they devastated the German air force wherever they found them. Mitchell and the Americans won a great victory that day which may have never occurred without the earlier exploits and instruction of the Lafayette Escadrille. As the sun set on Europe in 1918, the United States proudly rose to a place of new leadership and responsibility in the world. The legacy of Kiffin Rockwell and the Lafayette Escadrille was firm, but America did not yet have its own independent air force. It would take another world war and a few more brilliant minds to permanently etch the mark of the Lafayette Escadrille on the United States Air Force.

16

The Legacy of the Lafayette Escadrille

It is one of history's great ironies that air power was born during the First World War. The scale of destruction on the ground during the great conflict was unprecedented at the time. The war snatched one million lives from the British Empire, 1.7 million from France and about the same number from Russia, 1.5 million from the Hapsburg Empire, and two million from Germany. The United States suffered far less in comparison, but still lost over 100,000 lives and 200,000 wounded in its short contribution to the campaign. The number of wounded throughout Europe was nearly thirteen million people. Families and governments around the world were dumbfounded in the aftermath, and the scale of their grief was immeasurable as they realized they had lost almost an entire generation of men.[1] The Allies celebrated victory on Armistice Day, but most sensible people looked around at the carnage and wondered what the point was to all the previous madness.

One must view the birth of air power in the context of such suffering. From a strategic context, the advent of air power promised a new dimension of warfare in which soldiers would never have to endure a stalemated, immobile conflict again. From an individual perspective, the call of the air promised a permanent exit from the constraints of an infantry soldier. Many of America's first combat airmen came from the trenches of this desperate conflict. Counting the men of the American Ambulance, who also witnessed the war's horrors, the vast majority of the Lafayette Escadrille endured the worst conditions of the First World War. This fact is enormously significant. After tasting the freedom of the air, the pilots of the Lafayette Escadrille could never go back to their previous lives. Their distaste for hiding in holes during artillery bombardments and their love for the liberty of the skies were permanently embedded in the DNA of their famous squadron. The Americans who followed the Lafayette Escadrille airmen inherited this DNA and bestowed it upon their successors. The terrors and hopes following World War I are now eternally carved in the foundations of American air power.

So what, exactly, did the next generation of Americans inherit from the Lafayette Escadrille? What was this fighting spirit that seemed to characterize the pilots of the Lafayette Escadrille and their successors? The spirit they bequeathed to their fellow aviators is multifaceted and complex on the surface but relatively easy to explain. First and foremost, the pilots of the Escadrille had extreme confidence in their abilities. At times this appeared as recklessness (such as singlehandedly attacking multiple German aircraft), but the men refused to let their minds or fears limit themselves. The second aspect of their spirit was a nearly insatiable desire to improve. They did not accept failure—if something did not work, they tenaciously searched for the solution until they found it. This drive to improve was the foundation of their tremendous confidence. The men of the Lafayette Escadrille never lacked confidence because they knew they had the ability to eventually overcome any obstacle that arose. These two characteristics permeated the soul of the unit—the men were warriors above all else. Other qualities branded the unit as well, such as incredible acts of courage, idealistic attitudes, and a less formal, relaxed nature.

All of these qualities combined to create the soul and spirit of the Lafayette Escadrille, and the fighter pilots of succeeding generations inherited each one. But one final characteristic truly sets aerial warriors apart from their comrades on the ground. The speed required to make life-or-death decisions is far greater in the air than on the ground. This fact alone ensured the unique evolution of the fighter pilot culture. The speed of a dogfight in World War I was difficult to master, but today the amount of time a fighter pilot has to analyze and react to a situation is infinitesimally small. Aircraft hurtle towards each other with a closure rate of one thousand miles an hour. If this does not sufficiently explain the situation, picture this: A pilot realizes that an enemy aircraft is off his nose about twenty miles away. He has several courses of action available to deal with this enemy, but he better decide quickly. In just over a minute, that same enemy aircraft will be less than a mile away.

These speeds are extremely hard to fathom, but fighter pilots have successfully adapted to their grueling environment. They see their battlefield and make quick decisions in the same manner as a professional quarterback today. In both professions, those who take too long to make a decision are quickly out of a job. The ability to process information and make correct decisions in only seconds is a quality that has been demanded of a fighter pilot from day one. The pilots who lack this ability will not survive in a hostile environment, so the stakes in training are extremely high. To summarize, the harsh reality of aerial combat created a unique brand of lightning-fast decision makers who have little patience for failure.

Fighter pilots today have a reputation for being arrogant and overly sure of themselves. Individual pilots certainly feed this stereotype at times, but fighter pilots need a high level of confidence to survive in their environment. Unfortunately, this confidence often spills over into situations completely unrelated to the air. Nevertheless, all of the characteristics outlined above describe the soul and spirit of the Lafayette Escadrille. The pilots directed their energy and the soul of the squadron toward one supreme goal—absolute domination of the skies. Their gift to America was a fighting spirit in pursuit of air superiority. Looking back, one could ask for no greater gift from the first American combat aviators.

The transfer of Kiffin Rockwell and the Lafayette Escadrille's fighting spirit was a complicated, yet fascinating process involving many of the most famous air power personalities. The spirit has evolved over the years, but it has always played a central role in America's conflicts since 1918. The first major test occurred two decades after the close of the War to End All Wars. The massive conflict that ushered in the twentieth century spawned another titanic struggle far greater in scope, destruction, and significance. Less than four years after the Armistice, a young radical named Adolf Hitler zealously spelled out his nation's plight: "It cannot be that two million Germans should have fallen in vain.... No, we do not pardon, we demand vengeance!"[2] Hitler later prodded his country into a quest for revenge that dragged the rest of the world into another global conflict.

Preparing American aviators for the threat of Hitler and his Axis partners was a process that grew in fits and starts between the two world wars. The men most influenced by the

Lafayette Escadrille, the great American aces, largely faded into civilian life as the Air Service rapidly demobilized. Bill Thaw ended the war as the 3rd Pursuit Group commander and returned to Pittsburgh as a war hero. He never fully recovered from the scars of the war and died an early death at the age of forty-one in 1934. Thaw's personal legacy lived on through his nephew Russell William Thaw who became an ace in World War II and served in his uncle's old squadron, the 103rd. James Norman Hall returned to his previous passion of writing and became a famous novelist. Edwin Parsons, the only Lafayette Escadrille member to continue flying for France, finished the war as an ace with eight victories. He joined the FBI as a special agent in 1920 and then served on aircraft carriers in the U.S. Navy during World War II. Parsons retired as a rear admiral and wrote of his experiences in his book, *I Flew with the Lafayette Escadrille*. Eddie Rickenbacker left the Air Service as America's leading ace and started the Rickenbacker Motor Company in pursuit of his long passion for automobiles. He honored General Hap Arnold's request to tour Army Air Corps bases during World War II in order to inspire the pilots and bolster morale, but he did not serve in uniform during the war. After the war ended, Rickenbacker ran Eastern Air Lines until retiring as chairman of the board in 1963. Many other veterans of the Lafayette Escadrille and the Air Service squadrons lived equally exciting and adventurous lives after their great service to their country. As these remarkable men left the military, their spirit, like the spirit of the Lafayette Escadrille, lived on. They passed the torch to many others who carried it proudly during the lean interwar years.

The fighting spirit that characterized the Lafayette Escadrille continued to exist in the squadrons of the U.S. Air Service during the 1920s and the 1930s. Ironically, the ones most responsible for preserving the legacy of the Lafayette Escadrille were the same individuals who underestimated the American veterans in the first place. The Army regulars whom Billy Mitchell loved to hate—men like Bert Atkinson, Carl Spaatz, and Benjamin Foulois—eventually embraced the culture and spirit required to control the skies. During the uncertain period between the wars, these men, and others like them, did not extinguish the flame that had started in the battles above France.

Bert Atkinson finally appreciated the contribution of the Lafayette Escadrille in the waning months of the war. General Mitchell promoted him to lieutenant colonel and placed him in command of the 1st Pursuit Wing during the St. Mihiel offensive. The air power pioneer massed an armada of 1,481 aircraft from four different countries and successfully applied his theories in the victorious battle.[3] Atkinson witnessed the role that his individual squadrons played in the effort to control the skies, and the importance of the Lafayette Escadrille finally dawned on him. In December of 1918, he paid a special tribute to the famous squadron:

> The Lafayette Escadrille, organized long before the entry of the United States into the European War played an important part in bringing home to our people the basic issues of the war. To the French people of future generations, the names of its organizers and early pilots must mean what the names of Lafayette and Rochambeau mean to us Americans, of this generation.... In February last the Lafayette Escadrille of the French Army was transferred to the 103rd Aero Squadron, United States Army. It was the first, and for nearly two months it was the only American Air Service organization on the front. The Squadron produced two of America's four Pursuit Group Commanders as well as a very large proportion of the squadron and flight commanders. While giving thus liberally of its experienced personnel to new units the standard of merit of this squadron has not been lowered. No task was too arduous or too hazardous for it to perform successfully.[4]

Carl Spaatz, a Foulois protégé since the Mexican Punitive Expedition, played a significant role in transporting the spirit of the Lafayette Escadrille from one generation to the next. Spaatz was a West Point graduate who had little regard for formal military education. After watching Glenn Curtis fly over West Point in 1910, he only cared about flying, and his conduct ranking of 95 out of 107 cadets was just good enough to get him what he wanted.[5] He spent a tour in the 25th Infantry Regiment, but he graduated from flight training just in time to join Foulois's 1st Aero Squadron before it traveled to Mexico. When the U.S. joined the war in Europe, Spaatz took command of the 3rd Aviation Instruction Center at Issoudun, France, and built the complex into the largest training field in the world.[6] Spaatz remained in command until September of 1918 when Billy Mitchell let him have a short stint at the Front before he was ordered back to the United States to direct training efforts. In one short month, he managed to shoot down three enemy aircraft, and he gained Mitchell's highest commendation. The Air Service recognized Spaatz as one of the leading experts in training and pursuit aviation after the war, and his expert status drew him into the orbit of another future aviation powerhouse—Colonel Henry "Hap" Arnold.[7]

Arnold and Spaatz would eventually lead the Air Service into the next world war and beyond, but Benjamin Foulois and Billy Mitchell were still the foremost aviation pioneers after the war concluded. The two men continued their bitter rivalry, but both of them advanced the concept of air power and the fighting spirit that buttressed the idea. Foulois and Mitchell worked for Major General Mason Patrick, who was the highest-ranking aviation officer from 1918 until he retired as chief of the Air Corps in 1927. But General Patrick was less familiar with flying than his top-ranking subordinates, so he administered the organization while Foulois and Mitchell pushed their air power theories to anyone who would listen.

Towards the end of World War I, Foulois made a fateful decision. Despite the misgivings between them, Foulois actually recommended Mitchell as his replacement when General Patrick promoted Foulois to be his deputy. Foulois soon resented the outcome of his decision. Mitchell's performance as the primary operational air commander during the final few months of the war launched him into stardom while Foulois was largely forgotten. Foulois especially condemned the credit Mitchell received for his theories of air power and strategic bombardment because he claimed Mitchell never had any part in the development of the strategic bombardment plans.[8] Foulois believed that his staff officers should have received the credit because they had prepared the plans using air power theories from Douhet and Trenchard. There may be some truth to Foulois's claims, but in the end Mitchell is the man people remember.

Nevertheless, the two men had to try to work together after the war because they both believed in the same objective—an independent air force. Billy Mitchell immediately launched his air power crusade and left the others floating in his wake. Foulois wrote, "I have no quarrel about Mitchell's championing the need for air power before the American public. It was his methods and his lack of judgment about what he said that I deplored."[9] Mitchell had become an activist, though, and would listen to nothing Foulois or anyone else in the War Department had to say. The Secretary of War sent out a directive ordering Mitchell to clear all his speeches and articles with the War Department, but he circumvented the order and "went on his merry, fanatic way."[10] Foulois believed the real hero of air power was General Mason Patrick, who "was calmly and efficiently winning the battle for the Air

Service the only way a military man should—through proper channels and supported with overwhelming ammunition in the way of facts and clear logic."[11] Fed up with his loud-mouthed contemporary, Foulois left Washington to serve as the military attaché to Germany while Billy Mitchell continued his crusade.

When Mitchell's antics and insubordination finally resulted in his court-martial, the door opened for Foulois to reestablish himself as the leading proponent of air power. He testified before Congress on what became the 1926 Air Corps Act, and the Air Service formally transitioned to a new organization called the Air Corps. After the transition occurred, Foulois received a promotion to be the assistant chief of the Air Corps in December 1927. Four years later Foulois took command of the Air Corps in December 1931 and led the organization through one of its greatest periods of transition.[12] He relished the opportunity to command all the airmen in the United States, and he continued to powerfully advocate for an independent air force. Ironically, Foulois's fierce pursuit of a separate air force angered many of the same General Staff officers who had censored Billy Mitchell earlier. But Foulois did not wilt under the pressure of the General Staff. He continued the campaign for air power until he retired in 1935.

Foulois continued the legacy of his bitter rival and preserved the spirit of the Lafayette Escadrille in the process. One of his final statements echoed the heritage left by the men of the Lafayette Escadrille. He wrote, "But of all these [accomplishments] I have seen and done, the one achievement I want to be remembered for is the establishment of the 'can-do' spirit that has become traditional among our American airmen. It is that spirit that we need on a national level to accomplish the world peace we so earnestly seek."[13] The "can-do" spirit that Foulois spoke of started with the Lafayette Escadrille, and men like Mitchell, Foulois, and Atkinson kept the spirit alive in the years leading up to World War II.

The founding fathers of American air power passed the torch to the new generation represented by Hap Arnold, Carl Spaatz, Ira Eaker, and Claire Chennault. These men kept the flame of the Lafayette Escadrille burning hot until they finally witnessed the birth of an independent Air Force in the United States. Henry H. "Hap" Arnold was and is one of the most significant pioneers of American air power. He graduated from West Point in 1907, served for a few years in the infantry, and transferred to the Signal Corps in 1911. The Wright brothers instructed Hap Arnold in flying, and he became one of the earliest military aviators in June 1911.[14] After receiving his own flight training, Arnold taught other Signal Corps officers how to fly at the Corps' aviation school in College Park, Maryland. He continued flying for most of this period before the First World War, with a short stint back in the infantry. Arnold organized an air service in Panama and commanded it from February to May 1917, but the Signal Corps recalled him to Washington as a staff officer after the United States declared war on Germany. He remained on the Signal Corps staff until World War I ended.

When Carl Spaatz returned home in October 1918, he met Hap Arnold and the two quickly became great friends. As Mitchell and Foulois began leading the first generation of air power pioneers, Arnold and Spaatz were quietly developing the second generation. The two younger men commanded a number of units over the next two decades, but their careers slightly diverged during the first ten years. Hap Arnold commanded troops at various airfields, while Carl Spaatz commanded a pursuit group and graduated from the Air Corps Tactical School. Both of them were fierce advocates of Billy Mitchell's air power theories, and they courageously testified in Mitchell's defense during his famous court-martial proceedings. In 1929, Spaatz additionally piloted an aircraft called the *Question Mark* to a new world record for endurance. The aircraft stayed aloft for over 150 hours due to innovative aerial refueling procedures. Two members of his crew, Captain Ira Eaker and Lieutenant Elwood Quesada, would later become important players in the second generation of air power pioneers.

As the Roaring Twenties came to a close, Arnold and Spaatz were central figures in a controversy that, on the surface, seemed to threaten everything the Air Corps inherited from the Lafayette Escadrille. The Air Corps Tactical School that Spaatz had attended was right in the middle of the debate. The Air Service started the school after World War I in order to preserve and expand the tactics that aviators had developed during combat. The school focused primarily on observation, bombardment, pursuit, and attack, but from the start pursuit was king.

Over time, however, a number of instructors and former students of the Air Corps Tactical School began to believe in the superiority of the bomber. Several factors played into this shift in thought, but advances in bomber technology had the most significant influence. In the mid-thirties, the United States had bombers in development that flew at speeds above 200 miles an hour—an even match for most pursuit aircraft. Arnold and Spaatz both testified that pursuit no longer possessed a great advantage in speed or the ability to go all the way to the target with bomber aircraft.[15] This conundrum led to the development of heavily armed bombers that supposedly did not need a fighter escort. Some men took these theories to the extreme and developed the belief that nothing "could frustrate the accomplishment of a bombardment mission."[16] The "Bomber Mafia," as they became known, constructed the theory of unescorted daylight precision bombing that led to the deaths of thousands of bomber crewmen during World War II.

Even though the Bomber Mafia won the debate during the interwar years, there were still a few fierce advocates of pursuit aviation. The most vocal member of the opposition was Captain Claire Chennault, a pursuit instructor at the Air Corps Tactical School. Chennault believed that pursuit aircraft "could intercept bombers before they reached their target if the defensive area had sufficient depth and the defenders received timely warning."[17] He based his theories on several aerial exercises he conducted at the time, but his grating personality alienated many other aviators in the Air Corps. His colleagues found it more satisfying to ignore him, and Chennault retired from the Air Corps in 1937 after others drowned out his voice in the debate.[18] Pursuit aviation, and the spirit of the Lafayette Escadrille that served as its foundation, appeared to be dying a slow death in the years leading up to World War II.

In reality, the legacy of the Lafayette Escadrille never really dimmed during the interwar years. The story of the rise of the Bomber Mafia is far more nuanced than it seems on the surface. There were certainly some zealots who pushed the survivability of the bomber to the extreme, but many of the bomber advocates were originally pursuit men who never forgot the value of fighter aircraft. Spaatz is a perfect example of this type of advocate. He lived and loved the existence of a fighter pilot during World War I and several years after the war. He never forgot his former life even when he was temporarily blinded to the fact that the Air Corps had made too many assumptions about the bomber's superiority. *Furthermore, the legacy of the Lafayette Escadrille was never confined solely to pursuit tactics.*

The spirit they passed on to future aviators consisted of an attitude and a culture that always strived to dominate the skies by any means necessary. The Bomber Mafia's assumptions may have been faulty, but they certainly possessed the same spirit. Their goal was to control the skies once again over Europe. Unfortunately, the methods they pursued to attain their goal were misguided and nearly ended in complete disaster.

Hap Arnold, Carl Spaatz, and many others officially inaugurated the rise of the second generation of American aviators in the years just before World War II. Hap Arnold became chief of the Air Corps in 1938 and then chief of the Army Air Forces in June 1941. He named Spaatz as the first chief of the Air Staff in the same month. When the United States finally declared war on Japan, Germany, and Italy, Spaatz received command of the historic Eighth Air Force until General Eisenhower promoted him to be his air coordinator for the invasion of North Africa. Spaatz's protégé from the *Question Mark*, Ira Eaker, commanded the Eighth Air Force during its buildup phase and painstakingly prepared his inexperienced force to face the mighty German Luftwaffe. He fought incessantly with General Arnold, who demanded progress more quickly but then shifted needed bombers from the Eighth Air Force to North Africa. Eaker's preparation finally paid off after his promotion and departure from the Eighth. Under his successor, Jimmy Doolittle, the Eighth Air Force gained air superiority over the Luftwaffe, the invasion of France took place, and the Allies ultimately won their victory in Europe.[19]

Spaatz's other protégé on the *Question Mark* flight, Elwood Quesada, stayed in pursuit throughout the interwar years and commanded the 12th Fighter Command in North Africa during the war. He played one of the most significant roles on D–Day in command of the 9th Fighter Command by establishing air superiority for the Allied invasion of the European continent.[20] Even Claire Chennault, the old pursuit advocate, barreled back into the limelight during World War II. He traveled to China as an adviser to Chiang Kai-shek and created a group of volunteers called the Flying Tigers to help the Chinese fight the Japanese invaders. After the U.S. entered the war, Arnold made him the commander of the Fourteenth Air Force in Asia. He inspired many young aviators while he served in China, but he ultimately never gained the trust of senior Army leaders who did not approve of his command style.[21]

As World War II drew to a close, Spaatz and Arnold finished their work as leaders of the second generation of American aviation pioneers. Hap Arnold continued as the commanding general of the Army Air Forces until the defeat of Germany and Japan. He suffered a heart attack from all his toil and was forced to retire a year after the war ended. Carl Spaatz followed General Eisenhower throughout Europe and commanded the U.S. Strategic Air Forces in Europe until Germany capitulated. After a short stint on the Air Staff in Washington, he took command of the U.S. Strategic Air Forces in the Pacific and led the massive force until the unconditional surrender of the Japanese. After the war, Spaatz succeeded Arnold as commander of the Army Air Forces and then became the first chief of staff of the United States Air Force. General Eaker retired, but Elwood Quesada received a promotion to lieutenant general and was the first commander of Tactical Air Command, leading the vast majority of the fighter pilots in the newly formed Air Force.

The pilots and leaders described above kept the spirit of the Lafayette Escadrille alive from the close of World War I to the creation of the United States Air Force. Their ideas and feats inspired legions of additional young aviators who carried the torch through the gauntlet of the Second World War and the establishment of the United States Air Force. For every Bert Atkinson, Carl Spaatz, Ira Eaker, and Ben Foulois, there were also countless other unnamed and forgotten airmen who operated behind the scenes. They too inspired and instructed their own flying descendants between the wars. It would be impossible and unnecessary to catalogue the various ways the spirit of Kiffin Rockwell and the Lafayette Escadrille passed from the First World War generation to the Second World War generation. On the other hand, it is useful to examine one of these connections because it illustrates the powerful bonds that connect the earliest combat aviators to the fighter pilots of today.

One of the simplest ways to trace a direct line from the Lafayette Escadrille to the present is to follow the life of a man known as Robin Olds. Almost every fighter pilot from the last four decades knows the name of Robin Olds even if the general public may have a hard time remembering him. From a very early age, Olds was immersed in the drama described in the pages above. He was born in 1922 to a pursuit pilot named Robert Olds. His father went to France as a captain in 1918 and graduated from Carl Spaatz's Issoudun Pursuit School. Robin Olds grew up with an aircraft always on hand: "By the time I was five, I could name an airplane by the sound of its engine… [My father] and his pursuit buddies were gods to me, men of steel in planes of wood and cloth. I had to be a fighter pilot."[22] His dad was a great friend of Eddie Rickenbacker's, and his father also became an aide to General Billy Mitchell after the war. Robert Olds's Air Corps buddies were the famous World War I aces as well as Hap Arnold, Carl Spaatz, Ira Eaker, and many others.[23] Robin Olds wanted nothing more in life than the chance to be a pilot like his father and his buddies. Their ideas quickly permeated his thought: "As I grew I began to understand the dreams of these early pioneers. World War I made them determined to change things. If they could make air power prevail in future battles, the horror of the trenches, endless stalemate, and thousands of casualties with no discernible gain could be prevented. Airplanes could carry the war to the enemy, attack his industrial base and his lines of communication, destroy his transportation system, and quickly erode his will to fight. All this could happen from the air, but with aircraft not yet built. Such was the dream uniting these pilots."[24]

Robin Olds's father pursued these ideas like a zealot when he became an instructor at the Air Corps Tactical School. He was a bona fide member of the Bomber Mafia, but his story further illustrates the complexity of the situation. Robert Olds was not a dyed-in-the-wool bomber man. He was a pursuit man at heart, but his overarching interest was control of the skies like the others who had been influenced by the Lafayette Escadrille. Air superiority enabled bombers to attack the heart of the enemy before friendly forces on the ground even had to engage. The focus of men like Robert Olds shifted to bombers because they believed in the untapped capabilities provided by the new, powerful machines. When Robert Olds began to champion the new B-17 Flying Fortress all over the Western Hemisphere, his son Robin fully supported the endeavor but always maintained a desire to become a fighter pilot.

Robin Olds followed his dream by gaining a coveted appointment to West Point in 1940. He was a star football player in the class of '44, but world events ensured an atypical existence as a West Point cadet. America joined the war in 1941, and the cadets at the Military Academy learned that they would all graduate a year early (surely a welcome announcement for the young men). All the cadets had to choose the regular army or the

Army Air Corps (AAC) as their service branch, and: "To the great dismay of the old-time infantry and artillery guys who'd been running the Point for years, almost half the class chose AAC."[25] Robin attended primary flight school in the summer before his final year, when his father had recently been promoted to major general as the commander of the 2nd Army Air Forces Bomb Wing. His father surprised him by picking him up in a B-24 and flying him back to the Academy at the end of the summer. Sadly, Robert Olds died of a heart attack just before his son graduated from West Point. As his father lay dying, Robin told him that he would one day be a fighter pilot. Robert Olds smiled at his son and said, "Robbie, listen to me. I never once went up in the air without learning something new. Never, ever think you know it all."[26]

Robin Olds originally inherited the spirit of the Lafayette Escadrille from his father and his father's buddies who had fought in World War I, but he soon experienced everything himself. He fulfilled his promise to his father and shipped off to England in 1944 as a P-38 pilot in the 479th Group. Robin's descriptions of his squadron in World War II are remarkably similar to that of the Lafayette Escadrille—the spirit of the first American fighter squadron was alive and well. Robin roamed the skies over Normandy on D–Day, and in August of 1944 a famous pilot named Colonel Hubert "Hub" Zemke took command of his group. Robin's account of Zemke again echoes depictions of men like Kiffin Rockwell. "Hub was our kind of guy, aggressive, smart, relentless, and determined to hit the Luftwaffe where it hurt," he wrote. "He was already a triple ace and had created legends in the 56th [Group], like Gabreski, Mahurin, and Johnson. We in the 479th knew about their exploits and were in awe of their skill and good fortune."[27]

Olds certainly lived up to the expectations of Colonel Zemke. He ended his second and final tour in World War II as a P-51 pilot and commander of the 434th Squadron. He had flown 107 combat missions, shot down twelve enemy aircraft, and destroyed another 11 aircraft on the ground. At the end of April 1945, Olds proudly proclaimed his squadron's role in clearing the skies of German fighters: "Goring's Luftwaffe was largely crippled by this time. The mighty Huns had fallen to their knees under the daily Allied onslaught. By the end of the month, we knew it was all over."[28] After Germany surrendered, Robin Olds received a telegram ordering him to report to the office of General Carl Spaatz just outside Paris. Olds nervously flew to Paris and entered a room in a château prepared for a major gathering. He stared in disbelief as General Eaker, General Vandenberg, General Quesada, General Doolittle, and others walked into the parlor and mingled. When General Spaatz came down the stairs, everyone cheered in celebration of their great victory. Spaatz thanked them graciously, walked straight to Robin Olds, and pulled him into a side room. The famous general told the young pilot that Robin's father would have been proud of him and then proceeded to give Robin some advice that would stay with him the rest of his life.[29] General Spaatz had officially passed the torch, and Robin Olds carried it proudly to the end of his career.

His work in the air was far from over at the end of World War II. Olds joined the newly created U.S. Air Force and continued flying fighter aircraft. He flew for a time with Colonel Tex Hill, a top ace and member of the Flying Tigers under Clair Chennault. A short while later he joined an acrobatic team with Lieutenant Colonel John "Pappy" Herbst, a phenomenal pilot and the leading ace of the Fourteenth Air Force. He and Pappy flew P-80s in demonstrations all over the country until Pappy was killed performing a dangerous low-altitude maneuver with Robin on his wing. Olds eventually moved on to the Air Force's first premier fighter jet, the F-86. He served as the operations officer in the 94th Fighter Squadron—the same squadron that Lufbery had flown in with Eddie Rickenbacker and Douglas Campbell, and the squadron that Rickenbacker eventually commanded. It was an honor for Robin to serve in the squadron of the man who "was a good pal of my dad as I grew up, but in my eyes he had been a superhero. As a kid I sat at the dining table in total awe of the two of them."[30] Robin was not the only one who lived in awe of these great aces. Thousands of other pilots knew the reputation of the men who ruled the skies in the two world wars, and they all fought hard to model themselves after the distinguished aviators who served before them.

At the time, however, the young United States Air Force had a bit of an identity crisis. The Cold War with the Soviet Union captured the attention of the leaders in Washington, and after the Korean War the focus of the Air Force shifted from air superiority to nuclear superiority. Air Force generals spent a great deal of energy and money proving to Congress that they had an armada of nuclear bombers and intercontinental missiles capable of deterring a war with the Soviets. For a tactician like Robin Olds, this fundamental shift came with some dangerous costs. He believed the generals were disregarding critical facets of airpower in their pursuit of nuclear supremacy, and the prospects of the young force were not good if a shooting war did start. Olds wrote: "My dad and his buddies after World War I had fought for air power against all odds, against infantry and artillery generals and battleship admirals.... I began to realize that the infantry and artillery generals my dad had argued against still existed, but they had evolved into bomber generals, who had taken control of the USAF after World War II.... I knew what needed to be done to build a fighting force, and I determined to be the missionary for those concepts."[31] The problem was not necessarily that all the generals were bomber pilots, but that the generals had narrowed the focus of the Air Force to nuclear strike at the expense of all else. Olds's entire background convinced him that this approach was wrong and would cause significant negative consequences for the young men replacing the ranks of the World War II generation. He was right. The Air Force was woefully unprepared for the tactical challenges it faced in Vietnam, and the fighter force suffered severe losses in the early years of the war. Robin Olds had missed the Korean War, but he was determined not to miss the current conflict. His persistence paid off, and in September 1966 he received command of the 8th Tactical Fighter Wing at Ubon Royal Thai Air Force Base in Thailand.

Robin Olds transformed his wing into a legendary organization over the course of a year. He instilled all the qualities that members of the Lafayette Escadrille had bestowed on the pilots who succeeded them. With a spirit that rivaled that of Kiffin Rockwell and the other Escadrille prodigies, Robin Olds was supremely confident and demanded aggressiveness and excellence from every pilot under his command. He named his organization the Wolf Pack because the teamwork and fierceness of his men resembled a pack of wolves on the hunt in the air. Robin's vice commander was none other than the famous Daniel "Chappie" James, one of the great Tuskegee Airmen and a man destined to be the first African American promoted to the rank of four-star general in the Air Force.

The wing that Robin and Chappie built in the skies over Vietnam was as cohesive, aggressive, and successful as the Lafayette Escadrille from the First World War. The wing flew a total of 13,249 combat sorties over North Vietnam and Laos in the year Robin Olds commanded the organization. The Wolf Pack racked up a total of thirty MIG victories that year and became the top-killing unit in Vietnam at the time[32]. Robin Olds himself shot down four MIGs and flew a total of 152 combat missions as the wing commander. He left his beloved Wolf Pack with a heavy heart and some hearty encouragement: "You still have a helluva war ahead of you gang! … I know the 8th Wing is going to go at it with great spirit, high morale, superb skill, and the application of absolutely the best tactics.… So I ask you, give it everything you've got; enjoy it to the hilt! Be soldiers, be warriors, be men, not babies but men![33]" Even today it remains a great honor to serve in the 8th Fighter Wing—still known as the Wolf Pack.

Robin Olds went on to be the Commandant of Cadets at the U.S. Air Force Academy and a founding member of the Red River Valley Fighter Pilots' Association. As the commandant, Olds inspired a new generation of men who earned their spurs in Vietnam and led the Air Force during dominant performances in the Gulf War and the Balkans. After he retired, Olds continued his campaign through the work of organizations like the Red River Valley Association and speaking circuits among the Air Force's flying units. Robin preached on the necessity of preserving the spirit and the traditions of America's great aviators of the past. There are many young fighter pilots today who heard his words and took them to heart.

Robin Olds was just one man. His personal experience spanned from Eddie Rickenbacker to Operation Enduring Freedom and Operation Iraqi Freedom, but his direct influence continues today even after his death. A number of pilots who flew with him or learned from him are still serving their country right now. Robin was indeed legendary, but there are thousands of other pilots like him. The line started with the Lafayette Escadrille and every generation of pilots since has passed the torch to the new generation. The vast majority of these pilots were not legends like Robin Olds, but they influenced their sphere of protégés in the same way that Robin influenced his legion of followers. As long as this line continues and the United States preserves its commitment to controlling the skies, America's Air Force will play a critical role in protecting the freedom we all enjoy.

Edwin Parsons, one of the aces of the Lafayette Escadrille, wrote about the enduring legacy of his organization in his book. His words are still true today: "Those of us fortunate enough to have survived have witnessed tremendous strides made in military planes, armament and tactics; but inevitably, and doubtless necessarily with this progress, has come regimentation, and to a large extent, deprivation of individual initiative. Unquestionably, however, there remains the same love of country, spirit of self-sacrifice and burning desire to conquer new worlds that actuated the thirty-eight young Americans who served in the Lafayette Escadrille."[34]

17

Final Thoughts

About fifty kilometers to the northeast of Paris, off a lazy, meandering highway is a quaint village named Blérancourt. In the middle of the town, a beautifully landscaped estate dominates the scene with a stunning château centered among the green lawns and groves of trees. The estate used to be a royal residence, but now serves as the National Museum of Franco-American Cooperation. One room is dedicated to the Americans who proudly flew for the French during World War I. The shelves contain a number of items related to the Lafayette Escadrille, but in terms of significance a single item dominates all the others. The Bottle of Death sits prominently at its final resting place in France—the same bottle cracked open by Kiffin Rockwell on that cool spring evening in 1916 after he gained the squadron's first victory.

For many years the whereabouts of the Bottle of Death were unknown. People familiar with its contents and its story thought that it had disappeared. Yet on April 24, 1934, the bottle finally surfaced. William Thaw II, the great aviator, mentor, and member of the Lafayette Escadrille and commander of the 103rd Pursuit Squadron, died that day in Pittsburgh, Pennsylvania. As his relatives sifted through his belongings, they found the Bottle of Death with its many famous signatures inscribed upon it. Thaw had jealously guarded the treasure until he succumbed to pneumonia on that April day in 1934. The Bottle of Death eventually made its way to the museum in Blérancourt, where it rests among the famous pilots' other artifacts.

There were many men who put this bottle to their lips and drank. All of them are now gone like fleeting memories of years long ago. Their signatures are still inscribed on the sides of the bottle. Names such as Kiffin Yates Rockwell, Raoul Lufbery, William Thaw, Norman Prince, and James Norman Hall adorn the relic, but most of these names have long since been forgotten. The Bottle of Death should be a national treasure because it symbolizes the service and sacrifice of the very men who created the soul and spirit of the United States Air Force. Instead, it sits on the shelf as men and women visit year after year without truly understanding its significance. One day this symbol and these men should receive the recognition they deserve.

This book centered largely on one man who represented an idea much greater than himself. Kiffin Rockwell fought for a cause—the cause of all humanity—in the Great War that eventually took his life. He was the soul of the Lafayette Escadrille from its inception to his untimely death, but the bullet that snatched him from this world did not extinguish the spirit he left with his brother aviators. Kiffin was an exceptional man even among the legends of the air, and his name certainly needs to be restored to its place beside the other great American aerial warriors. On the other hand, the purpose of this book is not a campaign to restore the name of Kiffin Rockwell. The purpose of this book is to identify and document the roots that make our nation's Air Force great. The deepest roots of the United States Air Force are the men of the Lafayette Escadrille. The character and the spirit of today's premier air force are nearly identical to the character and the spirit of the Lafayette Escadrille. This book will be a success if this one simple fact is never forgotten again.

Comparing the spirit of one small unit to the vast organization of the United States Air Force is no accident. Despite its small size, the character of the Lafayette Escadrille percolated through the entire Air Force and now saturates all careers and all ranks throughout the organization. How did this occur? It started, of course, with the fighter squadrons. The influence of the Lafayette Escadrille was always the strongest in the fighter squadrons because the pilots shared the spirit of the original unit with each new generation. The confidence and quick decision-making required to succeed in aerial warfare created a truly unique culture and fighting spirit within the combat units. But while the fighter squadrons naturally transformed and evolved, the rest of the Air Force adapted at the same time. Every organization has a culture, and the Air Force is no exception. In a good organization, the culture supports and reinforces the mission. Since the core mission of the United States Air Force has always been air superiority, the entire organization developed a shared culture to achieve control of the skies.

In essence, the greater organization borrowed the culture and spirit that started with the Lafayette Escadrille. The drive to achieve air superiority required everyone to contribute. The legacy of the Lafayette Escadrille is potent because it demands excellence and constant improvement, but fighter pilots were never the only individuals demanding excellence and continuous progress. The other combat units and supporting entities eagerly seized and adopted the legacy as well. The culture of the Air Force is not identical to the culture of a fighter squadron, but the Air Force certainly acquired the drive for perfection and constant improvement that characterized the fighter squadrons. As the Air Force's culture absorbed the more significant aspects of the culture of the fighter squadrons, the nation's newest force quickly demonstrated its own exceptional nature.

The history of the United States Air Force attests to the fact that the spirit of the Lafayette Escadrille has always been present throughout the whole organization. Sometimes the efforts of the Air Force and its various elements were misguided, but a drive to excel was never one of the problems. I could list example after example to prove that the entire record of the Air Force demonstrates the commitment of all units to the idea of excellence, but such an exercise would be unnecessary. The Air Force of today provides sufficient proof of the fact that the fierce drive to succeed is part of the organization's DNA:

- Nowadays it is almost an afterthought when our national leaders expect the Air Force to transport hundreds of thousands of soldiers and their innumerable tons of equipment across the world and back every year.
- Security Forces flawlessly protect airbases vital to achieving and maintaining air superiority over dozens of battlefields across the globe.
- In amazing feats of generation and production, maintenance crews constantly work through the night to provide the aircraft required for the countless missions tasked to the U.S. Air Force.
- Medical doctors and nurses work with other services to ensure truly astonishing and historically unequaled survival rates among our wounded warriors.

- Space operators ensure continued access to information and navigation systems vital to our national security and our military's ability to wage war.
- The incredibly vast network of support personnel keep the organization functioning and enable it to achieve the results listed above.

The Lafayette Escadrille did not pass its spirit only to fighter pilots—the rest of the Air Force inherited the legacy as well. The list above is only a sample of how the Lafayette Escadrille's character has permeated the entire Air Force. The men and women of the U.S. Air Force, a relatively young military organization, should take great pride in what their service has achieved over the past sixty-plus years, but they should also understand what enabled their success.

Whether or not the legacy inherited from the Lafayette Escadrille will always drive the culture of the Air Force remains to be seen. The future is uncertain—we don't know how much new technologies or scenarios will affect the Air Force of tomorrow. It is certainly safe to say that the Air Force cannot go wrong by keeping this spirit central to the organization. For when the Air Force stops demanding excellence and continuous improvement, then disaster will surely follow.

The question at the end of every book should be "What now?" Unless a book is read purely for entertainment purposes, one should always question what the point of the exercise was. Now that we know about Kiffin Rockwell and his comrades in arms, what do we do with that knowledge? The answer to that question, of course, depends on the person. We can all learn from the sacrifices these men made for their country and for freedom. Every one of us can strive to meet life's challenges with the same energy and confidence exhibited by the pilots in the Lafayette Escadrille. And any employer or employee can certainly learn a great deal from these aviators about how to run an efficient and effective organization.

For other contemplative human beings, the question of "What now?" will hopefully stir something far deeper within their souls. It was not just the exciting stories, harrowing adventures, and fascinating personalities that drew me into the tale of Kiffin Rockwell and the Lafayette Escadrille. Instead, it was something far simpler. Kiffin's immediate reaction to a world crisis had me hooked from the start. Kiffin Rockwell was only one man—he knew he could not change the world on his own. When the war clouds gathered in the summer of 1914 and darkness set in, he immediately volunteered to fight for what he believed was an assault on freedom itself. Kiffin had no idea what he was getting into, but once he made the decision, he never looked back. How many of us would do the same if a new crisis threatened the liberties we hold dear? How many of us would instead choose to continue living in comfort while others answered the call?

Kiffin Rockwell and the men of the Lafayette Escadrille accomplished a great deal during the few years they spent in France. They created a squadron that laid the foundations for the United States Air Force. But I submit that their choice to fight for freedom was far more significant. They recognized the depth of the threat in Europe before their own country was willing to acknowledge it. And they were willing to fight for the cause when others were not. For this they deserve our highest praise.

So what do we do with the knowledge we now have? None of us can predict what the future holds. The years before us are shrouded in mystery, but one thing is certain. The

Kiffin Yates Rockwell (1892–1916) (from the Rockwell family collection, courtesy Sybil Robb).

country we love, the system we cherish, the liberty that sustains us, are not eternal. The United States of America will last only as long as men and women are willing to defend it. Kiffin Rockwell understood this and left for France knowing that he could not turn the tide on his own. Fortunately, there were others who answered the call and joined him in his quest. Kiffin gave his own life—his own existence on this earth—in pursuit of this cause. Think about that for more than just one or two seconds. There are many others who have made the same sacrifice, some very recently in our country's history. They deserve our honor, but the best way to exalt them is to join them. This does not mean everyone should join the military. There are many ways to defend the republic that we all treasure. Our country stands today because innumerable Americans chose to put the interests of our nation above their own interests. May we all have the courage to walk the same path that Kiffin Rockwell and the members of the Lafayette Escadrille blazed for us.

Chapter Notes

Preface

1. James Norman Hall and Charles Bernard Nordhoff, *The Lafayette Flying Corps*, vol. 1 (Boston: Houghton Mifflin, 1920), 410.

Prologue

1. The story of Kiffin Rockwell's duel and return to the field is found in the following reference: Edwin C. Parsons, *I Flew with the Lafayette Escadrille* (Indianapolis: E.C. Seale, 1963).

Chapter 1

1. Henry Ensign Rockwell, *The Rockwell Family in America: A Genealogical Record from 1630 to 1873* (Boston: Rockwell and Churchill, 1873), 14.
2. Paul Rockwell, *Three Centuries of the Rockwell Family* (Paris: Privately printed, 1930), 41–42.
3. Frances Harding Casstevens, *Clingman's Brigade in the Confederacy 1862–1865* (Jefferson, NC: McFarland, 2002), 117.
4. Rockwell, *Three Centuries*, 56.
5. Ibid.
6. Howard E. Covington and Marion A. Ellis, *Terry Sanford: Politics, Progress, and Outrageous Ambitions* (Raleigh, NC: Duke University Press, 1999) 1–4.
7. Glenn Tucker, "Rockwell, James Chester," in *The Dictionary of North Carolina Biography*, ed. William S. Powell (Durham: University of North Carolina Press, 1996), available from http://ncpedia.org/biography/rockwell-james-chester, accessed on June 29, 2013.
8. Ibid.
9. Ibid.
10. James Chester Rockwell still has a number of sermons and notebooks from his years at the Southern Baptist Seminary in Kentucky that are now stored in the archives of Wake Forest University, North Carolina.
11. Glenn Tucker, "Rockwell, James Chester."
12. Ibid.
13. R.B. House, "Kiffin Yates Rockwell," *The North Carolina Booklet* 19, 4 (April–July 1920): 150–155.
14. Paul Ayres Rockwell, *Kiffin Yates Rockwell: Foreign Legionnaire and Aviator, France 1914–1916* (Garden City, NY: Doubleday, Page, 1925), ix.
15. Rockwell, *Three Centuries*, 60.
16. Ibid.
17. James Chester Rockwell, "The Poet's Story," in *North Carolina Poems*, ed. E.C. Brooks (Raleigh: North Carolina Education, 1912), 109.
18. Rockwell, *Three Centuries*, 61–62.
19. Ibid., 78.
20. Ibid., 80.
21. Rockwell, *Kiffin Yates Rockwell*, x.
22. Ibid.

Chapter 2

1. Rockwell, *Kiffin Yates Rockwell*, xii.
2. Duay O'Neil, "Newport's Kiffin Rockwell Carried on Family's Military Traditions," *Newport Plain Talk* (January 28, 2010), available from http://www.newportplaintalk.com/tearsheets/editions/NPT_2010/npt_20100128_1_de/pdf/C-02.pdf, accessed on October 18, 2013.
3. Documented by Dr. George T. Winston in a memorial to Kiffin Rockwell. In R.B. House, "Kiffin Yates Rockwell," *The North Carolina Booklet* 19, 4 (April–July 1920): 150–155.
4. Nomination form for the National Registry of Historic Places Inventory, submitted in September 1986; available from http://www.hpo.ncdcr.gov/nr/BN0180.pdf, accessed on April 18, 2013.
5. W.B. Meacham, "Destiny of the Osteopathic Profession," *Journal of the American Osteopathic Association* 16, 1 (September 1916): 656.
6. "Ottari Sanitarium," available from http://www.nps.gov/nr/travel/asheville/text.htm#ott, accessed on April 18, 2013.
7. Thomas Waring, "A Most Unforgettable Character," *News and Courier* (December 16, 1979), available from http://news.google.com/newspapers?id=4WpJAAAA-IBAJ&sjid=2woNAAAAIBAJ&pg=1777,4348221&dq=loula+rockwell&hl=en, accessed on October 18, 2013.
8. Kate M. Herring, "If I Had a Dozen Sons I Should Want Them to Fight for France," *Atlanta Constitution* (June 16, 1918), 121.
9. From www.vmi.edu, accessed on April 25, 2013.
10. Rockwell, *Kiffin Yates Rockwell*, xii–xiii.
11. Ibid., xiii.
12. From www.vmi.edu, accessed on April 25, 2013.
13. Rockwell, *Kiffin Yates Rockwell*, xiii.
14. From www.wlu.edu/x52673.xml, accessed on April 25, 2013.
15. Ibid.
16. Ibid, xiv.
17. Rockwell, *Kiffin Yates Rockwell*, xv.
18. Ibid.

19. Allan Dunn, *Care Free San Francisco*, from http://www.sfgenealogy.com/sf/history/hbcare1.htm, accessed on April 25, 2013.
20. Paul Terry Cherington, *The Advertising Book 1916* (Garden City, NY: Doubleday, Page, 1916), i.
21. Ibid., viii.
22. From a discussion with Vance Brown, great-grandson of Paul Rockwell.
23. Rockwell, *Kiffin Yates Rockwell*, xviii.
24. Lucian Lamar Knight, *A Standard History of Georgia and Georgians*, vol. 5 (Chicago: Lewis, 1917), 2614.
25. Ibid., 2616.
26. Rockwell, *Kiffin Yates Rockwell*, xvii.
27. Ibid., xix.
28. Ibid., xviii.

Chapter 3

1. John Keegan, *The First World War* (New York: Alfred Knopf, 1998), 17.
2. Cecil Jenkins, *France: People, History, and Culture* (Philadelphia: Running Press, 2011), 267.
3. Michael Howard, *The First World War* (Oxford: Oxford University Press, 2002), 2.
4. "Szoegyeny's report to Berchtold, July 6, 1914, relating his talk with German chancellor Theobald von Berthmann-Hollweg," in *The First World War: An Eyewitness History*, ed. Joe Kirchberger (New York: Facts on File, 1992), 42.
5. Keegan, 59.
6. Ibid., 62.
7. Kirchberger, "Szoegyeny's report," 45.
8. "Field Regulations of the French Army, October 1913," in *The First World War: An Eyewitness History*, ed. Joe Kirchberger (New York: Facts on File, 1992), 29.
9. Jan Wilhelm Schulte-Nordholt, "The Peace Advocate Out of Touch with Reality," in *Major Problems in American Foreign Relations*, vol. 1: *To 1920*, ed. Dennis Merrill and Thomas Paterson (Boston: Houghton Mifflin, 2005), 451.
10. Ibid., 452.
11. Walter LaFeber, *The American Age: United States Foreign Policy at Home and Abroad*, vol. 1: *To 1920* (New York: W.W. Norton, 1994), 285.
12. Rockwell, *Kiffin Yates Rockwell*, 1–2.
13. Herring, "If I Had a Dozen Sons," 121.
14. Ibid., 3.
15. Philip J. Haythornthwaite, *The World War One Source Book* (London: Arms and Armour Press, 1992), 15.
16. Bouget, Boris, *The Invalides: The Army Museum, the Tomb of Napoleon* (Paris: Musée de l'Armée, 2014), 9.
17. Frederick Palmer, "My Year of the Great War (in Paris, August 1914)," in *The First World War: An Eyewitness History*, ed. Joe Kirchberger (New York: Facts on File, 1992), 61.
18. General Clergerie, "Memoir of the Battle of Ourcq River (5–8 September 1914)," from http://www.firstworldwar.com/source/ourcq_clergerie.htm, accessed on April 28, 2013. General Clergerie was the Chief of Staff to General Gallieni during the defense of Paris.
19. "General von Kluck's Account of the First Battle of the Marne, September 1914," from http://www.firstworldwar.com/source/marne_vonkluck.htm, accessed on April 28, 2013.
20. Marshall Joseph Joffre, *The Memoirs of Marshall Joffre*, vol. 1, trans. Colonel T. Bentley Mott (London: Billing and Sons, 1932), 205.
21. "September 3 Government Proclamation," in *Source Records of the Great War*: vol. 2: *A.D. 1914*, ed. Charles F. Horne and Walter F. Austin (New York: National Alumni, 1923), 199–200.
22. Horne, *Source Records of the Great War*, 201–208.
23. Ibid.
24. Ibid., 198.
25. Keegan, 112.
26. "Memoir of the Battle of Ourcq River," from http://www.firstworldwar.com/source/ourcq_clergerie.htm, accessed May 5, 2013.
27. Report from French Army Commander-in-Chief General Joseph Joffre to the Minister of War. From http://www.firstworldwar.com/source/marne_joffrereport.htm

Chapter 4

1. Paul Louis Hervier, *New York Times Current History: The European War*, vol. 11 (New York: New York Times, 1917): 470–472.
2. Ibid.
3. Herbert Molloy Mason, *The Lafayette Escadrille* (New York: Random House, 1964), 5.
4. "Charles Sweeny: Adventurer, Soldier of Fortune Fought in 7 Wars," *The Blade*, February 28, 1963, p. 32.
5. Philip D. Caine, *Eagles of the RAF: the World War II Eagle Squadrons* (Washington, DC: National Defense University Press, 1991), 22–26.
6. Douglas Porch, *The French Foreign Legion: A Complete History of the Legendary Fighting Force* (New York: Harper Perennial, 1992), 337. Douglas Porch's book on the French Foreign Legion is a thorough source covering the entire history of the Legion. It is highly useful for a detailed study of the French Foreign Legion and for an understanding of the Legion's unique culture.
7. Mason, 8.
8. Rockwell, *Kiffin Yates Rockwell*, 7.
9. Ibid.
10. Henry Ensign Rockwell, *The Rockwell Family in America: A Genealogical Record from 1630 to 1873* (Boston: Rockwell and Churchill, 1873), 11.
11. Mason, 9.
12. Porch, xi.
13. Ibid., 74.
14. Thomas Rid, "Razzia: A Turning Point in Modern Strategy," *Terrorism and Political Violence* 21 (2009): 622.
15. Porch, 151.
16. Ibid., 177–78.
17. Ibid., 194.
18. Ibid., 193.
19. Ibid., 301.
20. Ibid.., 289.
21. Ibid., 301.
22. Ibid., 305.
23. Ibid.
24. Mason, 13–14.
25. Ibid., 15.
26. Rockwell, *Kiffin Yates Rockwell*, 156.

27. Ibid.
28. M.A. DeWolfe Howe, *Memoirs of the Harvard Dead in the War Against Germany*, vol. 1 (Cambridge: Harvard University Press, 1920), 108–124. From http://net.lib.byu.edu/estu/wwi/memoir/Seeger/Harvard.htm, accessed May 15, 2013.
29. Ibid.
30. Ibid.
31. Ibid.
32. "American Volunteers in the French Foreign Legion, 1914–1917," from http://www.scuttlebuttsmallchow.com/phelizot.html, accessed on May 15, 2013.
33. Rockwell, *Kiffin Yates Rockwell*, 9.
34. Herring, "If I Had a Dozen Sons," 121.
35. Ibid.
36. Alan Seeger, *Letters and Diary of Alan Seeger* (New York: Scribner's, 1917), 3.
37. Ibid.

Chapter 5

1. Seeger, 4.
2. Ibid.
3. Ibid., 6.
4. Bert Hall, *En L'Air: Three Years On and Above Three Fronts* (New York: New Library, 1918), 14.
5. Ibid., 17.
6. Seeger, 6–7.
7. Rockwell, *Kiffin Yates Rockwell*, 10.
8. Hall, *En L'Air*, 17.
9. Mason, 23.
10. Seeger, 12.
11. Mason, 24.
12. Seeger, 15.
13. Mason, 25.
14. Keegan, 176.
15. Kirchberger, *The First World War: An Eyewitness History*, 66.
16. Mason, 25.
17. Hall, *En L'Air*, 36.
18. Mason, 27.
19. Hall, *En L'Air*, 25.
20. Rockwell, *Kiffin Yates Rockwell*, 12.
21. The Americans did develop lasting relationships with several of the men, but others were still thieves and murderers at heart—a fact that they would soon find out.
22. Seeger, 29–30.
23. Ibid., 47.
24. Rockwell, *Kiffin Yates Rockwell*, 12.
25. The Lafayette Flying Corps was a term used by the French to describe the entire group of American pilots fighting in the French Air Service. The Lafayette Escadrille was a full squadron of American pilots, but there were many more Americans serving in other squadrons in the French Air Service. In fact, most Americans who flew for France did not fly in the Lafayette Escadrille—the majority flew with other squadrons, and collectively they are all known as the Lafayette Flying Corps.
26. Hall and Nordhoff, *The Lafayette Flying Corps*, 458.
27. Rockwell, *Kiffin Yates Rockwell*, 15.

Chapter 6

1. Rockwell, *Kiffin Yates Rockwell*, 15.
2. Ibid., 17.
3. Ibid.
4. Ibid., 18.
5. Ibid., 22.
6. Ibid., 23.
7. Mason, 35.
8. Rockwell, *Kiffin Yates Rockwell*, 24.
9. Kiffin's concern was apparently well-founded. Morlae was wounded in the Battle of Champagne several months later and traveled back to the United States. He wrote a story in the *Atlantic Monthly* titled "A Soldier of the Legion," which his fellow American Legionnaires believed was inaccurate and full of fabricated tales of courageous acts that Morlae never performed.
10. Seeger, 72.
11. Rockwell, *Kiffin Yates Rockwell*, 29.
12. Ibid., 30.
13. Mason, 34.
14. Ibid.
15. Ibid.
16. Rockwell, *Kiffin Yates Rockwell*, 157.
17. Ibid., 32.
18. Ibid., 36.
19. Ibid., 33.
20. Russell A. Kelly, *Kelly of the Foreign Legion: Letters of Legionnaire Russell A. Kelly* (New York: Mitchell Kennerly, 1917), 63.
21. Howard, *The First World War*, 44.
22. Keegan, 187.
23. Howard, 46.
24. Marshal Joffre, *The Memoirs of Marshal Joffre*, vol. 2, trans. Colonel T. Bentley Mott (London: Billing and Sons, 1932), 349.
25. Interestingly, Italy would not officially declare war on Austria until a month later on May 23, 1915, but the captain of the Americans' company claimed that he had received a phone call about the declaration that night.
26. Howard, 62.
27. Rockwell, *Kiffin Yates Rockwell*, 39.
28. Ibid.
29. Ibid., 40.
30. Ibid., 41.
31. Ibid., 42.
32. Ibid., 43.
33. Joffre, vol. 2, 351.
34. Ibid., 352.
35. Martin Marix Evans, *Battles of World War I* (Ramsbury, UK: Crowood, 2004), 23.

Chapter 7

1. Rockwell, *Kiffin Yates Rockwell*, 44.
2. Ibid., 46.
3. Ibid.
4. Kelly, *Kelly of the Foreign Legion*, 86.
5. Ibid., 88.
6. Ibid., 89.
7. Joffre, Vol. 2, 354.
8. Rockwell, *Kiffin Yates Rockwell*, 48.
9. Ibid., 49–50.

10. Ibid., 47.
11. Ibid., 51.
12. Herring, "If I Had a Dozen Sons," 121.
13. Ibid., 55.
14. Kelly, 107–111.
15. Ibid., 111.
16. Ibid., 117.
17. Rockwell, *Kiffin Yates Rockwell*, 56.

Chapter 8

1. The National Weekly Corporation, *The Independent* 106 (October–December 1920): p. 53.
2. *New York Times*, December 5, 1916, p. 11.
3. Rockwell, *Kiffin Yates Rockwell*, 56.
4. Excerpt from Alice Weeks's book, *Greater Love Hath No Man*, from http://www.scuttlebuttsmallchow.com/aliceweeks.html, accessed on June 5, 2013.
5. Rockwell, *Kiffin Yates Rockwell*, 58.
6. Ibid., 59.
7. Ibid., 61.
8. Ibid., 66.
9. From the John F. Kennedy Library http://www.jfklibrary.org/Research/Ready-Reference/JFK-Miscellaneous-Information/I-Have-a-Rendezvous-with-Death.aspx, accessed June 5, 2013.
10. "Lost Poets, Alan Seeger," from http://www.english.emory.edu/LostPoets/Seeger.html, accessed June 5, 2013.
11. Georges Thénault, *The Story of the Lafayette Escadrille*, trans. Walter Duranty (Boston: Small, Maynard, 1921), 8.
12. Hall and Nordhoff, *The Lafayette Flying Corps*, 459.
13. Ibid., 100.
14. Ibid.
15. Ibid., 101.
16. James R. McConnell, *Flying for France: With the American Escadrille at Verdun* (Garden City, NY: Doubleday, Page, 1917), 142.
17. Ibid.
18. Ibid., 152.
19. Rockwell, *Kiffin Yates Rockwell*, 69.
20. Ibid., 70.
21. Ibid., 72.
22. Ibid., 77.
23. Victor Chapman, *Victor Chapman's Letters from France* (New York: Macmillan, 1917), 4.
24. Ibid., 14.
25. Ibid., 8.
26. Ibid., 16.
27. Ibid., 22.
28. Evans, *Battles of World War I*, 25.
29. Rockwell, *Kiffin Yates Rockwell*, 79.
30. Ibid., 85.
31. Ibid., 87.

Chapter 9

1. Hall and Nordhoff, *The Lafayette Flying Corps*, 392.
2. Ibid.
3. Mason, 48.
4. Hall and Nordhoff, *The Lafayette Flying Corps*, 392.
5. Ibid., 8.
6. "AFS Intercultural programs," from http://www.afs.org/afs-history-and-archives/about-the-archives/archival-collections/, accessed on June 8, 2013.
7. Hall and Nordhoff, *The Lafayette Flying Corps*, 9.
8. Mason, 51.
9. Ibid.
10. Rockwell, *Kiffin Yates Rockwell*, 88.
11. "Nieuport 11," from http://sped2work.tripod.com/neiuport11.html, accessed on June 9, 2013.
12. Chapman, 159.
13. Ibid.
14. Hall and Nordhoff, *The Lafayette Flying Corps*, 11.
15. Ibid., 12.
16. Ibid.
17. Mason, 52.
18. Philip M. Flammer, *The Vivid Air: The Lafayette Escadrille* (Athens: University of Georgia Press, 1981), 25.
19. Hall and Nordhoff, *The Lafayette Flying Corps*, 14.
20. Rockwell, *Kiffin Yates Rockwell*, 96.
21. Hall and Nordhoff, *The Lafayette Flying Corps*, 16.
22. Rockwell, *Kiffin Yates Rockwell*, 101.
23. McConnell, *Flying for France*, 17.

Chapter 10

1. Howard, *The First World War*, 75.
2. Erich von Falkenhayn, *The German General Staff and Its Decisions, 1914–1916* (New York: Dodd, Mead, 1920), 246.
3. Ibid., 249.
4. Ibid.
5. Ibid., 250.
6. Howard, 76.
7. Joffre, vol. 2, 437.
8. Ibid., 440.
9. Ibid., 442.
10. Ibid.
11. Ibid., 446.
12. Keegan, 281.
13. Joffre, 446.
14. Howard, 76.
15. Henri Philippe Pétain, *Verdun*, trans. Margaret MacVeagh (New York: Dial Press, 1930), 13.
16. Evans, *Battles of World War I*, 27.
17. Joffre, vol. 2, 449.
18. Ibid., 451.
19. Pétain, 64.
20. Later, in December 1916, the French changed the name of the *Escadrille Américaine* to the Lafayette Escadrille. The latter name is the name by which most people know the famous squadron, so I refer to the squadron by its more famous name for the remainder of the book.
21. McConnell, *Flying for France*, 20.
22. Ibid., 15.
23. Ibid., 23.
24. Thénault, 16.
25. Hall and Nordhoff, *Lafayette Flying Corps*, 82.
26. Ibid., 83.
27. McConnell, 22.
28. Mason, 56.
29. McConnell, 26.
30. Thénault, 18.

31. Ibid., 21.
32. Rockwell, *Kiffin Yates Rockwell*, 102.
33. Ibid., 104.
34. Thénault, 30.
35. Ibid., 34.
36. Rockwell, *Kiffin Yates Rockwell*, 106.
37. Ibid., 107.
38. Thénault, 36.
39. McConnell, 29.
40. Ibid., 30.
41. Ibid., 31.
42. Thénault, 38.
43. Ibid., 39.
44. Ibid.
45. McConnell, 34.
46. Elliot Cowdin was actually the first American to gain an aerial victory after he shot down a German aircraft on April 20, 1916, in N65, a French squadron. Bill Thaw, Bert Hall, and Norman Prince all had their chances earlier in their French squadrons, but success had always eluded them.

Chapter 11

1. Walter J. Boyne, *The Influence of Air Power Upon History* (Gretna, Louisiana: Pelican Publishing, 2003), 80.
2. Ibid.
3. Ibid.
4. Lee Kennett, *The First Air War 1914–1918* (New York: Free Press, 1991), 71.
5. Boyne, 81.
6. Thénault, 50.
7. Rockwell, *Kiffin Yates Rockwell*, 110.
8. Flammer, *Vivid Air*, 31.
9. Thénault, 50.
10. Ibid., 51.
11. Johannes Werner, *Knight of Germany: Oswald Boelke German Ace* (Havertown, PA: Casemate, 2009), 17.
12. Captain Manfred Freiherr von Richthofen, *The Red Battle Flyer*, trans. J. Ellis Barker (New York: Robert M. McBride, 1918), 80.
13. Thénault, 52.
14. Ibid.
15. Ibid.
16. Confronting discipline problems was a thorny issue for Captain Thénault throughout his tenure as commander of the Lafayette Escadrille. Due to diplomatic concerns, the French did not give him the authority to discipline the American pilots according to normal French military procedures. Thus, command of the squadron could be difficult at times since the Americans occasionally took advantage of Thénault's predicament.
17. Ibid., 53.
18. Ibid., 54.
19. Chapman, 181.
20. Thénault, 56.
21. Hall and Nordhoff, *Lafayette Flying Corps*, 332.
22. Ibid.
23. Ibid., 266.
24. Ibid., 356.
25. Ibid.
26. Rockwell, *Kiffin Yates Rockwell*, 113.
27. Thénault, 58.
28. Ibid.
29. Rockwell, *Kiffin Yates Rockwell*, 115.
30. McConnell, 39.
31. Rockwell, *Kiffin Yates Rockwell*, 116.
32. Thénault, 59.
33. His recovery took nearly a year and Balsley was forced to stay on his back for much of the time. It was a long and arduous recovery.
34. Rockwell, *Kiffin Yates Rockwell*, 118.
35. Ibid., 119–122.
36. Chapman, 18.

Chapter 12

1. Joffre, vol. 2, 457.
2. Keegan, 295.
3. McConnell, 46.
4. Ibid., 51.
5. Thénault, 22.
6. Ibid.
7. Ibid., 24.
8. Ibid.
9. Rockwell, *Kiffin Yates Rockwell*, 126.
10. McConnell, 61.
11. Hall and Nordhoff, *Lafayette Flying Corps*, 198. Hall includes an excerpt from Boelke's diary dated 4 July 1916.
12. Ibid.
13. Ibid.
14. Rockwell, *Kiffin Yates Rockwell*, 127.
15. Mason, 61.
16. McConnell, 67.
17. Ibid., 68.
18. Mason, 97.
19. Ibid., 98.
20. Hall and Nordhoff, *Lafayette Flying Corps*, 199.
21. Thénault, 64.
22. Ibid., 65.
23. Ibid., 64.
24. Ibid.
25. McConnell, 72.
26. Mason, 104.
27. Thénault, 67.
28. McConnell, 77.
29. Ibid., 82.
30. Ibid., 79.
31. Thénault, 75.
32. Ibid.
33. McConnell, 83.
34. Thénault, 76.
35. Thénault described their early frustrations with the Vickers gun: "The first trials of the Vickers machine-gun, as indeed of all of them, were very unsatisfactory for us, constantly jamming, due especially to the drums and the freezing of oil owing to the high altitude at which we flew. Only gradual improvements of detail could set that right" (Thénault, 78).
36. McConnell, 92.
37. Thénault, 78.
38. McConnell, 93.
39. Ibid., 95.
40. Ibid., 97–98.

41. Thénault, 79.
42. McConnell, 99.
43. Ibid.
44. Rockwell, *Kiffin Yates Rockwell*, 138–140.
45. Ibid., 144.
46. Ibid., 147.
47. Ibid., 148.
48. Herring, "If I Had a Dozen Sons," 121.
49. Ibid.
50. Brooks, *North Carolina Poems*.
51. McConnell, 96.

Chapter 13

1. McConnell, 100.
2. Ibid., 102.
3. Ibid.
4. Thénault, 84.
5. McConnell, 109.
6. Thénault, 86.
7. Ibid., 87.
8. Hall and Nordhoff, *Lafayette Flying Corps*, xi.
9. McConnell, 113.
10. Roger G. Miller, *Like a Thunderbolt: The Lafayette Escadrille and the Advent of American Pursuit in World War I* (Washington, DC: Air Force History and Museums Program, 2007), 16.
11. Ibid., 17.
12. Richthofen, 118.
13. Miller, 17.
14. Thénault, 91.
15. Ibid., 90.
16. Ibid., 90–91.
17. McConnell, 115.
18. Thénault, 93.
19. Ibid., 97.
20. Ibid., 98.
21. Hall and Nordhoff, *Lafayette Flying Corps*, 278.
22. Ibid., 242.
23. Ibid., 378.
24. Thénault, 104.
25. Hall and Nordhoff, *Lafayette Flying Corps*, 38.
26. Paul Rockwell, *Three Centuries of the Rockwell Family*, 72.
27. Evans, *Battles of World War I*, 34.
28. Ibid.
29. Thénault, 107.
30. Hall and Nordhoff, *Lafayette Flying Corps*, 325.
31. Thénault, 110.
32. Ibid.
33. Ibid., 113.
34. Ibid., 114.
35. Ibid., 118.
36. Hall and Nordhoff, *Lafayette Flying Corps*, 354.
37. Ibid., 223.
38. Ibid., 155.
39. Thénault, 123.
40. Ibid.
41. Miller, *Like a Thunderbolt*, 21.
42. Ibid., 22.
43. Evans, *Battles of World War I*, 37.
44. Keegan, 332.

Chapter 14

1. Keegan, 351.
2. Ibid., 372.
3. Lee Kennett, *The First Air War 1914–1918* (New York: Free Press, 1991), 21.
4. Irving B. Holley, Jr., *Ideas and Weapons*, (New York: Yale University Press, 1983), 31.
5. Alfred F. Hurley and William C. Hemdahl, "Roots of Military Aviation," in *Winged Shield, Winged Sword: A History of the United States Air Force*, vol. 1: *1907–1950*, ed. Bernard C. Nalty (Washington, DC: U.S. Government Printing Office, 1997), 30.
6. Ibid., 32.
7. Kennett, 73.
8. Thénault, 127.
9. Ibid., 128.
10. Hall, 258.
11. Thénault, 129.
12. Ibid., 157.
13. Evans, *Battles of World War I*, 40.
14. Ibid.
15. Keegan, 368.
16. Thénault, 141.
17. Hall and Nordhoff, *The Lafayette Flying Corps*, 40.
18. Ibid.
19. Thénault, 145.
20. Ibid., 147.
21. Hall and Nordhoff, *The Lafayette Flying Corps*, 495.
22. Thénault, 154.
23. Ibid., 152.
24. Ibid., 162.
25. Air University, "Billy Mitchell," from http://www.airpower.maxwell.af.mil/airchronicles/cc/mitch.html, accessed June 11, 2013.
26. William Mitchell, *Memoirs of World War I: From Start to Finish of Our Greatest War* (New York: Random House, 1960), 119.
27. Ibid., 140.
28. Flammer, 170.
29. Ibid., 172.
30. Mason, 235.
31. Ibid., 236.
32. Ibid.
33. Mitchell, 165.
34. U.S. Air Force, "Major General Benjamin Delahauf Foulois," from http://www.af.mil/information/bios/bio.asp?bioID=5445, accessed on June 12, 2013.
35. Mitchell, 165. This was a highly controversial move since it added significant delays into the process of bring American aviation units on line. The United States did not have aircraft or parts ready for sustained combat at the time, so America had to rely on French or British supplies initially. Cancelling orders for French material only delayed the process further. In his previous assignment, Foulois had been responsible for the production, maintenance, and organization of all American aeronautical material, which might have had something to do with his hasty decision.
36. Benjamin D. Foulois, *From the Wright Brothers to the Astronauts: The Memoirs of Major General Benjamin D. Foulois* (New York: McGraw-Hill, 1968), 161.
37. Thénault, 165.

38. Foulois, 162.
39. Mason, 281.
40. Thénault, 170.

Chapter 15

1. Miller, *Like a Thunderbolt*, 29.
2. Edwin C. Parsons, *I Flew with the Lafayette Escadrille* (Indianapolis: E.C. Seale, 1963), 73.
3. Parsons, 78.
4. Ibid., 89.
5. Ibid., 92.
6. Evans, *Battles of World War I*, 46.
7. Miller, 31.
8. Kennett, *The First Air War*, 170.
9. Hall and Nordhoff, *The Lafayette Flying Corps*, 461.
10. Kennett, *The First Air War*, 170.
11. Miller, 33.
12. Bert Frandsen, *Hat in the Ring: The Birth of American Air Power in the Great War* (Washington, DC: Smithsonian Books, 2003), 18.
13. Hall and Nordhoff, *The Lafayette Flying Corps*, 335.
14. Frandsen, *Hat in the Ring*, 23.
15. Ibid., 69.
16. Ibid., 77.
17. Eddie Rickenbacker, *Fighting the Flying Circus* (New York: Frederick A. Stokes, 1919), 6.
18. Ibid., 9.
19. Ibid., 15.
20. Ibid., 28.
21. Ibid., 34.
22. Ibid., 43.
23. Ibid., 63.
24. Ibid., 64.
25. Ibid., 96.
26. Ibid., 100.

Chapter 16

1. Keegan, 423.
2. Ibid., 3.
3. Miller, *Like a Thunderbolt*, 47.
4. Ibid., 56.
5. Richard Davis, "Spaatz," *Air Force Magazine* 83, 12 (December 2000): 68.
6. Ibid.
7. Ibid., 69.
8. Foulois, 181.
9. Ibid., 197.
10. Ibid., 200.
11. Ibid., 201.
12. John F. Shiner, "Benjamin D. Foulois: In the Beginning," in *Makers of the United States Air Force*, ed. John Frisbee (Washington, DC: U.S. Government Printing Office, 1996), 25.
13. Foulois, 296.
14. United States Air Force, "General Henry H. Arnold," from http://www.af.mil/information/bios/bio.asp?bioID=4551, accessed June 17, 2013.
15. Maurer Maurer, *Aviation in the U.S. Army, 1919–1939* (Washington, DC: U.S. Government Printing Office, 1987), 362.
16. Ibid.
17. Ibid., 364.
18. B. Chance Saltzman and Thomas R. Searle, *Introduction to the United States Air Force* (Maxwell AFB, Alabama: Airpower Research Institute, 2001), 34.
19. Ibid., 35.
20. United States Air Force, "Lieutenant General Elwood R. Quesada," from http://www.af.mil/information/bios/bio.asp?bioID=6575, accessed June 17, 2013.
21. Saltzman and Searle, 34.
22. Robin Olds with Christina Olds and Ed Rasimus, *Fighter Pilot: The Memoirs of Legendary Ace Robin Olds* (New York: St. Martin's Griffin, 2010), 5.
23. Ibid., 6.
24. Ibid.
25. Ibid., 11.
26. Ibid., 17.
27. Ibid., 77.
28. Ibid., 131.
29. Ibid., 135.
30. Ibid., 198.
31. Ibid., 229.
32. "Ubon Royal Thai Air Force Base Historical Brief," from http://vdha.us/stuff/contentmgr/files/e11de6ce9bb05c02204cd73464ac5302/docs/ubon_historical_brief.pdf, accessed June 18, 2013.
33. Olds, 336.
34. Parsons, *I Flew with the Lafayette Escadrille*, vi.

Bibliography

Bouget, Boris. *Les Invalides: The Army Museum, the Tomb of Napoleon.* Paris: Musée de l'Armée, 2014.

Boyne, Walter J. *The Influence of Air Power Upon History.* Gretna, La: Pelican, 2003.

Caine, Philip D. *Eagles of the RAF: The World War II Eagle Squadrons.* Washington, DC: National Defense University Press, 1991.

Casstevens, Frances Harding. *Clingman's Brigade in the Confederacy, 1862–1865.* Jefferson, N.C.: McFarland, 2002.

Chapman, Victor. *Victor Chapman's Letters from France.* New York: Macmillan, 1917.

Covington, Howard E., and Marion A. Ellis. *Terry Sanford: Politics, Progress, and Outrageous Ambitions.* Durham, NC: Duke University Press, 1999.

Evans, Martin Marix. *Battles of World War I.* Ramsbury, UK: Crowood, 2004.

Falkenhayn, Erich von. *The German General Staff and Its Decisions, 1914–1916.* New York: Dodd, Mead, 1920.

Flammer, Philip M. *The Vivid Air, the Lafayette Escadrille.* Athens: University of Georgia Press, 1981.

Foulois, Benjamin D. *From the Wright Brothers to the Astronauts; The Memoirs of Benjamin D. Foulois.* New York: McGraw-Hill, 1968.

Frandsen, Bert. *Hat in the Ring: The Birth of American Air Power in the Great War.* Washington, DC: Smithsonian Books, 2003.

Hall, Bert. *"En L'air!" (In the Air): Three Years on and Above Three Fronts.* New York: New Library, 1918.

Hall, James Norman, and Charles Nordhoff. *The Lafayette Flying Corps.* Boston: Houghton, 1920.

Haythornthwaite, Philip J. *The World War One Source Book.* London: Arms and Armour, 1992.

Holley, Irving B., Jr. *Ideas and Weapons.* New York: Yale University Press, 1983.

Horne, Charles F., and Walter F. Austin. *Source Records of the Great War.* Vol. 2: *A.D. 1914.* New York: National Alumni, 1923.

Howard, Michael. *The First World War.* Oxford: Oxford University, 2002.

Howe, M. A. De Wolfe. *Memoirs of the Harvard Dead in the War against Germany.* Cambridge: Harvard University Press, 1920.

Jenkins, Cecil. *France: People, History, and Culture.* Philadelphia: Running Press, 2011.

Joffre, Joseph Jacques Césaire, and Thomas Bentley Mott. *The Memoirs of Marshal Joffre.* London: Billing and Sons, 1932.

Keegan, John. *The First World War.* London: Alfred A. Knopf, 1998.

Kelly, Russell Anthony. *Kelly of the Foreign Legion; Letters of Légionnaire Russell A. Kelly.* New York: M. Kennerley, 1917.

Kennett, Lee B. *The First Air War, 1914–1918.* New York: Free Press, 1991.

Kirchberger, Joe. *The First World War: An Eyewitness History.* New York: Facts on File, 1992.

Knight, Lucian Lamar. *A Standard History of Georgia and Georgians.* Chicago: Lewis Pub., 1917.

LaFeber, Walter. *The American Age: United States Foreign Policy at Home and Abroad Since 1750.* New York: Norton, 1994.

Mason, Herbert Molloy. *The Lafayette Escadrille.* New York: Random House, 1964.

Maurer, Maurer. *Aviation in the U.S. Army, 1919–1939.* Washington, D.C.: Office of Air Force History, U.S. Air Force, 1987.

McConnell, James R. *Flying for France: With the American Escadrille at Verdun.* Garden City, N.Y.: Doubleday, Page, 1917. Bottom of Form

Merrill, Dennis, and Thomas G. Paterson. *Major Problems in American Foreign Relations: Documents and Essays.* Boston: Houghton Mifflin, 2005.

Miller, Roger G. *Like a Thunderbolt: The Lafayette Escadrille and the Advent of American Pursuit in World War I.* Washington, D.C.: Air Force History and Museums Program, 2007.

Mitchell, William. *Memoirs of World War I: "from Start to Finish of Our Greatest War."* New York: Random House, 1960.

Olds, Robin, Christina Olds, and Ed Rasimus. *Fighter Pilot: The Memoirs of Legendary Ace Robin Olds.* New York: St. Martin's Press, 2010.

Parsons, Edwin C. *I Flew with the Lafayette Escadrille.* Indianapolis, Ind.: E.C. Seale, 1963.

Pétain, Philippe, and Margaret MacVeagh. *Verdun.* New York: L. MacVeagh, The Dial Press, 1930.

Porch, Douglas. *The French Foreign Legion: A Complete History of the Legendary Fighting Force.* New York: Harper Perennial, 1992.

Rickenbacker, Eddie. *Fighting the Flying Circus.* New York: Fredrick A. Stokes, 1919.

Richthofen, Manfred, J. Ellis Barker, and C. G. Grey.

The Red Battle Flyer. New York: R.M. McBride, 1918.

Rockwell, Henry Ensign. *The Rockwell Family in America: A Genealogical Record from 1630 to 1873.* Boston: Rockwell and Churchill, 1873.

Rockwell, Kiffin Yates, and Paul Ayres Rockwell. *War Letters of Kiffin Yates Rockwell, Foreign Legionnaire and Aviator, France, 1914–1916.* Garden City, N.Y.: The Country Life Press, 1925.

Rockwell, Paul Ayres. *Three Centuries of the Rockwell Family in America, 1630–1930. Prepared for Françoise Jeanne Anne Loula Rockwell and Kiffin Yates Rockwell II.* Paris: Priv. Print, 1930.

Saltzman, B. Chance, and Tom Searle. *Introduction to the United States Air Force.* Maxwell AFB, Ala: Airpower Research Institute, CADRE, AU Press and Air Force History and Museums Program, 1999.

Seeger, Alan. *Letters and Diary of Alan Seeger.* New York: Scribner's, 1917.

Thénault, Georges, and Walter Duranty. *The Story of the Lafayette Escadrille.* Boston: Small, Maynard, 1921.

Werner, Johannes. *Knight of Germany: Oswald Boelcke German Ace.* Havertown, Pa: Casemate, 2009.

Index

Abd-el-Kader 36
advertising 21–22
aerial victories 107, 110
Afghanistan 3
air patrol tactics 111–113, 121, 136
air superiority 3, 109, 125, 134, 152, 171
aircraft: *Albatross* 128; *Avitik* 124; *B-17 Flying Fortress* 168; *B-24* 168; *Bleriot* 82; *Breguet* 133, 139; *Caudron G.2* 80; *Deperdussin Monoplane* 55; *F-86* 169; *Farman* 133; *Fokker* 121–122; *Maurice Farman* 83; *Morane Parasol* 93–94; *Morane Saulnier* 80; *Nieuport* 83, 93–95, 97, 103, 105, 121–122, 127; *P-38* 168; *P-51* 168; *P-80* 168; *Sopwith* 133; *Spad* 136
Aisne, Battle of 47
Aisne River 32, 64
Aisne Sector 146, 149
Albert, King of Belgium 47
Alexander 1
American Ambulance Service 91, 115, 136–138, 140, 142
American Expeditionary Force 144, 149
Antwerp, Belgium 47
Arnold, Gen. Hap 162–166
Artois, Battle of 70, 72, 99
Artois, France 64–65
Asheville, NC 16, 22
Atkinson, Bert 155, 162, 167
Atlanta, Georgia 22, 27, 72
Ayres, Enoch Shaw 14 16, 23

Bach, James 55, 79–81, 90–91
Bacon, Robert 91, 94
Balsley, Clyde 96, 101, 115–118
Bar-le-Duc, France 109–111
Bentonville, Battle of 14
Bernstorff, Amb. Count Johann von 95, 138
Besnard, Rene 92, 94, 96
Bigelow, Stephen 140
Blérancourt, France 171
Bliss, Robert 90
Boelke, Oswald 112, 117, 122, 134, 136
Bolling, Col. Raynal 149
Boston Institute of Osteopathy 18
Bottle of Death 8, 107, 132, 171

Bouttieaux, Col. Paul 90–91
Breckinridge, Gen. John C. 19
Bridgman, Ray 159
British Expeditionary Force 47
Brussels, Belgium 29
Bugeaud, Gen. Thomas 36
Bulow, Gen. Karl von 30

Camp d'Avord 83–84, 86, 94
Campbell, Andrew 142
Campbell, Douglas 156–157, 159, 169
Capdevielle, Ferdinand 40–41, 58, 61, 63, 79
Carstairs, Stewart 40, 42
Chambers, Reed 156
Champagne, France 49, 64, 85–86, 99
Champagne Sector 151
Chapman, John Jay 83
Chapman, Minna 83
Chapman, Victor 83–84, 88, 93–96, 101, 105–106, 110, 114, 116–119, 125, 151
Chatkoff, Herman 61–62
Chennault, Claire 164–166, 168
Cherington, Paul Terry 21
Chicago Daily News 71, 75
Civil War 9, 13–15, 19–20, 38
Cobb, Irvin 28
Cold War 3
comrade de combat 48
Cowdin, Elliot 90, 95–96, 101, 110–111, 122, 125
Craonnelle, France 53, 55, 57
Cuiry, France 56
Curtis, Frazier 90
Curtis, Glenn 163
Cyrus the Great 1

de Castelnau, Gen. Noël Édouard 100
de Laage de Meux, Lt. Alfred 102, 113, 116, 122–123, 129–130, 133, 141, 146
de Lesseps, Jacques 90
de Lesseps, Paul 90
de Sillac, Jarousse 90
Dolan, Charles 149, 159
Doolittle, Jimmy 166, 168
Doolittle raid 3
Dowd, Dennis 40–41, 61, 79
Dresser, Edith Stuyvesant 17

Dugan, William 142, 149
Dunn, Alan 21

Eaker, Ira 164–168
Eighth Air Force 166
8th South Carolina Regiment 14
8th Tactical Fighter Wing 169
Eisenhower, Gen. Dwight 166
Elting, John 36
Escadrille Américaine 90–92, 96, 97, 101, 138
excellence 3–5, 8

Falkenhayn, Gen. Erich von 32, 46–47, 98, 120, 139
Farnsworth, Henry 86
Féquant, Group Commander Philippe 136, 147
Fere-Champenoise, France 49
5th Pursuit Group 159
Fifty-first North Carolina Infantry Regiment 10
fighting spirit 3–5, 88, 109, 132, 151, 162–163, 171
1st Pursuit Wing 162
Fisk, John Earl (John Smith) 63, 70, 73, 76
Flanders, France 64, 146–147
Foch, Marshal Ferdinand 64
Fonck, René 123
Foulois, Brig. Gen. Benjamin 150–151, 153, 162–164, 167
Fourteenth Air Force 166
Franz Ferdinand, Archduke 25–26
French, Field Marshal Sir John 31–32
French Air Service 55, 81, 140, 142
French Consul, New Orleans, Louisiana 23
French Foreign Legion 33, 36–39, 45, 47–50, 63, 78, 88, 148
French Revolution 24

Gallieni, Gen. Joseph 30–31, 99
Genêt, Edmond 138, 141–142
George V, King of England 145
Green, Eddie 158
Grey, Sir Edward 26
Groener, Gen. Wilhelm 142
Gros, Dr. Edmund 91, 94, 138, 148–149
Gulf War 3

Index

Guynemer, Georges 123, 136, 147, 155

Hall, Bert 48–49, 52–55, 79, 81, 90–91, 95–96, 101, 110–111, 120–122, 126
Haig, Field Marshal Sir Douglas 120, 146
Hall, James Norman 90, 142, 145–146, 149, 156–158, 162, 171
Ham, France 141, 145–146
Happe, Capt. Maurice 103–104
Harmon, Millard 156
Harvard Monthly 40
Harvard University 40–42, 91, 140, 156
Haviland, Willis 136
Hayes, Kiffin Rockwell 139
Hayes, the Rev. Leonidas Braxton 138
Hayne, Paul Hamilton 11
Herbst, John "Pappy" 168
Herrick, Ambassador Myron T. 31, 34
Hewitt, Thomas 142
Hill, Dudley 94, 115, 126, 149, 159
Hill, Tex 168
Hindenberg, Field Marshal Paul von 98, 139, 146
Hinkle, Edward 140
Hirschauer, Gen. Auguste-Edouard 91
Hitler, Adolf 161
Holtzendorff, Adm. Henning von 144
Hoskier, Ronald 137, 141–142
House, Edward 26
Huffer, Jean 156

Immelmann, Max 112
Irwin, William Henry 28
Issoudun, France 155–156
Izac, Eduuard 147

Jackson, Thomas J. "Stonewall" 14, 19
James, Gen. Daniel "Chappie" 169
Jeanne d'Arc 35
Joffre, Gen. Joseph 30–32, 47, 64, 66, 70, 85–86, 92, 99, 101, 120
Johnson, Charles C. 96, 101
Johnson, Charles Chouteau 115, 141, 149
Johnson, Davenport 156
Jones, Henry 149, 159
Journal de Genève 131

Keegan, John 24, 142
Kelly, Russell 63–64, 69–70, 73, 76
Kenly, Brig. Gen. William 149
Kennedy, John F. 79
Kiffin, William 11
Kluck, Gen. Alexander von 29–30
Korean War 3, 169

Lafayette, Gilbert du Motier, Marquis de 24, 129
Lafayette Flying Corps 55
Lansing, Robert 95

Laurinburg, NC 10
La Valbonne, France 78
Lee, Gen. Robert E. 20
Leygues, George 75, 92, 138
Leygues, Jeanne 75, 138
London, England 28
Louis XIV, King of France 29
Louis-Philippe, King of France 36
Lovell, Walter 140
Ludendorff, Gen. Erich von 98, 146, 154
Lufbery, Raul 114–115, 118, 123, 125–129, 132–134, 136, 139, 142, 145, 147–151, 153, 155–159, 169, 171
Luxeuil-les-Baines 7, 101–102, 106–107, 126, 130
Lyon, France 65, 76–78

MacMonagle, Douglas 148
Mailly, France 47–49, 61
Marion County, SC 14
Marne, First Battle of 31, 47
Marne River 31
Marr, Kenneth 142, 149, 156
Massacre of the Innocents 47
Massengale, Elmo 22
Massengale Advertising Agency 22
Masson, Didier 116, 133, 137
McConnell, James R. 96, 101–103, 106–107, 115, 120–122, 126, 129, 138, 141
Meacham, Dr. William Banks 18
Menier, Senator Gaston 91
Menin, Belgium 47
Meuse River 99
Miller, James E. 156
Millerand, Alexandre 30, 75, 90
Mitchell, Gen. William "Billy" 2, 148–152, 159, 162–164, 167
mobilization 25–26, 154
Mohammad 1
Moltke, Gen. Helmuth von 31–32, 46
Mongolian Invasions 1
Mons, Belgium 29
Morlae, Edward 61
Morristown, TN 11
Murchison, Reverend C.M. 11

Napoleon Bonaparte 29
National Osteopathic Association 18
neutrality, American 27, 34, 90, 95
Neuvième Escouade (Ninth Squad) 40–41, 50, 57–58, 60–61
Neuville-Saint-Vaast, France 66
New Market, Battle of 19
New York Sun 52, 54
New York Times 33
Newport, TN 11–12, 16, 18
Newport Grammar School 16
Nieuport, Belgium 47
95th Aero Squadron 154–155
94th Aero Squadron 156–159
94th Fighter Squadron 169
9th Fighter Command 166
Nivelle, Gen. Robert 101, 139

Nordhoff, Charles 146
Nungesser, Charles 123

Olds, Robert 167
Olds, Robin 167–170
103rd Aero Squadron 153, 155, 162, 171
128th Pursuit Squadron 159
Operation Enduring Freedom 170
Operation Iraqi Freedom 170
Operation Michael 154
osteopathy 18
Ottari Sanitarium 18
Ottoman Empire 25
Oxford University 42

Paris, France 28–31, 34–35, 40–42, 55, 73, 89, 91, 94, 113, 126, 138, 147
Parsons, Edwin 138, 153–154, 162, 170
Patrick, Maj. Gen. Mason 163
Pau, France 90–91, 94
Pavelka, Paul "Skipper" 63–64, 66, 70, 73, 78–79, 86, 93, 123, 130
Peloux, Vicomte du 75
Perris, George 31
Pershing, Gen. John J. 144–145, 149–151
Pétain, Gen. Philippe 100–101, 109, 147
Peterson, David 156–157, 159
Phélizot, René 42, 61–62
Plessis-Belleville, France 96–97
Pourpe, Marc 115
Prince, Frederick H. 89–90
Prince, Frederick H., Jr. 134
Prince, Norman 89, 95–96, 101, 117–118, 120, 124–126, 132–134, 151, 171
Princeton University 41

Quackenbush, Professor W.G. 10
Quesada, Elwood 165–166, 168
Question Mark 165–166

Ravenel, France 139
razzia 36
Reber, Col. Samuel 28
Regnier, Col. Henri 96
Reims, France 47, 49–50, 52, 63
Rennes, France 69, 71
Revolutionary War 17, 20
Rheims, France 31
Richthofen, Baron Manfred von 112–113, 134, 136, 142, 145–146
Rickenbacker, Eddie 2, 156–159, 162, 169–170
Rochambeau, Jean-Baptiste Donatien de Vimeur, comte de 24, 72, 129
Rocheville, Sir Ralph de 35
Rockwell, Agnes 57, 138–139
Rockwell, Chester 9
Rockwell, Henry Clay 9
Rockwell, James Chester 10–13, 131
Rockwell, Loula (Ayres) 11, 13–20, 22, 27–28, 43, 72, 76, 131, 138–139
Rockwell, Norman 9

Index

Rockwell, Paul 4, 8, 11, 13–16, 18–30, 32–35, 39–40, 43, 53, 55, 60–61, 71, 73, 76, 91–93, 107, 111, 126, 129–130, 138–139
Rockwell, Robert "Doc" 126–127, 149, 159
Rockwell, William 9
Roosevelt, Quentin 156
Roosevelt, Theodore 156
Rouen, France 30, 35
Royal Flying Corps 134, 145
Rumsey, Lawrence 96, 101, 115, 141

Saint-Cyr, France 55, 80
St. Mihiel Offensive 159, 162
SS *St. Paul* 27
San Francisco, California 21, 25
Scanlon, Laurence 63, 70, 73–74, 79
Schlieffen, Count Alfred von 28
Schlieffen Plan 28, 30–31
Seeger, Alan 40–41, 43–44, 47–48, 50–52, 54, 61–63, 73, 78–79
Sigma Phi Epsilon Fraternity 20
Somerset County, England 9
Somme, Battle of 134, 136–137
Soubiran, Robert 136, 149, 159
Southern Theological Seminary 11
Spaatz, Carl 155, 162–168
Still, Dr. A.T. 18
Stone, Edward Mandell 61
Sweeny, Charles 34, 79
Szogyeny-Marich, Count Laszlo 26

Teresien, Sergeant 50, 58, 60
Thaw, Benjamin 41
Thaw, Harry Kendall 41
Thaw, William 41
Thaw, William II 40–41, 49, 55–56, 76, 79–81, 91, 95–96, 101–102, 110, 114, 120, 124, 126, 137, 141, 148–149, 153–154, 159, 162, 171

Thénault, Capt. Georges 96, 102–106, 109–110, 112–114, 116–117, 121–131, 134, 136–138, 141, 146–148, 151
3rd Pursuit Group 159, 162
Toulouse, France 35, 38–39, 42–44, 46–47
trench foot 52–53
trench warfare 33, 45–46, 52–54, 68
Trenchard, Maj. Gen. Hugh 134, 163
Tricornot de Rose, Major 109
Turner, Frederick Jackson 25
Tuskegee Airmen 3
12th Fighter Command 166
22nd Pursuit Squadron 159

United States Air Force 1, 3–4, 8, 46, 88, 131, 152, 159, 166, 171–174
United States Air Force Academy 1, 170
United States Air Service 2, 45, 88, 145, 151, 158
United States Army Air Corps 139, 164, 168
United States Army Air Corps Tactical School 164–165
United States Army Air Forces 166
United States Army Signal Corps 88
United States Naval Academy 20
United States Naval Air Service 136
University of Michigan 42
University of Pennsylvania 138
University of Virginia 115

Vandenberg, Gen. Hoyt 168
Vanderbilt, Anne Harriman 92
Vanderbilt, George 17
Vanderbilt, William K. 92, 94

Verdun, Battle of 97–108, 125
Verdun Sector 147
Vertus, France 49
Verzenay, France 49–50
Verzy, France 50
Viereck, George Sylvester 95
Vierzon, France 86
Vietnam War 3, 169
Villeneuve, France 155
Vimy Ridge 64–66
Virginia Military Institute 19–20

Wake Forest University 19
Washington, George 20
Washington and Lee University 19–21
Waynesville, NC 11
Weaver, the Rev. Charles 139
Weeks, Alice 63, 76, 77, 93
Weeks, Kevin 63, 70, 73, 76
Weidemann, Corporal 49–50, 57, 60
Wellesley College 19
Wheelock, John Hall 40
White, Stanford 41
Wilhelm II, Emperor Kaiser 31
Wilhelm, Crown Prince Friedrich 99
Wilkesboro, North Carolina 138
Williamson, Mary Walden 17
Willis, Harold 140, 147
Wilson, Woodrow 27, 72, 144–145
Winslow, Alan 157
World War II 1

Yates, Matthew 11
Ypres, Belgium
Ypres, First Battle of 47
Ypres, Second Battle of 65
Ypres, Third Battle of 146

Zemke, Col. Hubert "Hub" 168
Zinn, Frederick 40, 42, 58, 61, 79

www.ingramcontent.com/pod-product-compliance
Ingram Content Group UK Ltd.
Pitfield, Milton Keynes, MK11 3LW, UK
UKHW050524150426
5217IPUK00026B/1785